JOE LOUIS

JOE LOUIS

A BIBLIOGRAPHY OF ARTICLES, BOOKS, PAMPHLETS, RECORDS, AND ARCHIVAL MATERIALS

Compiled by Lenwood G. Davis
With the assistance of Marsha L. Moore

GREENWOOD PRESS
Westport, Connecticut • London, England

Library of Congress Cataloging in Publication Data

Davis, Lenwood G.
   Joe Louis: a bibliography of articles, books,
pamphlets, records, and archival materials.

   Includes index.
   1. Louis, Joe, 1914–   –Bibliography. 2. Boxing–
Bibliography. I. Moore, Marsha L. II. Title.
Z8519.7.D38 1983   016.7968'3'0924 [B]   83-1732
[GV1132.L6]
ISBN 0-313-23327-6 (lib. bdg.)

Library of Congress Catalog Card Number: 83-1732
ISBN: 0-313-23327-6

First published in 1983

Greenwood Press
A division of Congressional Information Service, Inc.
88 Post Road West, Westport, Connecticut 06881

Printed in the United States of America

10 9 8 7 6 5 4 3 2 1

TO
MARY A. LYNCH

Contents

Foreword

Throughout his time on earth Joe Louis represented the best that America had to offer: He was the symbol of things remembered; the conscience of things present; and the hope of things to come. Perhaps, what typifies the "Brown Bomber's" life best is the glow of integrity and the base level human compassion he had for fellow human beings.

Joseph Louis Barrow was one of America's most important figures during the 1930s and 1940s. Highly praised by both Blacks and Whites, Louis was the best example of a genuine folk hero. A much admired character, the "Brown Bomber" was not without tragedy in his life. Born under hard circumstances in Lexington, Alabama, Joe's family eventually made their way to Detroit to look for a better life. His rags to riches story has become a much revered part of American literary, social, and folk tradition.

Before Joe Louis began his reign in boxing, the controversial Jack Johnson had been stripped of his title and taunted by White America in such a manner that the "Golden Age" of Black pugilism seemed to be gone forever. It was almost unimaginable, after following such racial conflict, that another Black champion could survive the bigotry and hypocrisy of America's racialism. However, the course of history was changed as witnessed by Jack Orr in *The Black Athlete* (1969):

> Between 1915 and 1937 no black heavyweight was given the opportunity to wrest the title from the white champions. When one finally was allowed a shot at the crown, he was to be one of the genuine sports heroes of all time and he was to usher in an era in which black fighters all but dominated the game of fist-fighting. His name was Joe Louis.

Joe Louis represented America with a larger-than-life image during a time when Black Americans were struggling through various means to advance their case toward national recognition for full citizenry. Like Jackie Robinson of baseball's Hall of Fame, much was expected of the Black ringmaster. Although handicapped "by a lack of formal education," he was viewed as "a model for emulation." Louis did not shun this responsibility but carried it with such dignity that he ultimately gained the respect of the nation — White and Black alike.

Edwin B. Henderson, writing in *The Negro in Sports* (1948), provides some interesting insights into the life of Joe Louis. Expressing with authority, Henderson remarked "that the combination of Joe Louis, sportsman, boxer, American, has never been equalled." Louis's presence in the ring and out was an inspiration to all. He "never displayed the vices of an Uncle Tom" and openly "resented the segregation and discrimination against his race." His battle was fought in a gracious manner and bout after bout, working within the rules, Louis never failed to become a "generous and considerate victor at the end."

A strong contributor to the war cause, he aided America's troops by boosting their morale and by raising money for the relief funds for both the army and the navy. These personal feats "have never been equalled." E.B. Henderson comments:

> At the close of his army career the Brown Bomber had travelled over 30,000 miles all over the globe giving exhibitions, cheering the sick and wounded in the hospitals, and performing his duty under the usual hazards of war. He engaged in 196 exhibitions before millions of GIs. His courage under fire was undaunted. Twelve nights and continuous buzz-bombing in London failed to discourage him. One day after pulling the lanyard on a big gun of the 92nd division aimed against the German Gothic line, this same gun exploded killing several Negro artillerymen. He escaped death or injury several times when travelling by train, bus, truck or airplane. We are justified in repeating that no truer ideal American athlete ever lived than this greatest of all heavyweight boxers, Joe Louis.

Needless to say, in recent sports, at least, the athlete has become a sort of renaissance man, not judged "by ability alone," but by their "general and moral fitness" for representing themselves, their ethnic group, their hometown, their state, and their nation. For Joe Louis this was obviously the case. John Dizikes in *Sportsmen and Gamesmen* (1981) provides some testimony:

> The Brown Bomber was the symbol of the slowly awakening vision of racial harmony in the United States, and he inaugurated the present period of boxing history, in which the ring is dominated by black fighters.

The literature on the "Brown Bomber" is dominated by commentary on the importance of the boxer as symbol of a growing "democracy," whose time was yet to come. The climax of the unusual impact that prizefighting had on the American public and the world at large came during the second fight with Max Schmeling, the German fighter, allegedly representing the case for "a master race." All America cheered for Louis to "beat Schmeling to a pulp" and to end this nonsense of racial superiority. Louis won handily. Although the roots of American cries were clearly for nationhood, and not necessarily for the promotion of Black-White alliances, Louis's victory probably did more to bring the plight of Black Americans to the attention of the general public than any single occurrence at that time. Thus, the "realities of the ring" had its impact in the everyday life of American citizens.

If a central theme in the life of the "Brown Bomber" was to be mentioned, it is probably his concern for brotherhood. Writing in *My Life Story,* Louis expressed what brotherhood meant to him:

> Brotherhood should always be the symbol of America. We had that brotherhood during the war. With this brotherly spirit will come a new and stronger America, a united team of people from coast to coast who will pull together. A better tomorrow . . . that's what America means to me.

Louis's perception of life and his closeness to mankind gives an earnest picture of his true humanity. Biographer Gerald Astor finds an appropriate summation of Louis in " . . . *And a Credit to His Race.* " Astor remarks:

> Whatever his fears and ends, Joe Louis had carved out an identity for himself. In spite of all his associations with unsavory people, he had preserved his integrity. Against all the odds, he had taken the abilities given him by nature and turned them to the making of a champion.

Throughout life Louis also experienced "bouts" outside of the ring. Some were not pleasant; the marriages caused concern; the fear of "contracts on his life;" the tax problems; the mental breakdown; and the later demise to a "shadow of himself." However, despite the trials and tribulations, Louis trekked through life, much in the same "deliberateness" and "stalking" style he used in the ring. Perhaps this was his way of meeting life head on and taking "the blows as they came."

Although there are a number of books, articles, and other mass media-based materials about the remarkable life of Joe Louis, there are few sources, identifiable and in a single volume, that bring together those sources that provide the breadth and depth of this charismatic figure's life. The story of Joe Louis Barrow is an important facet of American life.

Therefore, it should be in its proper place in the annals of history. If this is to be done, in fact, then there must be special attention paid to those documents and materials that will ultimately assist us in a greater understanding of this towering figure who dominated a major segment of American life. The bibliographical work presented here by the indefatigable Renaissance bibliographer Dr. Lenwood G. Davis, is an excellent source that scholars, librarians, educators, and students will find available for their perusal. This compilation completes a commitment to fulfill a void in the life of another of America's heroes, whose years have gone by without a more searching investigation.

Professor Davis has rendered an invaluable service to us by painstakingly "digging up" the sources that make up this important work. Without a doubt it will serve as the basic source book for all who hope to seriously analyze the significance and interpret the results of one of America's genuine folk heroes — Joe Louis.

James E. Newton   February 1983
University of Delaware

Introduction

This is the first book-length bibliography on Joe Louis. Although much has been written about him, it has not been compiled in one place. He was one of the most popular boxers of all time, not only in the United States but throughout the world, giving exhibitions in both Europe and South America.

Although popular in most of the United States, he was criticized by some Black Americans because of his role in civil rights. Many thought he should have been more active, unaware that he gave financial support to several civil rights organizations. When asked about his involvement in the civil rights movement, he was reported to have replied: "I do my fighting in the ring." The fighter was implying that he could best represent Black people by using his boxing skills. He wanted to be a good role model for American citizens, both Black and White. Joe Louis was a man of honesty and integrity, and no scandal was every connected with his career. He lived a clean life in and out of boxing and did much to improve relations between the races. At the apex of his illustrious career, he was better known throughout the world than any American except Paul Robeson and President Franklin Roosevelt.

Mr. Louis held the heavyweight title for twelve years and defended it twenty-five times—more than any other heavyweight champion. Although he was given many nicknames, "The Brown Bomber" was the one that stuck with him and best described him because of his powerful punch and great boxing skill.

Joe Louis was born in 1914 in Alabama into a broken home and a poor family. His mother remarried when her son was seven years old, and the family moved to Detroit when Joe was ten. Louis had very little schooling during his early life, at one point attending a vocational school to become a cabinetmaker. Although the family was poor, money was found for Joe to take violin lessons. When he was sixteen years old, he joined a boxing club and fought a number of amateur fights. In his two years (1932–1934) as an amateur, he fought fifty-eight bouts. In April 1943, at age nineteen, he won the amateur light heavyweight boxing crown. In July 1934, he turned professional, earning only $59 in his first fight. Joe Louis fought a number of times between 1934 and 1937, knocking out Jimmy Braddock on June 22, 1937 to become "Heavyweight Champion of the World." Thus at age twenty-three he was the youngest fighter ever to hold the title. He continued to defend his title against all comers until 1942, then served in the United States Army until 1945. He continued to defend his title until his first retirement in March 1949, at which time he was still undefeated champion. Because of financial problems, Louis came out of retirement but was defeated in 1950 by Ezzard Charles and in 1951 by Rocky Marciano. During his career he had won seventy-three fights, including sixty-one knockouts, and he lost only three fights.

After Joe Louis retired from boxing he was plagued by a number of problems. Because of his generosity and unsuccessful business ventures he owed a large amount of federal income taxes. After many years of trying to pay his back taxes, the federal government realized that he would never be able to repay all of the money he owed, and a settlement was made. Joe also had a number of marriages that were unsuccessful. In 1970 he had to be committed to a psychiatric hospital for treatment and was later deemed "cured." Subsequently he was hired as a greeter at Caesar's Palace in Las Vegas. Joe Louis died of a heart attack on May 8, 1981, in Las Vegas.

Any work of this nature requires the assistance of many people. I would like especially to acknowledge a few who gave invaluable advice and assistance. Ernest Kaiser, of the Schomburg Center for Research in Black Culture, was most helpful in sharing with me a number of leads to sources on the topic. Janet L. Sims-Wood, of Howard University's Moorland-Spingarn Research Center, shared with me some of the references that I was missing and also sent me some citations that she had in her personal collection on Joe Louis.

I am indebted to my work-study students, Debra Stevenson and Pam McClain for helping with the proofreading and indexing. I would like also to thank Terri Welfare for typing the final copy of this manuscript and for making several grammatical and technical corrections. Doris Moore also assisted with the copying of citations and indexing. Several libraries also assisted me: the Schomburg Center for Research in Black Culture; the Moorland-Spingarn Research Center; University of Michigan, Michigan Historical Collection; Wake Forest University Library; New York Public Library; Winston-Salem State University Library; and the Library of Congress.

Although many people assisted me in this endeavor, I take full responsibility for any errors or omissions and for all of its shortcomings. I consulted all works that were available and attempted to give complete citation data. In a number of cases I saw only newspaper clippings of articles and not the complete newspapers. Many of the clippings did not give page numbers. Conversely, many of the papers are out of print and could not be located. In some instances, when several newspapers carried an identical story on Joe Louis, I did not list all of the newspapers because it would be redundant and serve no useful purpose. I would like to point out that I did cite several major newspapers such as the *New York Times, Washington Post,* and *Detroit Free-Press.* I also included most of the major Black newspapers such as the *New York Amsterdam News, Detroit Chronicle, Afro-American,* and *Pittsburgh Courier.* I believe that this volume is the most complete reference guide of works by and about the subject to date. It is my hope that it will help others to better understand the popular heavyweight who did so much to bring about better race relations between Black and White people in the United States and throughout the world.

JOE LOUIS

I
Works by Joe Louis

"Joe Louis is an honor to his race—naturally, I mean the human race."

Jimmy Cannon

A. BOOKS
(By Joe Louis and in Collaboration with Others)

1. 1947

1. Louis, Joe. My Life Story. Written with the editorial
aid of Chester L. Washington and Haskell Cohen. New
York: Duell, Sloan and Pearce, 1947. 188 pp.

2. 1948

2. Louis, Joe. How to Box. Edited by Edward J. Mallory.
Philadelphia: David McKay Co., 1948. 64 pp.

3. _____. Como Boxear. Mexico. D.F. La Aficion,
n.d. 64 pp. Translation of How to Box by Joe Louis
published in 1948.

3. 1953

4. Louis, Joe. The Joe Louis Story. Written with the
editorial aid of Chester L. Washington and Haskell
Cohen. New York: Grosset and Dunlap, 1953. 197 pp.

4. 1978

5. Louis, Joe. Joe Louis: My Life. With Edna and Art
Rust. New York: Harcourt Brace Javanovich, 1978.
277 pp.

5. 1981

6. Louis, Joe. Joe Louis: My Life. With Edna and Art
Rust. New York: Berkley Books, 1981. 304 pp.
(Paperback).

B. ARTICLES
(By Joe Louis and in Collaboration with Others)

1. 1935

7. Louis, Joe. As told to Norma Murray. "Life Story of
    Joe Louis In A Nut Shell," Washington Tribune, June 8,
    1935.

2. 1936

8. Louis, Joe. "I'll Beat Retzlaff to Punch"--Louis,
    Chicago Daily Times, January 13, 1936.

9. _____. "A Million 'N Then a Family, Says Joe",
    Chicago Daily Times, January 14, 1936.

10. _____. "Braddock No. Four in Louis' Rating!"
    Chicago Daily Times, January 15, 1936.

11. _____. "Louis Tells How It Feels To Be Rich,"
    Chicago Daily Times, January 16, 1936.

12. _____. "Honeymoon Before Next Kayo," Chicago
    Sunday Times, January 19, 1936.

13. _____. "Louis Predicts Kayo Within Three Rounds,"
    Detroit Evening Times, June 18, 1936.

14. _____. "Joe Says Delays Added Weight and Strength,"
    Detroit Evening Times, June 19, 1936.

15. Louis, Joe as told to Gene Kessler. "How I Shall Beat
    Max Schmeling," Liberty, June 20, 1936.

3. 1937

16. Louis, Joe. As told to Gene Kessler. "These Fighting
    Lessons Will Help Any Man," Liberty, February 20, 1937.

17. _____. "I'll Do Leading "n" Kayoing!"--Joe,"
    Chicago Daily Times, June 21, 1937.

18. _____. "I'm Going to Gamble on My Punch,"
    Cleveland News, June 21, 1937.

19. _____. "Louis' Own Story: Jim 'A Game Guy,'"
    Chicago Daily Times, June 23, 1937.

20. Louis, Joe. As told to Gene Kessler. "How I Shall Win
    the Championship," Liberty, June 26, 1937.

21. _____. "Farr Fooled Me--My Crown Is Doffed to Him,"
    Evening Standard (London), August 31, 1937.

4. 1941

22. Louis, Joe. As told to Ches Washington. "Army Camp
     Boxing Tour Starts," New York Post, October 9, 1941.

23. _____. "Nervous First Time in Draft Test,"
     New York Post, October 15, 1941.

24. _____. "He Hopes to Defend Title as Soldier,"
     New York Post, October 21, 1941.

25. _____. "Buddy Walker Is Promising Heavy,"
     New York Post, October 31, 1941.

26. _____. "Zivic 'Desperate' For Victory," New York
     Post, October 28, 1941.

5. 1946

27. Louis, Joe. "How I Will Win!" Time, Vol. 48, No. 1,
     July 1, 1946, pp. 25-27.

6. 1947

28. Louis, Joe. "My Life Story," Negro Digest, Vol. 6,
     No. 1, January, 1947, pp. 86, 93.

29. _____. "My Toughest Fight," Salute, Vol. 2, No. 12,
     December, 1947, p. 13.

7. 1948

30. Louis, Joe. "???????," New York Age, September 21,
     1948, p. 9. This was the first article by the boxer and
     he did not select a title for it. He announced that he
     would pay $100.00 for the best title for his column.

.31. _____. "???????," New York Age, September 24, 1948.
     He asked his readers to send him a name for his column.

32. _____. "???????," New York Age, September 28, 1948.
     He discusses Lena Horne.

33. _____. "???????," New York Age, October 1, 1948,
     p. 10. He discusses baseball and the title of his
     column.

34. _____. "???????," New York Age, October 9, 1948,
     p. 14. He discusses the New York Yankees and Cleveland
     Indians.

35. _____. "(Larry) Doby Plays Like Veteran Says
     Louis," New York Age, October 9, 1948, p. 1.

36. _____. "???????," New York Age, October 16, 1948,
     p. 15. He discusses Larry Doby and Satchel Paige.

37. Louis, Joe. "Joe Louis Says Doby Real Gone," <u>New York Age</u>, October 16, 1948, pp. 1, 15.

38. _____. "Brown Bomber Praises Doby's Work With Bat," <u>New York Age</u>, October 16, 1948, p. 15.

39. _____. "???????," <u>New York Daily</u>, October 23, 1948, p. 15. He discusses conditions in the United States and youths of today (1948).

40. _____. "Democracy Will Take a Stand," <u>New York Age</u>, October 30, 1948, p. 9.

41. _____. "Joe Louis Says Truman Elected by Negro Voice," <u>New York Age</u>, November 6, 1948, pp. 1, 8.

42. _____. "Joe's Write Hand," <u>New York Age</u>, November 6, 1948, p. 14. He discusses how his column got its name.

43. Louis, Joe. As told to Meyer Berger and Barney Nagler. "The Life Story of Joe Louis: His Early Years," <u>New York Times</u>, November 5, 1948, p. 27.

44. _____. "Life Story of Joe Louis: His First Fights," <u>New York Times</u>, November 6, 1948, p. 18.

45. _____. "Life Story of Joe Louis: First Big Money," <u>New York Times</u>, November 8, 1948, p. 31.

46. _____. "Life Story of Joe Louis: He Wins the Title," <u>New York Times</u>, November 9, 1948, p. 37.

47. _____. "Life Story of Joe Louis: Sees Roosevelt," <u>New York Times</u>, November 10, 1948, p. 41.

48. _____. "Life Story of Joe Louis: He Meets Jim Crow in the Army," <u>New York Times</u>, November 11, 1948, p. 41.

49. _____. "Life Story of Joe Louis: His Travels," <u>New York Times</u>, November 12, 1948, p.37.

50. Louis, Joe. "Joe's 'Write' Hand!" <u>New York Age</u>, November 13, 1948, p. 15. He discusses discrimination in the South and the previous elections.

51. Louis, Joe. "My Story," <u>Life</u>, Vol. 24, November 15, 1948, pp. 126-146.

52. Louis, Joe. "Joe's 'Write' Hand!: Bad News From <u>The New York Daily News</u>," November 20, 1948, p. 4.

53. Louis, Joe. "Joe's 'Write' Hand," <u>New York Age</u>, November 27, 1948, p. 17. He discusses professional football.

54. _____ . Joe's 'Write' Hand," New York Age, December 4, 1948, p. 17. He writes about Christmas and its meaning.

55. _____ . "Joe's 'Write' Hand," New York Age, December 11, 1948, p. 17. He discusses college sports.

56. _____ . "Joe's 'Write' Hand," New York Age, December 18, 1948, p. 17. He discusses the role of policemen.

57. _____ . "Joe's 'Write' Hand: Taking Sight of the New World," New York Age, December 25, 1948, p. 19. He discusses Human Rights and World Rights.

8.   1949

58. Louis, Joe. Joe's 'Write' Hand: '48 Reporting to '49," New York Age, January 1, 1949, p. 17. He summarized events that occurred in 1948.

59. _____ . "Joe's 'Write' Hand: That '49 Look," New York Age, January 8, 1949, p. 15. He discusses his hopes for 1949.

60. _____ . "Joe's 'Write' Hand: Thoughts in Paragraph," New York Age, January 15, 1949, p. 14. Louis discusses racial discrimination, democracy and sports.

61. _____ . "Joe's 'Write' Hand: 'The Quiet One,' Said Something," New York Age, January 22, 1949, p. 17. He discusses the movie, "The Quiet One," and surmises that it was about the best movie he had seen on juvenile delinquency.

62. _____ . "Joe's 'Write' Hand: 'The Quiet One' Continues to Talk," New York Age, January 29, 1949, p. 7. The writer continued to discuss the movie, "The Quiet One."

63 _____ . "Joe's 'Write' Hand: The Devil in God's Country," New York Age, February 5, 1949, p. 7. He contended that the Devil is the referee in the ring of race relations.

64. _____ . "Joe's 'Write' Hand: An Open Letter," New York Age, February 12, 1949, p. 7. This was an open letter to white sports writers. He told them they should speak up about discrimination in golf.

65. _____ . "Joe's 'Write' Hand: A Look in Our Own Backyard," New York Age, February 19, 1949, p. 7. He states that if those bigots on the green (golf) and in the bowling alleys continue to hold their un-American stand against any but the white race teeing off or striking the pins, then they should be removed from the sports roster with their games.

66. _____. "Joe's 'Write' Hand: An Open Letter to the Public," New York Age, March 12, 1949, pp. 13, 15. He thanks the public for supporting him over the years.

67. _____. "Joe's 'Write' Hand: From a Pencil Point of View," New York Age, March 19, 1949, p. 13. He discusses Westbrook Pegler column in the Journal-American and declares its guys like Pegler, who add to the Communist rank in America.

68. _____. "My Story: Joe Meets Roxborough, Launches Pro Career," Washington Post, March 23, 1949, p. 17.

69. _____. "My Story," Washington Post, March 29, 1949.

70. Louis, Joe. As told to Barney Nagler. "The Man Who Could Beat Me," Sport, March, 1949, pp. 10-11, 80.

71. Louis, Joe. "Joe's 'Write' Hand: What the Rent Bill Means to You," New York Age, April 2, 1949, p. 13.

72. _____. "Joe's 'Write' Hand: A Plan to Help Save Our Youth," New York Age, April 9, 1949, p. 7.

73. _____. "Joe's 'Write' Hand: Americans Aren't Second Class Citizens," New York Age, April 16, 1949, p. 7.

74. _____. "Joe's 'Write' Hand: It Takes Heart," New York Age, April 23, 1949, p. 13. Louis surmises that Dr. Ralph Bunche was about the greatest Negro of the century, as well as one of the greatest living Americans.

75. _____. "Joe's 'Write' Hand: The Senators Took a Walk," New York Age, April 30, 1949, p. 13. The writer states that the Senators in Washington took a walk from their offices in the nation's capital and witnessed human suffering, poverty and disease which existed right under their noses.

76. _____. "Joe's 'Write' Hand: The Answer Post," New York Age, March 5, 1949, p. 13. He discusses discrimination in sports.

77. _____. "Why I Retired," New York Age, March 5, 1949, pp. 1, 9.

78. _____. "Joe's 'Write' Hand," New York Age, May 14, 1949, p. 2. The author comments on the impact that his mother had on his life.

79. _____. "Joe's 'Write' Hand," New York Age, May 21, 1949, p. 14. He discusses the affects that mental illness has on people.

80.   _____. "Joe's 'Write' Hand: On Living for Today--
         Being Broke Tomorrow," New York Age, May 28, 1949, p.
         16.

81.   _____. "Joe's 'Write' Hand: Broadway Has Cousins
         All Over the World," New York Age, June 4, 1949, p. 16.

82.   _____. "Joe's 'Write' Hand: Irwinton's (Georgia)
         Idea of Memorial Day," New York Age, June 11, 1949,
         p. 16.

83.   _____. "Joe's 'Write' Hand: Open Season: Now
         Its Bombs Under the Bed," New York Age, June 18, 1949,
         p. 14. Louis writes about his father in this article.

84.   _____. "Joe's 'Write' Hand: Dear Congress: No
         Time for Vacation Now," New York Age, June 25, 1949,
         p. 14. Louis discusses the Ku Klux Klan in this
         article.

85.   _____. "Joe's 'Write' Hand: It's Over Now--And
         New Champ (Ezzard Charles) Is Real Stuff," New York Age,
         July 2, 1949, p. 16.

86.   _____. "Joe's 'Write' Hand: Twenty-Eight Years
         in Jail--A Mistake?" New York Age, July 9, 1949, p. 14.

87.   _____. "Joe's 'Write' Hand: 'Leaders' Can Make
         Road Easier for Us," New York Age, July 16, 1949,p. 14.

88.   _____. "Joe's 'Write' Hand: Louis Explains Why He
         Picked Gavilan to Win," New York Age, July 16, 1949,
         p. 32.

89.   _____. "Joe's 'Write' Hand: Busman's Holiday,
         Fight in Philly--Game in Brooklyn," New York Age,
         July 23, 1949, p. 14.

90.   _____. "Joe's 'Write' Hand: In Florida There's
         Some Un-American Activity Solidly in Evidence," New York
         Age, July 30, 1949, p. 14.

91.   Louis, Joe, "Joe's 'Write' Hand: A Lad Beats Me at
         Golf--I Visit Pompton Lakes and Start Reminiscing,"
         New York Age, August 6, 1949, p. 14.

92.   _____. "Joe's 'Write' Hand: Why Aren't Young
         Girls Answering the Urgent Call in Nursing Field?"
         New York Age, August 13, 1949.

93.   _____. "Joe's 'Write' Hand: Champ Ezzard Proved
         at Stadium--Classy Flesh in the Ring," New York Age,
         August 20, 1949, p. 14.

94.   _____. "Joe's 'Write' Hand: There's a Warm Spot in
         My Heart for the Ring--But I Shall Not Return!" New
         York Age, August 27, 1949, p. 12.

95.   _____ . "Joe's 'Write' Hand: The Dodgers and Ray Robinson Won Thursday But I Lost--At Golf," New York Age, September 3, 1949, p. 12.

96.   _____ . "Joe's 'Write' Hand: Baseball Has the Center of the Stage and Rightfully So," New York Age, September 10, 1949, p. 12.

97.   _____ . "Joe's 'Write' Hand: A Thing or Two, But Mostly About Old New York City," New York Age, September 17, 1949, p. 14.

98.   _____ . "Joe's 'Write' Hand: I Go West to See That Champ (Ezzard Charles) Is O.K.; I Mourn Death (of Harry T. Burleigh)," New York Age, September 24, 1949, p. 14.

99.   _____ . "Joe's 'Write' Hand: Cleanliness, After All Is Next to Godliness; Umpires Can be Unfair," New York Age, October 1, 1949, p. 14.

100.   _____ . "Joe's 'Write' Hand: Mainly About Subways and Women in Some Places," New York Age, October 8, 1949, p. 14.

101.   _____ . "Joe's 'Write' Hand: World Series Talk in Baltimore Like Everywhere Else," New York Age, October 15, 1949, p. 14.

102.   _____ . "Joe's 'Write' Hand: I Will Fight a Few Ten Round Bouts; Build Big Housing Project, and Hit Baltimore Jim Crow," New York Age, October 22, 1949, p. 14.

103.   _____ . "Joe's 'Write' Hand: Some Observations on the 69th Year of Our Oldest Negro Newspaper, and an Attack on Un-American Sports Ass.," New York Age, October 29, 1949, p. 14.

104.   _____ . "Joe's 'Write' Hand: Negro Tired Crying For His Civil Rights; Constitution Gives Them . . . .," New York Age, November 1, 1949, p. 14.

105.   _____ . "Joe's 'Write' Hand: About the New Cream-- Puff Boxing Rules and Dedication of the U.N.'s New Home," New York Age, November 5, 1949, p. 16.

106.   _____ . "Joe's 'Write' Hand: Much Pre-Election Fanfare Now Let's Watch For a Good Administration," New York Age, November 12, 1949, p. 14.

107.   _____ . "Joe's 'Write' Hand: The Fight Against Bias Must Be Fought on an Even Larger Scale," New York Age, December 3, 1949, p. 16.

108. _____. "Joe's 'Write' Hand: The Christmas Blues," New York Age, December 10, 1949, p. 19.

109. _____. "Joe's 'Write' Hand," New York Age, December 17, 1949, p. 19. He discusses several Black musicians.

110. _____. "Joe's 'Write' Hand," New York Age, December 24, 1949, p. 20. The writer states he hopes Santa put the Civil Rights vote in every Senator's stocking and enforces the Bill of Rights to the hilt.

111. _____. "Joe's 'Write' Hand," New York Age, December 31, 1949, p. 16. He discusses the major events of 1949 and previews the events of 1959.

9. 1950

112. Louis, Joe. "Joe's 'Write' Hand," New York Age, January 7, 1950, p. 15. He comments on the major events that took place in 1949.

113. _____. "Joe's 'Write' Hand," New York Age, January 14, 1950, p. 15. He discusses various types of people in society.

114. _____. "Joe's 'Write' Hand," New York Age, January 21, 1950, p. 17. He discusses crimes and insanity.

115. _____. "Joe's 'Write' Hand," New York Age, January 28, 1950, p. 17. He discusses segregation in sports, business, educational institutions and elsewhere.

116. _____. "Joe's 'Write' Hand," New York Age, February 4, 1950, p. 17. He states that he will not come out of retirement to box again.

117. _____. "Joe's 'Write' Hand," New York Age, February 11, 1950, p. 18. The writer discusses women's cry for equal rights.

118. _____. "Joe's 'Write' Hand," New York Age, February 18, 1950, p. 19. He discusses his exhibition in St. Petersburg, Florida and segregation in South Carolina.

119. _____. "Joe's 'Write' Hand," New York Age, February 25, 1950, p. 17. He discusses baseball, boxing, Albert Einstein, and children.

120. _____. "Joe's 'Write' Hand," New York Age, March 4, 1950, p. 19. The author asserts that there is a conspiracy in Congress against the American people and an investigation should be launched now.

121.   _____. "Joe's 'Write' Hand." New York Age,
        March 11, 1950, p. 1. In this article, Louis asks a
        number of questions concerning life in America as it
        affects Black people.

122.   _____. "Joe's 'Write' Hand," New York Age, March
        18, 1950, p. 18. He discusses the affects that base-
        ball had on female fans.

                        10. 1952

123.   Louis, Joe. "My Next Move," Quick, January 14, 1952.

124.   Louis, Joe. As told to A.E. Hotchner. "To Be a
        Champion You've Got to be Hungry!" New York Herald
        Tribune, May 18, 1952.

                        11. 1953

125.   Louis, Joe. As told to Barney Nagler. "Open Letter
        to Rocky Marciano as dictated by Joe Louis," Pageant,
        October 1953, pp. 36-39.

                        12. 1956

126.   Louis, Joe. As told to Edward Linn. "Oh, Where Did
        My Money Go?" Saturday Evening Post, Vol. 228, No. 28,
        January 7, 1956, pp. 22-23, 68-71.

II
Major Books and Pamphlets
about Joe Louis

''He can run but he can't hide!''

Joe Louis

127. Astor, Gerald. "...And A Credit To His Race": The
      Hard Life and Times of Joseph Louis Barrow, A.K.A. Joe
      Louis. New York: Saturday Review Press, E.P. Dutton
      & Co., Inc., 1974. 275 pp.

128. Bell, Norman. The Fighting Life of a Fighter: How Joe
      Louis Became the World's Greatest Heavyweight. London:
      The War Fact Press. 1943. 65 pp.

129. Edmonds, Anthony O. Joe Louis. Grand Rapids, Mich.:
      Eerdmans, 1973. 112 pp.

130. Fleishcher, Nathaniel S. The Louis Legend: The
      Amazing Story of the Brown Bomber's Rise To The
      Heavyweight Championship of The World and His Retirement
      From Boxing. New York: N.P., 1956. 181 pp.

131. Jones, Claudia. Lift Every Voice, For Victory! New
      York, 1942. 14 pp. This pamphlet discusses Joe
      Louis' role in World War II.

132. Kessler, Gene. Joe Louis, The Brown Bomber. Racine,
      WI: Whitman, 1936. .237 pp.

133. Libby, Bill. Joe Louis: The Brown Bomber. New York:
      Random House, 1980, 224 pp. Written for juvenile
      readers.

134. Miller, Margery. Joe Louis: American. New York: A.A.
      Wyn Publisher, 1945. 181 pp.

135. Miller, Margery. Joe Louis: American. Revised Edition.
      New York: Hill and Wang, 1961. 198 pp.

136. Nagler, Barney. Brown Bomber: The Pilgrimage of Joe
      Louis. New York: World, 1972. 236 pp.

137. Scott, Neil. _Joe Louis: A Picture Story of His Life_.
      New York: Greenberg, 1947. 126 pp.

138. Van Deusen, John G. _Brown Bomber_. Philadelphia:
      Dorrance & Co., 1940. 163 pp.

139. Van Every, Edward. _Joe Louis, Man and Superfighter_.
      New York: Frederick A. Stokes Co., 1936. 183 pp.

140. Vitale, Rugio. _Joe Louis: Biography of Champion_.
      Los Angeles: Holloway House Publishing Co., 1979.
      224 pp.

III
General Books and Pamphlets about Joe Louis

"I want to fight honest so that the next colored boy can get the same kinda break I got."

Joe Louis

141. Adams, Caswell, Editor. Great American. Philadelphia:
      David McKay Co., 1947. See "Louis vs. Baer, September
      24, 1935," pp. 247-251; "The Defeat of Joe Louis,
      Louis-Schmeling First Bout, June 19, 1936," pp. 252-
      256; "Louis vs. Braddock, June 22, 1937," pp. 257-260;
      "Louis vs. Schmeling Second Bout, June 25, 1938,"
      pp. 261-263; "First Louis-Conn Bout, June 18, 1941,"
      pp. 266-270; "Second Louis-Conn Bout, June 19, 1946,"
      pp. 271-275.

142. Andre, Sam and Nat Fleischer. A Pictorial History of
      Boxing. New York: Bonanza Books, 1981. Joe Louis,
      pp. 57, 86, 119-123, 125-147, 151-155, 172, 193-196,
      262, 299.

143. Associated Press Sport Staff. The Sports Immortals.
      Englewood Cliffs, N.J.: Rutledge Book, 1972. See,
      Earl Gerheim,"Joe Louis: America's Brown Bomber,"
      pp. 122-127.

144. Baldwin, James. Notes of a Native Son. Boston: Beacon
      Press, 1955. Joe Louis, pp. 64, 75. Author points out
      that Louis had succeeded on a level that white America
      indicates is the only level for which it has any respect.

145. Bardolph, Richard. The Negro Vanguard. New York:
      Vintage Books, 1961. Joe Louis, pp. 262, 270, 295, 453,
      454, 455.

146. Baskin, Wade and Richard N. Runes. Dictionary of Black
      Culture. New York: Philosophical Library, 1973. Joe
      Louis, p. 276.

147. Bromberg, Lester. Boxing's Unforgetable Fights. New
      York: Ronald Press Co., 1962. 351 pp. Joe Louis

pp. 218-228, 237-246, 259, 261-270, 280-285, 302, 304, 315, 338, 339.

148. Brooks, Thomas R. Walls Come Tumbling Down: A History of the Civil Rights Movement 1940-1970. Englewood Cliffs, N.J.: Prentice-Hall, Inc., 1974. Joe Louis, p. 10.

149. Burrill, Bob. Who's Who in Boxing. New Rochelle, N.Y.: Arlington House, 1974. Joe Louis, pp. 121-122. A short biographical sketch of Joe Louis is given in this collection.

150. Cannon, James. Nobody Asked Me. New York: Dial Press, 1951. "Louis and Conn, Second Fight," pp. 159-165; "Joe Louis Stay Retired!" pp. 184-194; "The Heavyweights and Damon Runyon."

151. Carpenter, Harry. Masters of Boxing. New York: A.S. Barnes & Co., Inc., 1964. "Headmaster" (Joe Louis, born 1914).

152. Clark, Patrick. Sports First. New York: Facts on File, 1981. The first heavyweight title fight to be televised was between Joe Louis and Billy Conn on June 19, 1946. This was also the first boxing match to have top price for tickets at $100.

153. Daily, Arthur. Sports of the Times, New York: E.P. Dutton & Co., 1959. See "(Joe Louis) Ten Years A Champion," pp. 129-131.

154. Darden, Anne. The Sports Hall of Fame. New York: Drake Publishers, 1976. Joe Louis, pp. 72-73. Short overview of Joe Louis as one of the greatest of heavyweight titleholders.

155. Davie, Maurice R. Negroes In American Society. New York: McGraw-Hill Book Company, Inc., 1949. Joe Louis, pp. 379, 445, 448, 507.

156. De Marco, Mario. Great American Athletes. Menlo Park, CA: Pacific Coast Publishers, 1962. Joe Louis, p. 49. Short biographical sketch of Joe Louis.

157. Dempsey, Jack. Dempsey, By The Man Himself. As told to Bob Considine and Bill Slocum. New York: Simon and Schuster, 1960. Joe Louis, pp. 144, 183, 211, 213.

158. Doren, Charles Van, Editor. Webster's American Biographies. Springfield, MA: G. & C. Merriam Co., 1974. Joe Louis, pp. 649-650.

159. Durant, John. The Heavyweight Champions. New York: Hasting House, 1967. Joe Louis, pp. 51, 58, 84, 115-117, 128, 150, 162, 163, 165. Chapter 9 is entitled,

"Brown Bomber," pp. 99-111.

160. _____ and Otto Bettmann. Pictorial History of
     American Sports: From Colonial Times To The Present.
     Revised Edition. New York: A. S. Barnes & Co., 1965.
     Joe Louis, pp. 228, 229, 230, 231, 266, 269.

161. Editors of Ebony. Ebony Pictorial History of Black
     America. Nashville, Tenn.: Southwestern Company, 1971.
     Volume II. Joe Louis, pp. 79, 222, 224-225, 229-230.

162. Edwards, Harry. The Struggle That Must Be: An
     Autobiography. New York: Macmillan Publishing Co.,
     1980. Joe Louis, pp. 27, 205.

163. Ellison, Mary. The Black Experiences: American Blacks
     Since 1865. New York: Harper & Row Publishers, Inc.,
     1974. Joe Louis, p. 144.

164. Embree, Edwin Rogers. 13 Against The Odds. New York:
     Viking Press, 1944. Joe Louis, pp. 534-545.

165. Fitzhugh, Harriet L. The Concise Biographical Diction-
     ary of Famous Men and Women. New York: Grosset &
     Dunlap, 1949. Joe Louis, pp. 798-799.

166. Fleischer, Nathaniel S. 50 Years At Ringside. New York:
     Fleet Publishing Corp., 1958. Joe Louis, pp. 4, 6, 80-
     81, 140-141, 146-155, 158, 171, 174, 176, 265, 273, 277,
     279-283. He states that Joe Louis would have stood out
     in any era, and his record as a heavyweight is one of
     the best.

167. _____. The Heavyweight Championship: An Informed
     History of Heavyweight Boxing From 1719 to the Present
     Day. New York: G. P. Putnam's Sons, 1949. Joe Louis,
     pp. 177, 203-205, 211, 221, 232, 233, 241-269.

168. Foner, Eric, Editor. America's Black Past: A Reader
     in Afro-American History. New York: Harper & Row,
     Publishers, 1970. Joe Louis, p. 390.

169. Franklin, John Hope. From Slavery to Freedom: A
     History of Negro Americans. New York: Alfred A.
     Knopf, 1980. Joe Louis, pp. 423, 443.

170. Frommer, Harvey. Sports Roots: How Nicknames,
     Namesakes, Trophies, Competitions, and Expressions in
     the World of Sports Came to Be. New York: Atheneum,
     1979, pp. 26, 28, 67, 76. States why Joe Louis was
     called "Brown Bomber," fought "Bum of the Month" and
     Louis' saying "He (Billy Conn) Can Run But He Can't
     Hide."

171. Galesworthy, Maurice. Encyclopaedia of Boxing.
     London: Robert Hale & Co., 1975. Joe Louis, pp. 17,

21, 34, 54, 61, 90, 132, 135, 142, 145, 147, 164, 186-188, 218, 236, 248. A short biographical sketch of Joe Louis is included in this work.

172.   Grombach, John V. The Saga of Sock: A Complete Story of Boxing. New York: A. S. Barnes and Co., 1949. Joe Louis, pp. 14, 16, 83-95, 120, 132, 164, 181-182, 193, 245, 257, 290.

173.   Henderson, Lenneal J., Jr. Black Political Life in the United States: A Fist as the Pendulum. San Francisco: Chandler Publishing Company, 1972. Joe Louis, p. 60.

174.   Heyn, Ernest V. Twelve Sport Immortals. New York: Bartholomew House, 1949. One section entitled "Brown Bomber, The Saga of Joe Louis" is included in this collection.

175.   Hirshberg, Al and Joe McKenney. Famous American Athletes of Today. Boston: L. C. Page & Co., 1947. Joe Louis, pp. 286, 358-360.

176.   Hughes, Langston, Milton Meltzer, and C. Eric Lincoln. A Pictorial History of Black Americans. New York: Crown Publishers, Inc., 1956. Joe Louis, p. 288.

177.   _____. A Pictorial History of the Negro American. New York: Crown Publishers, Inc., 1968. Joe Louis, pp. 288, 360, 372.

178.   Johnston, Alexander. Ten--and Out!--The Complete Story of the Prize Ring in America. New York: Ives Washburn, Publishers, 1936. Joe Louis, pp. 238-245, 329, 360.

179.   Kaese, Harold, et al. Famous American Athletes of Today. Boston: L. C. Page & Co., 1943. See LeRoy Atkinson, "Joe Louis: The Brown Bomber," pp. 133-167.

180.   Kamm, Herbert. The New Junior Illustrated Encyclopedia of Sports. Indianapolis: Bobbs-Merrill Co., 1975. Author states that there is no doubt that Joe Louis was one of the best-loved fighters ever to enter the ring, pp. 253-254.

181.   Levine, Lawrence W. Black Culture and Black Consciousness: Afro-American Folk Thought From Slavery to Freedom. Joe Louis, pp. 411, 420, 429, 433-438, 440; compared to Jack Johnson, 433; as representative figure, 433-436.

182.   Liebling, Abbott J. The Sweet Science. New York: Viking Press, 1956. Joe Louis, pp. 5, 6, 15, 25-47.

183. Lightfoot, Claude M. Ghetto Rebellion to Black Libera-
      tion. New York: International Publishers, 1968. Joe
      Louis, p. 182.

184. Low, Nat. The Negro in Sports. San Francisco, CA:
      Daily People's World, 1953(?). Joe Louis, pp. 3-5, 14,
      16.

185. Marsh, Irving T. and Edward Ehre, Editors. Best Sports
      Stories. New York: E. P. Dutton & Co., 1949. James
      P. Dawson, "Potent Punch Joe Louis," pp. 185-192.

186. _____. Best Sports Stories. New York: E. P.
      Dutton & Co., 1951. James P. Dawson, "Bomber Bombed
      (Joe Louis)," pp. 23-27.

187. _____. Best Sports Stories. New York: E. P.
      Dutton & Co., 1952. Joseph C. Nichols, "Joe Louis Was
      Knocked Out Last Night," pp. 211-213.

188. _____. Best Sports Stories. New York: E. P.
      Dutton & Co., 1966. Morris Siegel, "The Born Loser
      (Joe Louis)," pp. 144-146.

189. Maxwell, Jocko. Great Black Athletes. New York: Pendulum
      Press, 1981. Short biography of Joe Louis is included
      in this collection. It was pointed out that Louis
      had a brilliant amateur career in which he won 43 bouts
      by knockouts and 7 by decision, while losing 4.

190. McCallum, John D. The Encyclopedia of World Boxing
      Champions Since 1882. Radnor, PA: Chilton Books.
      Joe Louis, pp. 1-2, 17, 22, 35-36, 43, 45-53, 55, 58,
      75, 80, 86, 96, 103-107, 156-157, 166-167, 214, 298.

191. Martin, Fletcher. Our Great Americans: The Negro
      Contribution to American Progress. Chicago: Gamma
      Corp., 1954. Joe Louis, p. 58.

192. Matney, William C., Editor. Who's Who Among Black
      Americans, 1975-1976. Northbrook, IL: Who's Who
      Among Black Americans, Inc., 1976. Joe Louis, p. 396.

193. McAdam, Robert. Viva Gonzalez. Glendale, CA: Bourmar,
      1972, 63 pp. A short biography of Joe Louis is
      included. Written for young people.

194. McWhirter, Norris, et al. Guinness Book of Sports
      Records: Winners & Champions. New York: Sterling
      Publishing Co., 1980. Joe Louis held the longest
      reign of any world champion (any weight) for 11 years,
      8 months, 7 days. p. 66.

195. Menke, Frank G. The Encylcopedia of Sports. Garden
      City, NJ: Doubleday & Co., 1977. Joe Louis, pp. 273-
      274, 293.

196. _____. The All-Sports Record Book. New York: A.
      S. Barnes & Co., 1950. Writer discusses Joe Louis'
      title defense fights and Louis' ring earnings, 1934-
      1949, pp. 85, 92, 94.

197. Morsbach, Mabel. The Negro in American Life. New York:
      Harcourt, Brace & World, Inc., 1966. Joe Louis, pp.
      224, 225.

198. Myrdal, Gunnar. An American Dilemma: The Negro
      Problem and Modern Democracy. New York: Harper &
      Row, Publishers, 1944. Joe Louis, pp. 734, 903n,
      988, 1184, 1396.

199. Nagler, Barney. James Norris and The Decline of Boxing.
      Indianapolis: Bobbs-Merrill Co., 1964. Joe Louis,
      pp. 3-18, 34-59, 65, 73, 76-77, 81-84, 116-119, 143-
      144, 149-151, 156, 188, 248. Author discusses the
      rise and fall of Joe Louis and his financial problems.

200. Negro History in the Home, School, and Community: A
      Handbook, 1966. Washington, D. C.: Association for
      the Study of Negro Life and History, Inc., 1966, p. 40.
      Short biographical sketch of Joe Louis. It was stated
      that Joe Louis conducted himself as a gentleman in all
      situations.

201. Nelson, Robert L. The Negro in Athletics. New York:
      Bureau For Intercultural Education, 1940. Joe Louis,
      p. 11. Author states that Joe Louis was the first
      boxer to be chosen by the Associated Press Sports
      Writers as "The Outstanding American Athlete" (1935).

202. Oliver, Paul. The Blue Tradition. New York: Oak
      Publications, 1968. Section 5 is entitled "Joe
      Louis and John Henry," pp. 148-163.

203. Ottley, Roi. Black Odyssey: The Story of the Negro
      in America. London: John Murray, 1949. Joe Louis,
      pp. 261, 262, 270, 278.

204. Pratt, John Lowell and Jim Benagh. The Official
      Encyclopedia of Sports. New York: Franklin Watts,
      1964. Joe Louis, pp. 12, 89, 92, 93, 97, 98.

205. Quarles, Benjamin. The Negro in the Making of America.
      New York: Collier Books, 1964. Joe Louis, p. 246.

206. Redding, Saunders. They Came in Chains: Americans
      from Africa. Philadelphia: J. B. Lippincott Company,
      1950. Joe Louis, p. 290.

207. Rice, Grantland. The Tumult and the Shouting: My Life
      in Sports. New York: A. S. Barnes & Co., 1954. Joe
      Louis, pp. 133, 248, 249, 250.

208. Richardson, Ben. Great American Negroes. New York:
      Thomas Y. Crowell Co., 1945. Joe Louis, pp. 278-290.

209. Richardson, Ben and William A. Fahey. Great Black
      Americans. New York: Thomas Y. Crowell Co., 1976. Joe
      Louis, pp. 279, 289-299.

210. Robinson, Wilhelmena S. Historical Afro-American
      Biographies. New York: Publishers, 1968. Joe Louis,
      pp. 223-224.

211. Rogers, Joel A. World's Great Men of Color. Vol. 2.
      New York: J. A. Rogers, 1947. "Joe Louis: The
      Superman of the Prize Ring," pp. 530-534.

212. Rywell, Martin, Editor. Afro-American Encyclopedia.
      North Miami, FL: Educational Book Publishers, Inc.,
      1974. Joe "Brown Bomber" Louis, Vol. 5, pp. 1504-1505.

213. Santa Barbara County Board of Education. The Emerging
      Minorities in America. Santa Barbara, CA: American
      Bibliographical Center-Clio Press, 1972. Joe Louis,
      p. 53.

214. Silverman, Al. More Sports Titans of the 20th Century.
      New York: G. P. Putnam Sons, 1969. 224 pp. Joe
      Louis is included in this work.

215. Sitkoff, Harvard. A New Deal for Blacks: The Emergence
      of Civil Rights as a National Issue, Volume II: The
      Depression Decade. New York: Oxford University Press,
      1978. Joe Louis, p. 299.

216. Soderberg, Paul, et al. Compilers and Editors. The
      Big Book of Halls of Fame in the United States and
      Canada. New York: R. R. Bowker Co., 1977. Joe
      Louis, pp. 176, 775.

217. Synnestvedt, Sig. The White Response to Black Emanci-
      pation. New York: The Macmillan Company, 1972. Joe
      Louis, p. 161; defeats Max Schmeling, p. 145.

218. Talamini, John T. and Charles H. Page. Sport and
      Society: An Anthology. Boston: Little, Brown & Co.,
      1973. Joe Louis, pp. 250-255.

219. Thomas, Jesse O. My Story in Black and White. New
      York: Exposition Press, 1967. Joe Louis, pp. 143,
      152, 153.

220. Toppin, Edgar A. A Biographical History of Blacks in
      America Since 1528. New York: David McKay, 1971.
      Joe Louis, pp. 186, 241, 306, 354, 355, 356, 357, 358.

221. Van Deusen, John G. The Black Man in White America.
      Washington, D.C.: Associated Publishers, Inc., 1938.

Joe Louis, pp. 11, 239, 314.

222. Walton, Hanes. The Negro in Third-Party Politics.
Philadelphia: Dorrance Publishing Co., 1969. Joe Louis,
pp. 56-57. Author states that Joe Louis financially
and morally supported Henry A. Wallace and the
Progressive Party.

223. Weisboro, Robert G. Ebony Kinship: Africa, Africans,
and the Afro-American. Westport, Connecticut: Greenwood Press, Inc., 1973. Joe Louis, p. 96.

224. Wesley, Charles H. The Quest for Equality: From Civil
War to Civil Rights. New York: Publishers Co., 1976.
Joe Louis, p. 199.

225. Who's Who In America. Chicago: Marquis Who's Who,
Chicago, 1980: 41st Edition 1980-1981. Vol. 2, L-Z,
Joe Louis, p. 2070.

226. Wilson, W. Rollo. Fifty Years of Progress in the World
of Sports. Pittsburgh: Pittsburgh Courier, 1950.
Joe Louis, pp. 2-3. Author states that Joe Louis held
the heavyweight title for twelve years, longer than any
other fighter.

227. Young, A. S. "Doc." Negro First in Sports. Chicago:
Johnson Publishing Co., 1963. Joe Louis, pp. 5, 6, 8,
11, 15, 19, 20, 22, 24-25, 31, 33, 43-44, 98-100, 105-
115, 137, 163, 165, 178, 185, 191, 222, 225-228.

IV
Articles about Joe Louis

"We can't lose [World War II] because we're on God's side!"

Joe Louis

1. 1935

A. BOXER

228. Adams, Caswell, "Louis Bears Out Fan's Praise by
      Decisive Victory Over Brown," New York Herald Tribune,
      March 31, 1935.

229. Allen, Stookie, "Above the Crowd: Joe Louis, The Brown
      Bomber," New York Daily Mirror, Tuesday, April 2, 1935,
      p. 2.

230. "A New School of Etiquette: The Prize Ring," New York
      Sun, June 27, 1935.

231. Blackburn, Jack, "How I Trained Joe Louis to Beat
      Primo," Louisiana Weekly, July 27, 1935.

232. _____, "How I Trained Joe Louis to Beat Carnera,"
      Pittsburgh Courier, July 20, 1935; July 27, 1935.

233. "Braddock Selects Carnera on Points," New York World-
      Telegram, June 25, 1935.

234. Bradley, Hugh, "Louis Far From Crown," New York Post,
      June 26, 1935, p. 1.

235. "Brown Bomber Has Set Record: Rapidity of Louis' Rise
      to Fame Unparalleled in Ring Annals," New York Sun,
      June 25, 1935.

236. Brown, Earl, "'I Could Take Baer's Blows All Day'--
      Louis," New York Daily News, September 25, 1935.

237. "Brown Bomber Earns His Largest Purse, $333,994,"
      Jamaica (B.W.I.) Daily Gleaner, October 3, 1935.

238. "Brown, Swathed In Bandages Says Louis is a Terrific Hitter; 'Best Since Schmeling'--Experts," Journal and Guide, April 6, 1935.

239. Buck, Al, "Braddock is Bound by Garden Contract," New York Post, June 26, 1935.

240. _____, "Joe Louis Rests; Dreams of Title," New York Post, September 10, 1935.

241. _____, "Louis Wants Champ Next: Bomber to Get Either Schmeling or Baer," New York Post, June 27, 1935, p. 1.

242. Burchard, James A. "Doyle New Ring Killer (?): Irish Nightengale Amazes Fistic World with Shoulder Plexus Kayo in New York De-Boo." New York World-Telegram, June 25, 1935.

243. "Carnera Weighs 260½ Pounds . . . .: If the Colored Boy Scares Easily, 'He's in for a Fierce Night--,'" New York World-Telegram, June 25, 1935, p. 21.

244. "Carnera Will Win, Declared the Yanks," New York World-Telegram, June 25, 1935.

245. "Condition Perfect, Louis Eases Grind," New York Times, September 11, 1935, p. 29.

246. Cowans, Russell J, "Kid Ellis, Ex-Philly Pug, Trained Joe Louis," Afro-American, January 12, 1935.

247. _____, "Louis-Baer Fight Has Struck Fancy of Boxing Fans," Afro-American, September 21, 1935.

248. _____, "Writer Calls Joe Louis Tonic to Fight Game.'" Washington Tribute, April 20, 1935.

249. Dawson, James P. "Louis Favored to Triumph Over Carnera in Heavyweight," New York Times, June 24, 1935, p.2.

250. _____. "Louis Stops Baer in 4th At Stadium (Yankee) As 95,000 Look On," New York Times, September 25, 1935, pp. 1, 27.

251. _____, "70,000 See Louis Vanquish Carnera By Knockout in 6th," New York Times, June 26, 1935, p. 24.

252. Dayton, Alfred, "Louis Seeks Quick Knockout (Over Baer)," New York Sun, September 5, 1935.

253. Dougherty, Romeo L., "The Astuteness of the Managers of Joe Louis," New York Amsterdam News, July 6, 1935, p. 14.

254. "Experts Still Busy Sizing Up Ring Sensation: Joe Louis One Topic of Sidewalk Debating Clubs Today." New York

World-Telegram, June 26, 1935, p. 21.

255. "57,000 Fans Pay for Six Rounds of Louis," New York World-Telegram, June 26, 1935, p. 21.

256. "Fight Looked Good From Subway," New York Sun, June 26, 1935.

257. "Fight (Carnera-Louis) Sale Is Said To Be $200,000 Now," New York Sun, June 23, 1935.

258. "Fixers Want a Slice of Profits of Joe Louis But His Managers Say No," Afro-American, July 13, 1935.

259. Fleischer, Nathaniel, "Can Joe Louis Take It?" The Ring, Vol. 14, No. 9, October 1935, p. 3.

260. _____, "Louis' Rise Revives an Old Topic," The Ring, Vol. 14, No. 10, November, 1935, pp. 2-4, 49.

261. _____, "Max Is Knocked Out By Louis," The Ring, Vol. 14, No. 11, December, 1935, pp. 2-11, 15.

262. _____, "(Joe Louis) The Black Menace," The Ring, Vol. 14, No. 4, May, 1935, pp. 14-15, 45.

263. "Frothy Facts," New York World-Telegram, June 25, 1935.

264. "T. Galento's Promoters Seek Bout with Louis," New York Times, October 12, 1935, p. 22.

265. Gallico, Paul, "Aftermath: Max Is Slug-Stricken," New York Daily News, September 26, 1935.

266. _____, "Joe Louis: Husban-Executioner," Washington Post, September 25, 1935, pp. 18-19.

267. _____, "Plaintive Note: Who Tells Whom," New York Daily News, September 27, 1935.

268. "Geiger On Louis," Chicago Defender, January 5, 1935.

269. "Giants of Ring Have Not Been Fearsome Lot: Bigger They Are Harder They Fall Is Still Holding Good." New York World-Telegram, June 25, 1935.

270. Graham, Frank, "Setting the Pace: Boom--Boom--Boom--It's Deafening Now," New York Sun, September 16, 1935.

271. _____, "Setting the Pace: Jack and Gene Don't Believe It." New York Sun, December 16, 1935.

272. _____, "Setting the Pace: Paulino Comes to Journey's End," New York Sun, December 14, 1935.

273. _____, "Setting the Pace: The Chances Are He Can Take It," New York Sun, June 27, 1935.

274.   _____, "Setting the Pace: They're Coupling His Name With Dempsey's." New York Sun, June 26, 1935, p. 30.

275.   Grayson, Harry, "Dempsey Reveals He Will Second Baer Against Louis," New York World-Telegram, September 17, 1935.

276.   "Heavy-Weight Crown Now Worn By Max Baer Has Eyes of Louis; Depends on Bouts," Southern Broadcast, December 8, 1934.

277.   Hemingway, Ernest, "Million Dollar Fight (Between Max Baer and Joe Louis)," Esquire, December 5, 1935.

278.   "How The Brown Bombshell From Detroit, J. Louis, Beat Carnera," Daily Gleaner, July 3, 1935.

279.   "Ideal Fighter Stops Carnera," New York Post, June 26, 1935.

280.   Igoe, Hype, "Louis Should Develop Into Boxing's Greatest Hitter," New York Evening Journal, June 27, 1935, p. 31, ff.

281.   _____, "Maxie-Louis Bout Up To Doctors," New York Evening Journal, July 16, 1935.

282.   Inglis, William, "Can Louis Tame The Baer?" New York Tribune, September 22, 1935.

283.   "Irate Louis Pounds Partners In Drill," New York Times, September 12, 1935.

284.   "Jack Blackburn (Louis' Trainer) Challenges Jack Johnson's Statement Concerning Young Louis," Southern Broadcast, May 11, 1935.

285.   "Jacobs in Fear of Cuban Kidnappers (of Joe Louis). That's Real Reason Why Promoter Called Off Louis-Gastanaga Fight Scheduled For Havana," New York Sun, December 23, 1935.

286.   "Joe Louis a One-Man Revolution in Action," New York Daily News, December 5, 1935.

287.   "Joe Louis Did It. Can Ethiopia Do It?" New York Sun, June 27, 1935.

288.   "Joe Louis Gets Ready For Pirroni," Chicago Defender, December 29, 1934.

289.   "Joe Louis Is 2-17 Favorite to Defeat Carnera in N.Y." Chicago Defender, June 15, 1935.

290.   "Joe Louis: Knocked Down 7 Times, He Came Back For More," Afro-American, July 27, 1935.

291. "Joe Louis' Life Story Starts Tomorrow," New York Daily Mirror, April 2, 1935.

292. "Joe Louis: New Heavyweight Contender," New York Age, January 12, 1935.

293. "Joe Louis Ties Up Fight Fund in Washington, D.C.," Philadelphia Independent, September 8, 1935.

294. "Joe Louis Too Competent As a Fighter, Says (Heywood) Brown," Afro-American, July 6, 1935.

295. "Joe Louis Visits White House," Jamaica (B.W.I.) Daily Gleaner, September 6, 1935.

296. "Joe Louis Vs. O. Barry," New York Times, March 9, 1935.

297. "Joe Louis Vs. B. Benneh," New York Times, April 23, 1935, p. 29.

298. "Joe Louis Vs. H. Birkie," New York Times, January 12, 1935, p. 20.

299. "Joe Louis Vs. N. Brown," New York Times, March 30, 1935, p. 20.

300. "Joe Louis Vs. W. Davis," New York Times, May 4, 1935, p. 8.

301. "Joe Louis Vs. R. Lazar," New York Times, April 13, 1935, p. 18.

302. "Joe Louis Vs. L. Ramage," New York Times, February 22, 1935, p. 31.

303. "Joe Louis Vs. G. Stanton," New York Times, May 8, 1935, p. 26.

304. "Joe Louis Vs. R. Toles," New York Times, April 26, 1935, p. 26.

305. "Joe Louis Will Do No Boxing Today: Negro Heavyweight Floors Two Sparring Mates," New York Sun, June 30, 1935.

306. "Joe Louis Wins," Chicago Defender, June 29, 1935, p. 35.

307. "Johnson Only Negro to Win Heavy Crown: Louis Conceded Chance to Succeed Where Other Stars Failed," New York World-Telegram, June 25, 1935.

308. Johnson, Hugh S., "Johnson Points Out Moral In Louis Victory Over Baer," New York World-Telegram, September 30, 1935.

309. "(Jack) Johnson Only Negro To Win Heavy Crown: Louis Now Conceded a Chance To Succeed In Scaling Height," Philadelphia Tribune, June 27, 1935.

310. Langford, Sam, "Joe Louis Is Another Joe Gans," Chicago Defender, July 20, 1935.

311. Left, Straight, "Joe Louis Defeated Paulino Uzcudun Last Night in N.Y. By Technical K.O. in 4th Rd.," Jamaica (B.W.I.) Daily Gleaner, December 14, 1935.

312. Leonard, Lank, "Louis Revealed As Perfect Fistic Machine In Stopping Carnera," New York Sun, June 26, 1935.

313. Lewin, Murray, "Joe's Speed, Punch, Youth May Earn Him a Knockout (Over Carnera)," New York Daily Mirror, June 23, 1935.

314. Lewin, Murray, "Louis King Will Clash In Chicago," New York Daily Mirror, June 28, 1935.

315. Lewin, Murray, "Primo, Louis End Sparring Drills," New York Daily Mirror, June 24, 1935, p. 27.

316. "Louis Awarded Technical K.O. In 8th Round," Pittsburgh Courier, December 22, 1934.

317. "Louis Certain To Win Title States Primo," New York World-Telegram, June 26, 1935, p. 21.

318. "Louis Confident of Victory," New York Times, March 26, 1935, p. 26.

319. "Louis Hits Harder Than Baer, Carnera Declares," Afro-American, June 29, 1935, pp. 20-22.

320. "Louis Is Chosen Best Athlete In America," New York Daily, December 17, 1935.

321. "Louis Kayoes Red Barry In Three Rounds," Louisiana Weekly, March 16, 1935.

322. "Louis Knocks Out Pareda In The First Round," Afro-American, November 24, 1934.

323. "Louis Learns How to Feint," New York Post, September 17, 1935.

324. "Louis' Rise Spectacular One: Clouts Way From Crude Novice Into World's Outstanding Heavyweight In Three Years," New York Sun, June 26, 1935.

325. "Louis Scores Technical K.O. Over Carnera," Daily Gleaner, June 26, 1935.

326. "Louis Stops Lazer By K.O.," New York Amsterdam News, April 20, 1935, p. 32.

327. "Louis Too Rough With His Mates: Sparring Partners Rebel At Training Ordeal," New York Sun, 1935.

328. "Louis Tops Braddock in Rankings," New York Sun, December 30, 1935.

329. "Louis Trains," New York Times, September 21, 1935, p. 9.

330. "Louis Whips 8th Pro Foe,'" St. Louis Argus, October 26, 1934.

331. "Louis Wins (over Biff Bennett) In 75 Seconds," Boston Chronicle, April 27, 1935.

332. "Louis Won't Be Suspended (For Failure to Fight Isadoro Gastanaga)," New York Sun, December 20, 1935.

333. McLemore, Henry, "Outcome of Louis-Baer Bout Shown When Joe Hits Maxie Hard Wallop," New York World-Telegram, September 11, 1935.

334. Meany, Tom, "Carnera Is Still World Champion--As A Target!: Da Preem Bows Out Before Largest Fight Crowd In Years," New York World-Telegram, June 26, 1935, p. 21.

335. "Michigan's Governor (Frank D. Fitzgerald) Pens 'Literary Classic' To Joe On Evening of Big Battle," Pittsburgh Courier, June, 1935.

336. Miley, Jack, "A Vote for Primo!--And Baer Casts It," Daily News, June 10, 1935.

337. Mullin, Willard, "Louis Hopes To Take On Both Maxes Here This Fall: What Makes The Brown Bomb Tick," New York World-Telegram, June 27, 1935, p. 28.

338. Neil, Edward J., "Californian Counted Out On Knees After Negro Lands Right." Washington Post, September 25, 1935.

339. "Nicknames Coined Before and After Great Stadium Battle," Philadelphia Tribune, June 27, 1935.

340. Parker, Dan, "Blackburn Is Engaged As Trainer Of Joe Louis," Daily Mirror, April 6, 1935.

341. _____, "Joe Louis' Wardrobe Grows as Massera, Poreda Fall," Daily Mirror, April 8, 1935.

342. _____, "Louis Earns Over $18,000 For 5 Bouts As Fame Grows," Daily Mirror, April 10, 1935.

343. _____, "Louis Resembles Gans, Langford," New York
      Daily Mirror, April 12, 1935.

344. _____, "Louis Tells of Ring Bow: Joe Takes
      Pummeling In First Amateur Bout," New York Daily Mirror,
      Thursday, April 4, 1935.

345. Parton, Lemuel F., "Who's News Today: Behind the Build-
      Up of a Heavyweight Prize Fighter." The New York Sun,
      June 27, 1935.

346. Pegler, Westbrook, "Fair Enough: Plan to Stage Italian-
      Negro Prizefight at Very Door of Embittered Harlem is
      Called New High in Stupid Judgment," New York Sun,
      1935.

347. Perry, Lawrence, "Board is Urged to Make Louis Wear
      Pillows: Scheme to Handicap Boxing Superman by
      Different Sizes of Gloves," New York Sun, May 8, 1935.

348. Powers, Jimmy, "Baer Shouts Defi At Louis As He Leaves,"
      Daily News, September 27, 1935.

349. "Primo (Carnera) Has No Fear of Louis, Believes His
      Experience Will Offset Power of Negro's Punch,"
      New York Sun, June 24, 1935.

350. "Primo's Bones May Crumble His Erstwhile Manager Fears,"
      New York World-Telegram, June 25, 1935.

351. Reilly, Byron "Speed," "Baer Thinks Louis Great Fighter,
      Says He Did Not Let Color 'Howl,'" Journal and Guide,
      March 9, 1935.

352. "Grantland Rice Ranks Joe Second Only to Max Baer,"
      Washington Tribune, April 27, 1935.

353. Rice, Grantland, "The Sportlight: Carnera Crushed,"
      The New York Sun, June 26, 1935.

354. _____. "The Sportlight: The Answer Is 'Yes'!"
      New York Sun, June 27, 1935.

355. Rosa, Pat, "That Joe Louis! He Sure Can Hit! Mob
      Wonders, Can He Take It!" New York Post, July 26, 1935.

356. "Schmeling Watches Joe Louis in Workout," Pittsburgh
      Courier, December 14, 1935, p. 4.

357. "Seconds Allow Victor to Box In His Own Way," New
      York Sun, June 26, 1935.

358. "Sports Writers Chose Louis By Knockout," New York Times,
      September 15, 1935, p. 5.

359. Stewart, Walter, "Bomber Picked to Flatten Kingfish
      Levinsky in Chicago Scrap," New York World-Telegram,

August 6, 1935.

360.   _____, "Carnera Weighs 260-1/2 and Louis Makes
196: Doctor Says Both Battlers Are In Finer Trim Than
Were Braddock and Baer--Bomber Pulls a Wisecrack at
Gag of Primo's Aid," New York World-Telegram, June 25,
1935.

361.   _____, "Louis a Softy At Heart!" New York World-
Telegram, September 16, 1935.

362.   _____, "Louis Appears On Road To Rate With Ring's
Greatest: Promoters Frantically Seek To Get Bouts
For Joe Here," New York World-Telegram, June 26, 1935,
p. 21.

363.   _____, "Louis-Baer Battle Expected to Break New
York Record For Crowd and Gate," New York-World
Telegram, September 20, 1935.

364.   _____, "Louis Laughs, And How! As Tigers Rally,"
New York World-Telegram, September 13, 1935.

365.   _____, "Louis' Manager Will Seek Sealed Vote,
With Ballots Dropped After Each Round," New York
World-Telegram, September 11, 1935.

366.   "The Fight-Blow By Blow," Washington Post, September 25,
1935.

367.   "The Louis Brand of Dynamite," Sunday News, September
29, 1935.

368.   "This Primo Victory . . . Makes Joe Think . . . So
Does This Defeat," New York World-Telegram, June 25,
1935.

369.   "Trainer (Jack Blackburn) Says Louis Could Whip Jack
Johnson In His Prime," Washington Tribune, May 11,
1935.

370.   Turcott, Jack, "A Step Toward Fame: 2 to 1 Offered
Lee Would Last Route vs. Louis," New York Daily News,
October 14, 1935.

371.   _____, "But 64 Kayoes Made Folks Change Their
Minds," New York Daily News, October 9, 1935.

372.   _____, "Joe Louis Called Sissy As Boy," New
York Daily News, October 9, 1935, p. 68.

373.   _____, "Joe Louis Gave Up Fiddling For Fighting!"
New York Daily News, October 10, 1935, pp. 73, 76.

374.   _____, "Joe Louis Repeated K.O. Over Ramage,"
New York Daily News, October 16, 1935.

375. _____, "Louis Calm, Baer Scared Before Fight,"
      New York Daily News, October 18, 1935.

376. _____, "Louis Got $50 for Professional Debut,"
      New York Daily News, October 11, 1935.

377. _____, "Louis Inherited Strength," New York Daily
      News, October 15, 1935.

378. _____, "Louis K.O.'s His First Big Shot," New
      York Daily News, October 12, 1935.

379. _____, "Primo a Target for Louis!" New York Daily
      News, October 17, 1935.

380. Uhlmann, Gus, "Reports by Pack Train from Distant
      Reaches of Yankee Stadium: Man Who Picked Both
      Braddock and Louis Sees, Hears Fight," New York Post,
      July 26, 1935.

381. Van Every, Edward, "Baer-Louis Sale Is $400,000," New
      York Sun, September 11, 1935.

382. _____, "Basque Praises Conqueror," New York Sun,
      December 14, 1935.

383. _____, "Deny Louis Is Growing Stale," New York Sun,
      September 10, 1935.

384. _____, "Louis Devoid of Imagination: Coming Bout
      with Baer Is Just Another Fight to Sensational Ring
      Robot," New York Sun, September 4, 1935.

385. _____, "Louis Is Almost a Langford: Trainer
      Blackburn Says Joe Needs Two More Bouts to Reach Peak
      of Greatness," New York Sun, September 25, 1935.

386. _____, "Louis Turns Down Fortune: Ring Robot,
      Whose Aim Is above Money, Is Not Permitted to Peddle
      Signature," New York Sun, June 24, 1935.

387. _____, "No Color Line Says Braddock: Manager
      Holds Champion's Last Year, Like Louis', Was Impressive,"
      New York Sun, June 28, 1935.

388. _____, "Where Louis Gets His Punch: Something in
      Negro's Muscular Equipment Gives His Blows Tremendous
      Recoil," New York Sun, July 1, 1935.

389. Van Ness, Fred, "Detroit Heavyweight Seeks to Correct
      Minor Faults as He Drills Indoors," New York Times,
      September 17, 1935, p. 30.

390. _____, "Louis Outpoints Brown in Detroit: Heavy-
      weight Sensation Gains 17th Victory in a Row before
      13,000 Fans," New York Times, March 29, 1935, p. 20.

391. _____, "Louis Practices Counter Punching," New York Times, September 15, 1935, p. 5.

392. _____, "Louis Victory Seen as Boon to Boxing: Experts Hail Detroiter," New York Times, September 24, 1935, pp. 1, 7.

393. Vidmer, Richards, "All Louis Needs to Wear Crown Is Chance to Win It, Experts Feel: Boxing Leaders Acclaim Negro's Victory as Boon to Long-Suffering Sport," Daily Gleaner, July 3, 1935.

394. _____, "Richards Vidmer's Classic Comment on Joe Louis," Pittsburgh Courier, July 6, 1935.

395. Wallace, Francis, "'Tis Title Tilt Tonight: Milanese Mastodon Matches Might Muscles Against Inky Iceberg in--Aw, Nuts!" New York World-Telegram, June 25, 1935.

396. Washington, Chester ("Chess"), "Frank Sutton, Who Helped (Jack) Johnson Before Title Fight, to Be Dietitian in Joe Louis Camp," Pittsburgh Courier, April 6, 1935.

397. _____, "New Heavyweight Hope Looms on Fistic Horizon," Pittsburgh Courier, December 22, 1935.

398. "'Watch Joe Louis,' Warns Jimmy Johnston," Pittsburgh Courier, January 12, 1935.

399. Williams, Joe, "Black Menance on Louis 'Sucker for a Left Hand' And He's No Langford," New York World-Telegram, September 17, 1935.

400. _____, "Carnera Quits to Louis: Let's Hope It's for Keeps; Negro Repeats Baer Act," New York World-Telegram, June 26, 1935, p. 21.

401. _____, "If Two Maxes Are Signed Garden Strenghens Hand Hearst Faces Boxing War," New York World-Telegram, July 16, 1935.

402. _____, "Negro Star on the Spot; Louis by Early Kayo, or--Carnera to Outmaul Him," New York World-Telegram, June 25, 1935.

403. _____, "Saw Only Half of Louis! So Chicago Expert Says Unnatural Against Freak," New York World-Telegram, June 27, 1935.

404. _____, "What if Louis Connects--and Mr. Baer Stays Up? The Negro Can Still Win," New York World-Telegram, September 6, 1935.

405. "Wills Says Joe Louis Should Kayo Carnera," New York Daily News, June 14, 1935.

406. Wood, Wilbur, "Bans Baer's Fist Protector: Louis Will Not Approve Any Request Max Be Allowed to Wear Special Device," New York Sun, September 17, 1935.

407. _____, "Bomber Has Made $371,645," New York Sun, December 17, 1935.

408. _____, "Experts Dubious Louis," New York Sun, August 2, 1935.

409. _____, "His Defense Good as Attack: Brown Bomber Probably Could Have Ended It Earlier Had He Cared to Take Gamble," New York Sun, June 26, 1935.

410. _____, "His Fighting Nearly Perfect: Bomber's Only Mistake Was in Dropping Guard too Soon as Bell Ended Second," New York Sun, December 8, 1935.

411. _____, "Louis Is Strongest Ring Card: His Allegiance Gives Mike Jacobs Edge Over Garden, Though Letter Has Champion," New York Sun, July 6, 1935.

412. _____, "Louis Never Forfeits Poise," New York Sun, September 12, 1935.

413. _____, "Louis Real Brown Panther," New York Sun, December 16, 1935.

414. _____, "Louis' Ring Earnings Already Average $3,071 a Round," New York Sun, December 17, 1935.

415. _____, "Louis Tabbed as Future Great: Brown Bomber May Go Down in Boxing History as Ring Marvel of All-Time," New York Sun, August 9, 1935.

416. _____, "Schmeling Gets an Eyeful," New York Sun, December 14, 1935.

417. Wright, Richard, "Joe Louis Uncovers Dynamite," Daily World, October 8, 1935.

418. _____, "Joe Louis Uncovers Dynamite," New Masses, October, 1935.

419. "Writers Pick Louis to Stop Baer; Early Finish Is Forecast by Poll," New York Times, September 15, 1935, p.5.

420. Young, P. Bernard, "Louis Tells Guide Reporter Carnera Didn't Hurt a Bit," Journal and Guide, June 29, 1935.

421. "Young Joe Is Jinx to Perroni, Hans Next," Pittsburgh Courier, January 12, 1935, p. 25.

B. FAMILY

422. Brooks, Mrs. Lillie and John McNulty, "Joe's Behavior Mother's Care," New York Daily Mirror, June 7, 1935.

423. _____, "Joe in Church Sunday Under Mother's Care," New York Daily Mirror, July 8, 1935.

424. _____, "Joe's Mother Fighter, Too," New York Daily Mirror, June 24, 1935.

425. _____, "Mother Cooks for Joe, Tells How She Prepares Cornbread, Steak," New York Daily Mirror, July 1, 1935.

C. FOLK HERO

426. Abramson, J. P., "1st Big N.Y. Mixed Bout Draws 15,000 Negroes and 1,300 Police," New York Herald Tribune, June 23, 1935.

427. Cooke, Marvel, "Mrs. Paul Robeson, Manager and Mate (of Paul Robeson)," New York Amsterdam News, October 5, 1935, p. 9. States that Paul Robeson and Africans in London almost went wild when Joe Louis defeated Max Baer in 1935.

428. Cowans, Russell, J., "Detroit Looks to Joe Louis to Pull Its Fight Game Out," Chicago Defender, November 10, 1935.

429. _____, "Joe Louis Fan Mail Comes from Australia, Philipines and China," Afro-American, November 9, 1935.

430. _____, "Louis-Baer Fight Has Struck Fancy of Boxing Fans," Afro-American, September 21, 1935.

431. "East Eyes Joe Louis, New Negro Heavy Hope," Louisiana Weekly, December 29, 1935.

432. Editorial, "Joe Louis a Good Example," Chicago Defender, July 13, 1935.

433. Gibson, Bill, "Live Clean Life, Louis Advises Ring Hopefuls," Afro-American, June 15, 1935.

434. "Harlem Celebrates in Friendly Way: Crowds Along Lenox Avenue, While Somewhat Noisy, Make Police Laugh with Their Horseplay," New York Sun, June 26, 1935.

435. "'He'll Stand Wtih Kings,'--Amen Congregation Greets
      Joe Louis," New York World-Telegram, September 30, 1935.

436. "How Proud Should We Be of Joe Louis' Victory?" Afro-
      American, July 6, 1935 , p. 4.

437. "Joe Louis: Symbol of Equality," Black Dispatch,
      September 28, 1935.

438. Johnson, Hugh. Johnson Points Out Moral in Louis
      Victory Over Baer," New York World-Telegram, September
      30, 1935.

439. Lane, French. "Joe Louis Looms As World's Heavyweight
      Menace," Journal and Guide, January 5, 1935.

440. Lee, George, "Sporting Around: 'Poker Face' Joe
      Louis Is the Greatest Amateur Fighter in the World,"
      Chicago Defender, April 21, 1935.

441. "Louis Cheered by Crowd in Church: Boxer Is Hailed as
      Excellent Example of Clean Living Habits," Washington
      Post, September 29, 1935.

442. McMillan, Allan, "Joe Louis Drew Fans From All Sections
      to New York," Chicago Defender, July 13, 1935.

443. Mitchell, Joseph, "Harlem Argues Itself to Sleep About
      Joe Louis and How He'll Tear the Stadium to Pieces
      Tonight," New York World-Telegram, June 25, 1935.

444. _____ , "Harlem Is Wild About Joe Louis, Don't
      Folks Here Sleep? He Asks," New York World-Telegram,
      June 26, 1935, p. 1, ff.

445. "New 'Black Hope' Looms on Heavyweight Fistic Horizon:
      Joe Louis Newest Fistic 'Hope'," Pittsburgh Courier,
      December 22, 1935.

446. "No Race Riot," New York Age, July 6, 1935.

447. Perry, Lawrence, "Harlem Elite in Pilgrimage to Hail
      Louis," New York Sun, June 10, 1935.

448. "Police Appeal Defers Harlem Fete for Louis: 20,000
      in Lenox Avenue Wait Hour for Victor; Tongue-tied
      upon Arrival," New York Herald Tribune, June 23, 1935.

449. Poston, Tom R., "The Fan Didn't Riot! Tch! Tch! Mr.
      Pegler," New York Amsterdam, June 29, 1935.

450. Stewart, Walter, "Wedding Suit Bothers Joe Louis More
      Than Style of Fight Baer Will Put Up," New York World-
      Telegram, September 11, 1935.

451.   Van Every, Edward, "Louis Aspires to More Than Boxing
        Honors: Ring Robot's Sponsors Bind Him to Be Model
        for Negro Race," New York Sun, June 17, 1935.

452.   Wallace, Francis, "Brewing Storm Breaks as Crowd Yells
        With Joy: All Emotions Released as Explosion Finds Only
        Primo's Chin," New York World-Telegram, June 26, 1935,
        p. 21.

453.   Williams, Joe, "Kingfish Levinsky Versus Louis, No
        Racial Test--Good!: Old White Hope Speaks," New York
        World-Telegram, August 5, 1935.

454.   _____, "Louis Is New Harlem Rage: Negro Heavy
        Here for Go. May Equal Jonson's Rise," New York
        World-Telegram, May 16, 1935.

455.   Winsten, Archer, "There's Only Joy in Harlem as Joe
        Louis Is Acclaimed: Wildest Night Ever Climaxed as
        Boxer Faces 'Mike'--And Says Not a Word!" New York Post,
        June 26, 1935.

456.   Wood, Wilbur, "Louis Iceberg in Ring or Out: Bomber
        Abhors Flattery and Flatterers and Girls Don't Interest
        Him," New York Sun, August 12, 1935.

D.   PERSONAL LIFE

457.   Allen, Cleveland, "East Hears Louis Seeks
        Divorce from His Wife," Chicago Defender, April 28, 1935,
        p. 8.

458.   Ferguson, Edna and Rosaleen Doherty, "Louis' Bride's
        Happy--P.S.: and Maxie's Too," New York Daily News,
        September 26, 1935.

459.   Burchard, James A., "Louis Will Fight Every Night--
        With Arithmetic," New York Post, June 26, 1935.

460.   "Brown Bomber Buys Xmas Seals," Pittsburgh Courier,
        December 14, 1935.

461.   "Following Joe Louis Around the City: From Ringside
        to Bedside," Chicago Defender, July 13, 1935.

462.   Hall, George, "Reporters Storm Love Nest of Joe and
        Bride," Philadelphia Tribune, September 26, 1935.

463.   Jacobs, Frank, "Louis, Bride Depart, Harlem All Forlorn,"
        Sunday News, September 29, 1935.

464.   "Joe Louis Buys $12,500 Building Out in Chicago,"
        Journal and Guide, October 12, 1935.

465.   "Joe Louis to Represent Michigan at Economic Confab
        Here Sept. 26," Philadelphia Independent, September 8,
        1935.

466. "Joe Louis Called Sissy As Boy," Daily News, October 9, 1935.

467. "Joe Louis Delights to Play with Children When Leisure Permits: Thinks the Practice Will Aid Him as Family Man," New York Amsterdam News, October 19, 1935.

468. "Joe Louis Statue and Ash Tray," Pittsburgh Courier, December 14, 1935, p. 4.

469. "Joe Louis' Sweetheart Buys Gowns From Colored (Mae's Dress Shoppe) Shop," Philadelphia Tribune, September 19, 1935.

470. Jones, Julia B., "Joe and I Belong to the Public," Pittsburgh Courier, December 7, 1935, p. 9.

471. Kenney, George, "Kidnap Fear Halts Louis' Cuba Bout," New York Daily News, December 24, 1935, p. 32.

472. Lane, French, "Joe Louis Never Changes Expression When Fighting: Poker Face Stays with Detroit Lad," Chicago Tribune, December 27, 1935.

473. Lardner, John, "Joe Louis Sleeps and Sleeps But He's Happy, Family Say So: Bomber Doesn't Know What to Do with All His New Wealth," New York Post, June 27, 1935.

474. McLemore, Henry, "Negro Heavy Receives All Sorts of Get-Rich Quick Plans, But Passes Them By," New York World-Telegram, September 6, 1935.

475. Mitchell, Jonathan, "Joe Louis Never Smiles," New Republic, October 9, 1935, pp. 239-240.

476. "Movies Okayed, Fighters' Bit Is Increased: Louis-Primo Film Was Taken After All, Mike Jacobs Reveals." New York World-Telegram, June 29, 1935.

477. Nunn, William G. and Chester L. Washington, "The Life Story of Joe Louis," Pittsburgh Courier, April 6, 1935; April 20, 1935; March 2, 1935; March 16, 1935; March 23, 1935; March 30, 1935.

478. Turcott, Jack, "Joe Louis Gave Up Fiddling for Fighting!" New York Daily News, October 19, 1935.

479. Van Every, Edward, "Brown Bomber Is Cool Baseball Fan," New York Sun, September 13, 1935.

2.   1936

A.   BOXER

480.   Adams, Caswell, "Louis Likely to Dominate Boxing Again," New York Herald Tribune, January 16, 1936.

481.   "Al Ettore's Charges Smashed by Joe's Power Blasts," Pittsburgh Courier, September 26, 1936, Section Two, p. 5.

482.   "Argentine Boxer Proves Only Chopping Block for Chocolate Soldier," Winnipeg (Canada) Free Press, October 10, 1936.

483.   "As the Doctors Declared Them Fit and Ready," New York Sun, June 19, 1936.

484.   Baron, A. I., "Says Joe Will Win Title, Retire Unbeaten to Farm," Afro-American, July 25, 1936.

485.   "Beating Hurt Joe, Says Braddock," New York Sun, June 23, 1936.

486.   Berger, Meyer, "Portrait of a Strong, Very Silent Man: Joe Louis, Whose Strength Is in His Wallop, Is Already a Champion at Saying Nothing," New York Times Magazine, June 14, 1936, pp. 1-4.

487.   "Big Guns of Joe Louis Pound (Al) Ettore into Helpless Submission," Pittsburgh Courier, September 26, 1936, Section Two, p. 5.

488.   "Black Bomber's Target: Max Schmeling," Hamilton (Canada) Spectator, June 19, 1936.

489.   "Blackburn Says Louis Is Not a Born Killer," Honolulu Advertiser, June 18, 1936.

490.   Blackwell, Lincoln, "Experience and Schmeling's 'Gamule' Defeated Joe Louis," Louisville (KY) Defender, June 27, 1936.

491.   "Bomber Clean Boxer, He Says, Rapping Yussel Jacobs," New York Amsterdam News, June 6, 1936.

492.   "Bomber Does Some Boxing with Mates," Chicago Defender, May 16, 1936.

493.   "'Bomber' Is 10-1 Choice to Win Chicago Contest: Negro Hopes to Score 23rd K.O. in 27 Fights," Schenectady (N.Y.) Gazette, January 17, 1936.

494.   "Bomber Kayoes Sharkey in 3rd," New York Daily News, August 19, 1936.

495. "Bomber May Down Maxie (Schmeling)," New York Amsterdam News, October 31, 1936.

496. "Bomber Sees Max As Real Tough Rival," Chicago Defender, May 2, 1936, p. 1.

497. "Bomber Still Explodes His Special Dynamite," New York Amsterdam News, October 19, 1936.

498. "Bomber 10 to One Choice Over Rival in Contest Tonight," Ithaca (N.Y.) Journal, January 17, 1936.

499. "Bomber to Explode Dynamite Quickly on Al Ettore at Phila.," New York Amsterdam News, September 19, 1936.

500. "Bomber-Uhlan Clash in New York Tonight Will Draw Gate of $750,000," Butte (Montana) Daily Post, June 19, 1936.

501. "Both Fighters End Training in Fine Shape," Detroit Free Press, January 16, 1936.

502. Bowker, Joe, "Joe Louis is Too Tough for Len Harvey," Empire (London) News, December 27, 1936.

503. "Boxing Rancher Pits His Hopes on Right to Jaw," Idaho (Boise) Statesman, January 16, 1936.

504. Braddock, James J., "The World's Champion Picks-- Joe Louis to Beat Max Schmeling," This Week, June 14, 1936, pp. 10-11.

505. "Braddock Attends Joe Louis' Birthday Party," Detroit Free Press, May 14, 1936.

506. "Braddock Given Aid by Johnson: Lil' Arthur to Train Him for Louis Go," New York Amsterdam News, January 4, 1936.

507. "'Braddock K.O.'s Joe Louis' In Talk, However, in Florida," Chicago Defender, February 1, 1936.

508. "Braddock Says Louis Has Reached Peak of Trainings." New York Times, January 27, 1936, p. 24.

509. Bradley, Hugh, "Customers Must Be Wrong in Opinion on Tonight's Fight," New York Post, August 18, 1936.

510. _____, "Ettore Valor Wins Praise Unmarred by Louis' Great Show," New York Post, September 23, 1936, p. 1.

511. Brancher, Bill, "This May Be the Shower Before the Storm For Max," Davenport (Iowa) Democrat and Leader, June 3, 1936.

512. Brietz, Eddie, "Bout Delayed Until Tonight by Rainstorm," San Diego (California) Union, June 19, 1936.

513. _____, "Louis to Clash with Argentine," Winston-Salem (N.C.) Journal, October 9, 1936.

514. _____, "Max and Joe Will Meet June 18,' Colorado Springs Gazette, April 21, 1936.

515. _____, "Schmeling to Be Offered as Another Sacrifice to Louis," Duluth (Minn.) News-Tribune, June 18, 1936.

516. Brown, Heywood, "Joe Looks Pretty Languid, Jack Sharkey Even More So, Bomber's Victory Routine. Two Tired Business Men," New York World-Telegram, August 20, 1936.

517. Brown, Ned, "Boxing War Perile Ties Louis' Chance at Title," National Police Gazette, Vol. 143, No. 11, November, 1936, p. 8.

518. _____, "Who Can Lick Louis Now!" National Police Gazette, Vol. 143, No. 9, September, 1936, p. 2.

519. "Brown Bomber and Opponent Scrap Friday: Fifteen Rounder," Augusta (Georgia) Herald, January 16, 1936.

520. "Brown Bomber Asserts Ready," The State (Columbia, S.C.), January 16, 1936.

521. "Brown Bomber Is Honored--Gets Belt Signifying Position in Game," New York Amsterdam News, May 16, 1936.

522. "Brown Bomber Nets $150,000 in 27 Fights," Journal and Guide, July 20, 1936.

523. "Brown Embalmer Rest Until June: Managers Agree Louis Needs Rest Before Meeting Schmeling," San Antonio Express, January 19, 1936.

524. "Brown Foresees Louis as Champ: Points to Rebirth of Game Since Advent," New York Amsterdam News, January 4, 1936.

525. Brumby, Bob, "It's Long Road Back, Louis' Boxing Shows," Daily News, August 13, 1936.

526. Buck, Al, "Blood's Lone Sharkey Woe, Begs Medicos to Stay Away," New York Post, August 15, 1936.

527. _____, "Bomber's Out for Landon Tigers, Ettore to Place 2nd," New York Post, September 14, 1936.

528. _____, "Brescia Bout to Fill Hipp, But No Bets Can Be Found," New York Post, October 8, 1936.

529. _____, "Brescia Go Not Threat with Ettore K.O. Victim," New York Post, September 23, 1936.

530. _____, "Garden Okays Jacobs' Terms," New York Post, December 31, 1936.

531. _____, "Result Break for Schmeling," New York Post, August 19, 1936.

532. _____, "Well, Anyway, Louis, Sharkey and Mike Jacobs Are Satisfied," New York Post, August 17, 1936.

533. Burton, Lewis, "Mike Jacobs Plans Louis, Baer Battle," Detroit Sunday Times, June 21, 1936.

534. Cameron, Stuart, "Argue Farmer Hits Harder Than Any of Louis' Previous Foes; 15-Round Bout Scheduled Tonight in Chicago," Baton Rouge State Times, January 17, 1936.

535. _____, "Detroit Bomber Says 'At Guy Just Couldn't Take It' After Finish," Sacramento Bee, January 18, 1936.

536. _____, "Joe Louis Scores One Round Victory," Freemont (Nebraska) Evening Tribune, January 18, 1936.

537. _____, "Little Chance Given to Foe of Bomber," Washington Herald, January 17, 1936.

538. _____, "Louis Hangs Up Easy Knockout," The Punxsutawney (Pa.) Spirit, January 18, 1936.

538a. _____, "Odds Say 3 to 1 Charley Retzlaff Will BE Initiated in Heavyweight Battle at Chicago Tomorrow Night," Baton Rouge State Times, January 16, 1936.

539. _____, "Retzlaff Hopes to 'Connect'," San Francisco Chronicle, January 16, 1936.

540. _____, "Scribes of Opinion Joe Louis Will Send Charlie Retzlaff to Showers Within Five Rounds," Punxsutawney (Pa.) Spirit, January 17, 1936.

541. Cavagnaro, Bob, "Schmeling Elated at Unexpected Victory," Helena (Montana) Daily Independent, June 20, 1936.

542. "Champ Says Bomber Has Real Punch," Chicago Defender, May 23, 1936.

543. Ching, Harold, "Another Victory for Louis," Hawaii Press, June 18, 1936.

544. "Claim Bomber Will Conquer Foeman Early," Detroit Free Press, January 18, 1936, p. 1.

545. Collins, Bill, "I Didn't Know What Hit Me . . . Retzlaff," Austin (Tex.) Dispatch, Janaury 18, 1936.

546. "Comfort Theme For Louis' Bout," New York Amsterdam News, May 9, 1936.

547. Coe, Charles Francis, "Joe Is Back! Clear-Cut Knockout of Kid Psychology Convinces Coe," New York World-Telegram, August 19, 1936.

548. "Comments on Louis-Sharkey Prospects," New York Times, August 9, 1936, p. 7, sec. 5.

549. Cook, Alton, "Tom Manning Makes a Hit: Broadcasting of Brief Joe Louis-Eddie Sims Fight Makes Good Impression," New York World-Telegram, December 15, 1936.

550. Corum, Bill, "And He'll Be Champion Before HE Is 34," Detroit Evening Times, August 19, 1936.

551. _____, "Sports: The Bomber Can Still Bomb," New York Evening Journal, August 17, 1936.

552. Cuddy, Jack, "German Deals Crushing Defeat to 'Unbeatable' Louis in Amazing Upset," Peoria (Ill.) Transcript, June 20, 1936.

553. _____, "Joe Louis Is Knocked Out by Max Schmeling," Honolulu Advertiser, June 20, 1936.

554. _____, "Little Betting on Big Fight," Los Angeles Times, June 4, 1936.

555. _____, "Max Schmeling Looks Bad in Training," Denver (Colorado) Rocky Mountain News, June 4, 1936.

556. _____, "Title Chance Is Seen Likely for Winner Tonight," Hawaii Press, June 18, 1936.

557. Dawson, James P., "Crowd of 5,200 Sees Louis Knock Out Brescia in Third Round at Hippodrome," New York Times, October 19, 1936, p. 22.

558. _____, "Delay Is Expected to Help Fight Gate," New York Times, June 19, 1936, p. 24.

559. _____, "Ring Rivals Ready for Stadium Clash," New York Times, August 18, 1936, p. 22.

560. _____, "Schmeling and Louis End Training, Both in Fine Condition for Fight," New York Times, June 17, 1936.

561. Dayton, Alfred, "Bomber Wants Quick Victory," New York Sun, June 17, 1936.

562. _____, "Manager Says Delay Helps Schmeling," New York Sun, June 17, 1936.

563. _____, "Dempsey Was Not in Class of Joe Louis," New York Amsterdam News, January 18, 1936.

564. "Detroit Bomber Predicts Quick Victory Friday," Fort Smith (Arkansas) Times Record, January 16, 1936.

565. "Detroit Negro 5-1 Favorite to Top German," Butte (Montana) Daily Post, June 18, 1936.

566. "Did (Charley) Retzlaff Call Joe a Dirty Name?" Afro-American, Janaury 25, 1936.

567. Duffy, Edward P., "Is Louis Sport's Superman?" New York Sun, January 30, 1936.

568. Dunkley, Charles, "Brown Bomber Is Ready For Retzlaff Bout," Sioux City (Iowa) Journal, January 16, 1936.

569. _____, "Bomber Is Favored to Ruin Rival," New Haven Journal-Courier, January 17, 1936.

570. _____, "Dakotan Says He Is Ready for Big Test: Not Afraid of Negro Fighter's Lethal Blows, He Declares," Georgia Journal, January 12, 1936, p. 1.

571. _____, "Detroit Bomber Gets Quick K.O. 1" Morning Oregonian (Portland), January 18, 1936.

572. _____, "Heavyweight Bout Tonight Promies to Attact 20,000," Calgary Daily Herald, January 17, 1936.

573. _____, "Louis Ends Battle in One Round," Salt Lake (City, Utah) Tribune, January 18, 1936.

574. _____, "Louis Has Never Tried 'Sunday Punch' on Foe," Worcester Evening Post, January 16, 1936.

575. _____, "Retzlaff Has Opportunity to Deliver Million-Dollar Punch in Bout with Louis," Buffalo Courier-Express, January 12, 1936.

576. _____, "Retzlaff to Test Dynamite of Joe Louis Tonight: Bomber 10 to 1 Favorite in Boxing Battle," Sioux City (Iowa) Journal, January 17, 1936.

577. Dyer, Braven, "The Sports Parade: Tossing Retzlaff in with Louis Means Sudden Death for Joe's Foe Tonight," Los Angeles Times, January 17, 1936.

578. Edgar, W. W., "Bomber Scores Quickest Kayo of His Pro Career," Detroit Free Press, January 18, 1936.

579. _____, "Experts Think Opening Punch May End Fight," (Springfield) Illinois State Register, January 17, 1936.

580. _____, "Louis Favored to Knock Schmeling Out in Early Round," Detroit Free Press, June 18, 1936.

581. _____, "The Second Guess," Detroit Free Press, June 18, 1936.

582. _____, "Max Fists Reveal Bomber's Feets of Clay," Detroit Free Press, June 21, 1936.

583. _____, "Joe Was Cocky, Pilots Reveal," Detroit Free Press, June 21, 1936.

584. _____, "Sharkey Added to Louis' List of Badly Beaten Victims," Detroit Free Press, August 19, 1936.

585. _____, "The Second Guess--the Condemned Man Speaks," Detroit Free Press, January 17, 1936.

586. _____, "The Second Guess--Mike Jacobs' Fanfare Would Surprise Even Tex," Detroit Free Press, June 19, 1936.

587. Edmond, George, "Weakness of Foes Fails to Detract from Louis' Fame," St. Paul (Minn.) Dispatch, June 18, 1936.

588. "Editorial in Dixie Daily (Raleigh, N.C.) News and Observer) Lauds Jesse Owens, Joe Louis," Pittsburgh Courier, September 5, 1936, Section Two, p. 4.

589. Editorial. "Joe Louis," Louisville (KY) Defender, June 27, 1936.

590. "Expect Record Indoor Gate for Louis - Retzlaff Battle," Charleston (S.C.) News and Courier, January 17, 1936.

591. "Experts on Fight Adhere to Views," Salt Lake Tribune, June 21, 1936.

592. "Experts String with Joe Louis After Sharkey Win," Chicago Defender, August 29, 1936.

593. "Forget Braddock Now, Louis Managers Plead," New York Amsterdam News, May 23, 1936.

594. Gallico, Paul, "What If Joe Gets Smacked? Gallico Worries for the Brown Bomber," Detroit Free Press, January 16, 1936.

595. "German Writer Says Louis Defeat Needed by Nordics," Chicago Defender, October 3, 1936.

596. Goodman, Murray., "Kayo Follows Big Attack By Loser," Detroit Evening Times, October 10, 1936.

597.   Gould, Alan, "Bout to be Held Friday in New York: Joe
       Is 10 to 1 Favorite," Davenport (Iowa) Daily Times,
       June 18, 1936.

598.   _____, "Detroit Bomber Is Knocked Out by Max
       in Twelfth Round," Winnipeg (Canada) Free Press, June
       20, 1936.

599.   _____, "Negro Is Heavy Favorite against Teuton
       Fighter," Joplin (Missouri) News Herald, June 19, 1936.

600.   _____, "Schmeling Knocks Out Louis in 12th,"
       The Ottawa (Canada) Citizen, June 20, 1936.

601.   _____, "$600,000 Gate Is Seen for Joe Louis--
       Max Schmeling Bout," Davenport (Iowa) Daily Times,
       June 19, 1936.

602.   _____, "'Wise Money' Shifting to Louis as Fight
       Nears; Both Are Ready," Washington Post, June 21, 1936.

603.   Graham, Frank, "Setting the Pace: But It May Be
       Exciting," New York Sun, June 18, 1936.

604.   _____, "Setting the Pace: Drama at the Scales
       Sometimes," New York Sun, June 19, 1936.

605.   _____, "Setting the Pace: It Shouldn't Take Joe
       Louis Long," New York Sun, October 9, 1936.

606.   _____, "Setting the Pace: Newspaper Men Built
       Louis Up," New York Sun, June 22, 1936.

607.   _____, "Setting the Pace: Schmeling Destroys a
       Myth," New York Sun, June 20, 1936.

608.   _____, "Schmeling Learns more about Louis,"
       New York Sun, August 20, 1936.

609.   Grayson, Harry, "Joe Louis Remains Big Question Mark
       to Grayson Despite K.O. over Sharkey," New York World-
       Telegram, August 19, 1936.

610.   _____, "Louis' K.O. Gives Maxie Chance to Set
       Precedent," The Halifax (Canada) Mail, December 26,
       1936.

611.   _____, "Story of Dope Expose Told," Detroit News,
       July 19, 1936.

612.   Greene, Sam, "Louis' Payoff $42,000; Title Hopes Soar
       Again," Detroit News, August 19, 1936.

613.   Grieve, Curley, "Max' Blood Pressure Rises; Dempsey
       Refuses to Visit Park for Bout," San Francisco Examiner,
       June 19, 1936.

614.   Grumich, Charles, "Joe Louis Can Be Hit," Bangor
        (Maine) Daily News, September 29, 1936.

615.   "Hamas to Return: Wants Louis Bout," Washington Post,
        February 8, 1936.

616.   "Hand Trouble Comes to Joe: But Bomber Goes on
        Undisturbed," Detroit Free Press, October 6, 1936.

617.   "Handlers Striving to Steam Up Louis' Foe: Retzlaff Is
        Advised to 'Go out There and Slug with Negro,'" Baton
        Rouge State Times, January 16, 1936.

618.   Hentoff, Nat, "Odyssey of a Black Man," Commonweal,
        January 28, 1936.

619.   Harris, Ed R., "Max (Schmeling) Right Hand Sends Joe
        away in Twelfth Setto," Philadelphia Tribune, June 25,
        1936.

620.   "Haynes Bests Joe Louis' Time Again; Victim Is Natie
        Brown," Chicago Defender, April 25, 1936.

621.   "He's Unterrified by Louis," Independence (Kansas)
        Daily Reporter, January 17, 1936.

622.   "Hitler Still Frowns on Max Fighting Joe Louis in U.S.,"
        Chicago Defender, May 2, 1936.

623.   Hoffman, John C., "Louis-Levinsky Bout May Reach
        $100,000 Goal," Lewistown (Pennsylvania) Sentinnel,
        January 17, 1936.

624.   _____, "Louis Scores Knockout in First
        Round," Everett (Wash.) News, January 18, 1936.

625.   _____, "$100,000 Gate Expected for Louis-
        Retzlaff Bout," Los Angeles Evening Herald and Express,
        January 16, 1936.

626.   _____, "Retzlaff Goes Down for Ten Count in
        Round One," (Nebraska) Lincoln Star, January 18, 1936.

627.   Igoe, Hype, "Joe Gets by Big Gamble of Retzlaff,"
        Des Moines (Iowa) Tribune, January 18, 1936.

628.   _____, "Now Considers Sport Thrilling Adventure,
        Not 'Fool's Errand'," New York Evening Journal, June 1,
        1936.

629.   "I'll Peg Right Hand in Louis Tilt--Retzlaff,"
        Philadelphia Inquirer, January 8, 1936.

630.   "'Indian Sign' Would Stop Louis for Me, Says Ettore,"
        Chicago Defender, May 9, 1936.

631. "'It Ain't Gonna Rain No Mo'--Well, Maybe," New York Sun, June 17, 1936.

632. "Items of Interest on Louis-Schmeling Bout," Journal and Guide, June 27, 1936.

633. "Jack Johnson Rips Joe Louis Apart: Ex-Champ Sure Bomber Is too Highly Rated by Critics," Chicago Defender, June 13, 1936.

634. Jacobs, Joe, "Joe Jacobs Sees Same Old Louis," New York Post, September 23, 1936.

635. "Jeffries in Good Shape," Bridgeport (Conn.) Times-Star, January 18, 1936.

636. "Joe-Braddock Talk Is Bunk, Says Johnston," New York World-Telegram, September 25, 1936.

637. "Joe's Fame Overshadows Gen. Grant," New York World-Telegram, June 16, 1936.

638. "Joe Louis," Jamaica (B.W.I.) Daily Gleaner, August 20, 1936.

639. "Joe Louis, Al Ettore Primed for Philly Fight," Pittsburgh Courier, September 19, 1936, Section Two, p. 5.

640. "Joe Louis Announces Ready for Another Blast Tonight," The State (Columbia, S.C.), January 17, 1936.

641. "Joe Louis Doped, Chicago Hears: But Boxer Denies He Was Needled Before Bout," New York World-Telegram, July 14, 1936.

642. "Joe Louis Faces Acid Test Against Ettore," Pittsburgh Courier, September 19, 1936, p. 1.

643. "Joe Louis Fights Again: 'Brown Bomber' to Start Comeback Campaign Against Sharkey," Jamaica (B.W.I.) Daily Gleaner, July 22, 1936.

644. "Joe Louis Knocks Out Retzlaff in First Round at Chicago: 17,000 Watch Negro Pound Foe to Floor with Vicious Blows," Washington Post, January 18, 1936.

645. "Joe Louis' Record," Pittsburgh Courier, January 19, 1936.

646. "Joe Louis Scores Knockout in Third," Victoria (Canada) Daily Times, October 10, 1936.

647. "Joe Louis' Showing in Workouts Fails to Please Trainer: 'He's Being Hit Too Often,' Is Camp's Plaint," Detroit Free Press, June 9, 1936.

648. "Joe Louis Signs to Fight Johnny Risko in Cleveland," Chicago Defender, November 7, 1936.

649. "Joe Louis vs. Max Schmeling," Irish Press (Dublin, Ireland), June 20, 1936.

650. "Joe Louis Wins by Kayo in First Round of Bout," Evening Sun (Hanover, Pa.), January 18, 1936.

651. "Joe May Find Al Ettore Hard Foe," Pittsburgh Courier, September 5, 1936, Section Two, p. 4.

652. "Joe Takes Work Outs Seriously," New York Evening Journal, June 1, 1936.

653. Jones, Kevin, "Max Sees Himself Annihilate Louis," New York Daily News, June 22, 1936.

654. "Just Another $40,000 for Louis," New Orleans States, January 17, 1936.

655. Kellum, David W., "Says Goodbye to the Ring; Schmeling Next," Chicago Defender, January 25, 1936.

656. Kessler, Gene, "Fighters Eye Kayo! So Do 20,000 Fans," Chicago Daily Tribune, January 14, 1936.

657. _____, "Jim Mullen Saves Day for Retzlaff," Chicago Daily Times, January 15, 1936.

658. _____, "Louis 4 to 1 Choice to K.O. Retzlaff," Chicago Daily Times, January 17, 1936.

659. _____, "Surprise Left Hook Is 'Double Cross' Louis Must Watch," Chicago Daily Times, January 14, 1936.

660. Kieran, John, "Sports of the Times: Keeping Joe Louis Dark," New York Times, August 14, 1936, p. 24.

661. _____, "Sports of the Times: Merely Postponed," New York Times, June 19, 1936, p. 24.

662. _____, "That Man (Joe Louis) Is Back Again," New York Times, August 20, 1936, p. 17.

663. "'Killer' Louis Wins by K.O. (Over Al Ettore)," Pittsburgh Courier, September 26, 1936, p. 1.

664. Kirksey, George, "Boxing World Still Stunned by Upset," Hawaii Hochi, June 20, 1936.

665. _____, "Max Certainly Not Afraid of Brown Bomber," Minneapolis (Minnesota) Star, April 22, 1936, p. 1.

666. _____, "Schmeling Soars into Fame with Kayo over Louis," Ogden (Utah) Standard-Examiner, June 20, 1936.

667. _____, "Schmeling's Unexpected Victory over Louis Rocks Hall of Boxing," Oregon Daily Journal, June 20, 1936.

668. Lane, French, "Joe Shoots for 27th Straight in Stadium Ring," Chicago Daily Tribune, January 17, 1936.

669. _____, "Puts Retzlaff Away in Minute and 25 Seconds," Chicago Daily Tribune, January 18, 1936.

670. _____, "Retzlaff Boom is On! 5 or 6 Fans Pick Him: What if Louis Bout Proves 'Em Right?" Chicago Daily Tribune, January 14, 1936.

671. _____, "Retzlaff and Louis Wind Up Fight Chores," Chicago Daily Tribune, January 16, 1936.

672. Lardner, John, "Bomber's Barrage Lands in Round One," San Francisco Chronicle, January 18, 1936.

673. _____, "Champion Helping Build up for Uhlan's Match with Bomber," Lincoln Evening Journal (Nebraska), June 4, 1936.

674. _____, "Louis Quoted at Even Money to Score K.O. in Four Rounds," Providence (R.I.) Journal, June 18, 1936.

675. _____, "Charley Gots His $$$ However the Bout Goes," San Francisco Chronicle, January 17, 1936.

676. Left, Straight, "How Joe Louis Finished Jorge Brescia in 3rd Round of Last Friday Night's Bout in New York: Dusky Destroyer's (Joe Louis) Left Hooks, Said by Experts to Be Most Famous and Most Powerful in Fistiana, Caught El Gaucho's Jaw," Jamaica (B.W.I.) Daily Gleaner, October 12, 1936.

677. _____, "Joe Louis at 22, Accepted as the Reigning Sensation in World's Heavyweight Ranks," Jamaica (B.W.I.) Gleaner, May 26, 1936.

678. _____, " . . . Joe Louis Concedes Max Has a Right to Go after Title--Holder Before Fighting Anyone Else," Jamaica (B.W.I.) Daily Gleaner, July 13, 1936.

679. _____, "Joe Louis Getting 'Ring Smart' at Fast Rate, Unbelievers Say: Showing Against Ettore Proves Schmeling Bout Has Benefited Him," Jamaica (B.W.I.) Daily Gleaner, August 27, 1936.

680.   _____, "Schmeling Says He Saw Another Weak
        Spot in Joe Louis' Defense in the Sharkey Bout,"
        Jamaica (B.W.I.) Daily Gleaner, August 27, 1936.

681.   Lesperance, Zotique, "Louis Par Mise Hors De Combat
        a la 4e! (Louis by Knockout in 4th Round), La Patrie
        (Montreal), June 18, 1936.

682.   Lewis, Fred, "Jack Dempsey Talks of Joe Louis' Right,"
        Chicago Defender, February 1, 1936.

683.   Lewis, Perry, "Louis Finishes Ettore in 5th Round,"
        Philadelphia Inquirer, September 23, 1936.

684.   "Louis and Schmeling," Jamaica (B.W.I.) Daily Gleaner,
        April 15, 1936.

685.   "Louis and Victim Are Set for Go," The Bee (Sacramento,
        Calif. , January 16, 1936.

686.   "Louis Awaits Biggest Test in Next Bout," New York
        Amsterdam News, August 8, 1936.

687.   "Louis Awaits Call to Face Max in Setto," New York
        Amsterdam News, June 13, 1936.

688.   "Louis-Braddock Bout Now Topic of Fight Crowd,"
        New York World-Telegram, June 17, 1936.

689.   "Louis Beats Down Retzlaff in First Round at Chicago,"
        Arkansas Gazette, January 18, 1936.

690.   "Louis Can Now Dictate to Champion," Los Angeles Evening
        News, May 14, 1936.

691.   "Louis Ended Simms' Rush with but Sing: 11,000
        Cleveland Spectators Pay $49,827 to See Scrap that
        Lasted Only 26 Seconds," Washington (D.C.) Daily News,
        December 15, 1936.

692.   "Louis Defeat Nordic Triumph--Say Nazis," New York
        Amsterdam News, October 3, 1936, p. 17.

693.   "Louis Eases up in Drill for Retzlaff," Chicago Daily
        Tribune, January 6, 1936.

694.   "Louis Faces Test in Sharkey Fight," New York Times,
        August 16, 1936, p. 10.

695.   "Louis Flashes Old Form as He Hits Peak for Bout,"
        Detroit Free Press, January 15, 1936.

696.   "Louis Gets His Quickest K.O.," Dodge City (Kansas)
        Daily Globe, January 18, 1936.

697.   "Louis Gets $60,150 for Ettore Fight," New York Times,
        September 24, 1936, p. 35.

698. "Louis Impressive in Sparring Drill," New York Times, August 16, 1936. p. 10.

699. "Louis in East; Silent on Plans as Quiz Continues," Chicago Defender, July 11, 1936.

700. "Louis Is Heavy Favorite to Win Over Retzlaff Tonight," Kansas City Kansan, January 17, 1936.

701. "Louis Is Lighter Than Formerly," New York Sun, June 19, 1936.

702. "Louis Is Still 'Amateur' in Max's Opinion," New York Sun, May 22, 1936.

703. "Louis Knocks Out Retzlaff in First," The State (Columbia, S.C.), January 18, 1936.

704. "Louis Laughs!: Jewish Boycott Against Maxie May Hurt Gate," Detroit Free Press, June 16, 1936.

705. "Louis May Box Schmeling for Crown if Braddock is Unable to Defend Title," New York Times, August 20, 1936.

706. "Louis Only Got $30 for 1st Pro Ring Battle (against Jack Kracken on July 4, 1934)," Chicago Defender, June 20, 1936.

707. "Louis Out to Regain Glory Via Al Ettore," New York Amsterdam News, August 29, 1936, pp. 1, 15.

708. "Louis Passes 500 G's Mark," New York Post, June 18, 1936.

709. "Louis Picks Pompton to Prep for Ettore," Pittsburgh Courier, September 5, 1936, Section Two, p. 4.

710. "Louis Planning Heavy Program, Says He'll Be Champion by Next Christmas: Big-Fight-A-Month Being Mapped for Joe to Keep Him in Tip-Top Shape," Washington (D.C.) Daily News, December 25, 1936.

711. "Louis Plans Early Kayo of Ring Foe," Decatur (Illinois) Herald, January 16, 1936.

712. "Louis Primed to Breeze by Ettore Fight," New York Amsterdam News, September 19, 1936.

713. "Louis Punch Gone, Easy for Max," Chicago Defender, June 27, 1936.

714. "Louis Remains Prohibitive Favorite to Topple Schmeling Tonight," Providence (R.I.) Evening Bulletin, June 19, 1936.

715. "Louis, Retzlaff in Brisk Drills," Detroit Free Press, January 14, 1936.

716. "Louis Seeks Quick Kayo: Brown Bomber Hopes to Put Retzlaff Out Early in Battle Tomorrow," Los Angeles Times, January 16, 1936.

717. "Louis Set for Quick Victory over Retzlaff," Chattanooga (Tenn.) News, January 16, 1936.

718. "Louis Should Pop Retzlaff Friday Night," New Haven (Conn.) Journal-Courier, January 16, 1936.

719. "Louis Shows His Punches," Detroit News, June 8, 1936.

720. "Louis Starts Comeback in Late Summer: Will Fight Unnamed Opponent; More Valuable Man Now," Philadelphia Tribune, June 25, 1936.

721. "Louis Starts New Training," New York Amsterdam News, May 2, 1936.

722. "Louis Starts Ring Grind," Los Angeles Evening Times, April 7, 1936.

723. "Louis Starts Training For Max on Birthday," Milwaukee Journal, May 14, 1936.

724. "Louis to Meet Jorge Brescia," Beckley (W. Va.) Post-Herald, October 9, 1936.

725. "Louis Superior to Dempsey in His Prime," Boston Guardian, January 11, 1936.

726. "Louis to Fight Braddock!" New York Amsterdam News, November 14, 1936.

727. "Louis to Fight Ettore; Fans Want Schmeling," Chicago Defender, August 29, 1936.

728. "Louis Will Get Million by Autumn," Chicago Defender, June 6, 1936.

729. "Louis Yearns for Schmeling Again," New York Amsterdam News, August 22, 1936.

730. Lyman, Winthrop, "Brown Bomber Kayos Retzlaff with Deadly Right Smash to Jaw in First Round of Fight," Great Falls (Montana) Tribune, January 18, 1936.

731. McCarthy, Marvin, "Dead Cinch," Chicago Sunday Times, January 19, 1936.

732. _____, "K.O.'s Pull," Chicago Daily Times, January 15, 1936.

733. McKinley, A. B., "The Sporting Vista: Kaplan Discusses the Kayo," Hartford (Conn.) Daily Times, January 16, 1936.

734. McKinney, Bob, "5,500 Fans Pay $7,500 to See Joe Knock Out 2 in Exhibition Bouts," Pittsburgh Courier, November 28, 1936.

735. _____, "Harry Wills Gives a New Impression of Joe Louis," Chicago Defender, August 1, 1936.

736. McLemore, Henry, "German Boxer Caused One of Greatest Surprises in History," Hamilton (Canada) Spectator, June 20, 1936.

737. _____, "'I'll Nail Him As Soon As I Can,' Says Louis to His Public," Detroit News, January 17, 1936.

738. _____, "Joe Had Heart But Max Dished Out More of It," Detroit News, June 20, 1936.

739. _____, "Louis Fight Weekly, What Garden Needs," Louisville (Ky.) Times, May 8, 1936.

740. _____, "Mac Prepares to Issue His 'Can't Lose' Tip on Fight," Detroit News, June 16, 1936.

741. _____, "Roving Reporter Asserts Retzlaff Will Win Fight Due to Urge for Tractor," Utica (N.Y.) Observer-Dispatch, January 17, 1936.

742. _____, "Schmeling's Courage Apt to Prove His Best Asset," Salt Lake (Utah) Telegram, June 18, 1936.

743. MacDonnell, Frank, "Louis Wins: 30,000 at Bout Pay $150,000," Detroit Evening Times, June 16, 1936.

744. MacNamara, Harry, "Bomber Became a Fighter to Make Fortune and He's Well on Way with $160,000 in Annuities Almost Paid Up," Philadelphia Record, January 15, 1936.

745. _____, "Joe Believes He Was Born at Exactly Right Time," Des Moines (Iowa) Register, January 16, 1936.

746. Mastro, Frank, "Louis Is Glad He Ducked That 1st Right Hand," Chicago Daily Tribune, January 18, 1936.

747. "Max (Schmeling) Follows Plan Outlined in Liberty (Magazine) to Beat Joe," Journal and Guide, June 27, 1936.

748. "Max Is Certain of Financial Gains Anyhow," Detroit Free Press, May 13, 1936.

749. "Max to Taper Off Tuesday," Detroit Evening Times,
      June 11, 1936.

750. Meany, Tom. "Louis Still in Fight, But Glamour of
      Old Is Gone," New York World-Telegram, August 19, 1936.

751. "Meisterleistung!: Schmeling Torpediert den braunen
      Bomber in Grund und Boden Louis in der 12," Box-Sport
      (Berlin, Germany), June 22, 1936.

752. "Merry White Hope Hunt Goes 'Round and 'Round,"
      New York Amsterdam News, January 18, 1936.

753. Michelson, Paul, "Boys Quit Hiding As Joe Loses,"
      Daily Oklahoman, June 22, 1936.

754. _____, "Joe Louis Wins Over Al Ettore by
      Fifth Round Knockout," Arkansas City (Kansas) Daily
      Traveler, September 23, 1936.

755. _____, "Louis Can Name Round When He'll Score
      Kayo," Akron (Ohio) Beacon Journal, June 13, 1936.

756. _____, "Max Has No Fear of Brown Bomber,"
      Evening Bulletin (Providence, R.I.), June 11, 1936.

757. Miley, Jack, "Gob's Last Fight," New York Daily News,
      August 19, 1936.

758. _____, "Jim Braddock Asks for It!" New York
      Daily News, May 14, 1936.

759. _____, "Knock, Knock!" New York Daily News,
      August 14, 1936.

760. _____, "Palm Beach to Pier 6," Democrat and
      Chronicle (Rochester, N.Y.), January 18, 1936.

761. _____, "Sepia Sour Grapes: Jack Johnson Criticism
      of Joe Louis," New York Daily News, May 22, 1936.

762. _____, "The Road Back," New York Daily News,
      August 7, 1936.

763. Monroe, Al, "Bomber Fails to Slay 'Em in Workouts,"
      Chicago Defender, May 30, 1936.

764. _____, "Champion Eager to Mix with Joe,"
      Chicago Defender, February 8, 1936.

765. _____, "'Ducking' Trainer Is His Best Fun,"
      Chicago Defender, March 28, 1936.

766. _____, "Fan May Yet Learn Peal Story," Chicago
      Defender, March 28, 1936.

767.   _____, "Intended Punch Stopped by Bomber's Strong Arms," *Chicago Defender*, January 25, 1936.

768.   _____, "Joe Louis Never Picks 'Bomber'," *Chicago Defender*, May 2, 1936.

769.   _____, "Joe Should Win in the Fourth," *Chicago Defender*, January 18, 1936.

770.   _____, "Louis Batters Way Back to Glory with Smashing Rights," *Chicago Defender*, August 22, 1936.

771.   _____, "Louis Picks Tigers--Detroit Names Bomber: And Both May Be Right in the End," *Chicago Defender*, April 25, 1936, p. 1.

772.   _____, "Man Who Directs Louis Sees Ex Middle King in Action," *Chicago Defender*, January 11, 1936.

773.   _____, "Schmeling Has but Three to Go with Louis," *Chicago Defender*, June 6, 1936.

774.   _____, "What's Happened to Louis' Hand Injury?" *Chicago Defender*, July 25, 1936.

775.   "More Careful Training, Plan of Joe Louis," *New York World-Telegram*, August 5, 1936.

776.   Murphy, Bob, "Delay Aids Max, Says Doctor," *Detroit Evening Times*, June 18, 1936.

777.   _____, "Letter to Joe Louis," *Detroit Evening Times*, June 22, 1936.

778.   _____, "'Miracle' Proves Louis Can Lose--And Take It," *Detroit Evening Times*, June 20, 1936.

779.   _____, "Bob Tales," *Detroit Evening Times*, June 20, 1936.

780.   Murphy, Mike, "Record as Prophet Guarded by Louis," *Chicago Daily News*, January 14, 1936.

781.   Nichols, Joseph C. "Crowd of 50,000 Sees Louis Knock Out Ettore in Fifth Round at Philadelphia," *New York Times*, September 23, 1936, p. 31.

782.   _____, "Louis 1-3 Choice to Stop Brescia," *New York Times*, October 9, 1936, p. 32.

783.   "No Opponent Held as Easy Picking by Brown Bomber," *New York Daily Mirror*, January 22, 1936.

784.   "Nobody Can Beat Louis, Says Jack (Dempsey), *Washington Evening Star*, September 25, 1936.

785. "North Dakotan, Brown Bomber, Box Tomorrow," Seattle
      (Washington) Daily Times, January 16, 1936.

786. "North Dakotan Unable to Get up Second Time," Baltimore
      Sun, January 18, 1936, p. 1.

787. Nunn, William, "Louis, His Handlers Take 'Witness
      Stand' for Courier Readers, Pittsburgh Courier, July 11,
      1936.

788. _____, "Louis Winner!" Pittsburgh Courier,
      August 22, 1936.

789. _____, "Managers and Trainer Reveal What Louis
      Did During 'Mystery Hours'," Pittsburgh Courier, July
      11, 1936.

790. _____, "Writes a Letter to Joe--Asks Why He
      Didn't Listen to Blackburn," Pittsburgh Courier,
      June 27, 1936.

791. O'Brien, Jack, "On the Level," Bridgeport (Conn.)
      Times-Star, January 17, 1936.

792. "Odds Favor Louis by Knockout," Chicago Defender,
      June 20, 1936.

793. "Only Ex-Champs and Joe Louis in N.Y.: Heavyweight
      Clique, Charges Gus," Pittsburgh Courier, August 29,
      1936, Section Two, p. 6.

794. Ottley, Roi, "Good Business Knows No Race," New York
      Amsterdam News, June 20, 1936.

795. _____, "Louis Carded with Sharkey on August 18,"
      New York Amsterdam News, July 25, 1936.

796. _____, "Joe Louis No Longer Terror to Boxers,"
      Chicago Defender, July 11, 1936.

797. _____, "Louis-Ettore-Battle of Wits," New York
      Amsterdam News, September 12, 1936.

798. _____, "Sidetracking of Louis-Braddock Fight
      Stirs Strong Protest," New York Amsterdam News,
      December 19, 1936.

799. _____, "Sportopics: Bomber Starts Priming,"
      New York Amsterdam News, May 16, 1936.

800. Owens, Evan, "Brown Beaten Badly by Detroit Bomber,"
      Muncie (Indiana) Evening Press, January 16, 1936.

801. Pastor, Bob, "Pastor Platform Has Louis Fight as Its
      Main Plank," New York Post, October 27, 1936.

802. Penn, William, "Here Is Why Jack Johnson Doesn't Like Joe Louis," Chicago Defender, January 11, 1936.

803. Perry, Lawrence, "Baer Bears Down," Jersey Journal, January 2, 1936.

804. Powers, Francis J., "Longest 1935 Go 6 Rounds," Morning World-Herald (Omaha, Neb.), January 16, 1936.

805. Powers, Jimmy, "Bomber's Attack Gives Gob a Night of Agony," Detroit Free Press, August 19, 1936.

806. _____, "Joe Louis Kayoes Brescia in Third," New York Daily News, October 19, 1936.

807. _____, "Louis Knocks Out Sharkey in Third; 4th Down Does It!" New York Daily News, August 19, 1936.

808. _____, "The So-Called Fight Experts Also Made 'Bums By' Schmeling," Arkansas Gazette, June 21, 1936.

809. "Probe Report That Joe Louis Was Doped," Chicago Defender, June 27, 1936.

810. "Promoters Book Heavy Schedule for Joe Louis," Washington (D.C.) Tribune, November 6, 1936.

811. "Rain Causes Delay in Louis' Go with Max," Wyoming State Tribune-Cheyenne State Leader, June 18, 1936.

812. "Rancher Says He Will Carry Battle to Joe," Des Moines (Iowa) Register, January 17, 1936.

813. Ray, Bob, "The Sports X-Ray," Los Angeles Times, January 17, 1936.

814. Rea, E. B., "Brown Bomber Courageous But Was Not Ready," Journal and Guide, June 27, 1936.

815. "'Ready for Retzlaff,'" Says Joe Louis on Eve of Fight; Advance Sales Hit $50,000," Galveston (Tex.) Tribune, January 16, 1936.

816. "Repeat the Chorus," New York Times, June 17, 1936, p. 33.

817. "Retzlaff and Louis Drill for Bout," Chicago Defender, January 11, 1936, p. 1.

818. "Retzlaff Gets Chance to Punch Louis; Will He?" Chicago Sunday Tribune, January 12, 1936.

819. "Retzlaff Gets Order to Slug with Bomber," Ithaca (N.Y.) Journal, January 16, 1936.

820. "Retzlaff Given Only Slim Chance, To Win," (Jacksonville) Florida Times-Union, January 17, 1936.

821. "Retzlaff Has Only Slight Chance to Win," Galveston
      (Tex.) Tribune, January 16, 1936.

822. "Retzlaff Hears Familiar Refrain," Boston Globe,
      January 16, 1936.

823. "Retzlaff's K.O. Punch Threat," Boston Daily Record,
      January 17, 1936.

824. "Retzlaff Pins Hope on Million-Dollar Punch," (Syracuse)
      Post-Standard, January 12, 1926.

825. "Retzlaff Pins Hope on Terrific Left; Betters Like
      Louis," Courier-Post (Camden, N.J.), January 16, 1936.

826. "Retzlaff Ready for Louis Fight," Charleston (S.C.)
      News and Courier, January 16, 1936.

827. "Retzlaff to Get Chance at Fame in Chicago Ring,"
      Utica (N.Y.) Observer-Dispatch, January 17, 1936.

828. "Retzlaff Will Rely on Right: Intends to Carry Fight
      to Brown Bomber," Boston Post, January 7, 1936.

829. Rice, Grantland, "Baer's Beating (by Joe Louis) Worst
      Suffered by Any Heavyweight in History," Washington
      Evening Star, September 15, 1936.

830. _____, "Select a Round from 1 to 6!: If German
      Stays Longer, It Will Be Miracle," Daily Oklahoman,
      June 18, 1936.

831. _____, "The Sportlight: Fight's Postponement
      Failed to Change the Original Setup," Detroit Free Press,
      June 19, 1936.

832. _____, "The Sportlight: Twenty-Four Hours
      Later," New York Sun, June 19, 1936.

833. _____, "The Sportlight: Where Anything Can
      Happen," New York Sun, June 22, 1936.

834. _____, "Then and Now, Chicago Daily News,
      January 7, 1936.

835. "Risko Only One with Chance with Louis, Old Timer Says,"
      Nashville Tennessean, January 7, 1936.

836. Robinson, Pat, "Max Promises He'll Put Louis on Floor,"
      Canton (Ohio) Repository, June 4, 1936.

837. Rochie, Fillie, "What I Think About Joe Louis," The
      Barbados Herald, January 4, 1936.

839. "Rumor Untrue of Louis Being Doped by Aide,"
      Philadelphia Tribune, June 25, 1936.

840. "Runyon Lauds Joe for Sock," New York Amsterdam News,
      May 9, 1936.

841. Runyon, Damon, "'Condemned Man' Is Victor over Bomber,"
      Omaha (Neb.) Bee-News, June 20, 1936.

842. _____, "Experts Agree Max Won't Be Afraid,"
      Detroit Evening Times, June 18, 1936.

843. _____, "Joe Louis' Ice Cold Nature Saved Him
      From Damage in His Bouts Among Amateurs," St. Louis
      Post-Dispatch, May 13, 1936.

844. _____, "Louis Is Forced to Drop Ex-Gob Four
      Times," Detroit Evening Times, August 19, 1936.

845. Ryan, Ida Mae, "Jack Johnson Challenges Joe Louis,"
      New York Amsterdam News, October 24, 1936.

846. "Salient Facts on the Bout (Louis vs. Schmeling),"
      New York Times, June 14, 1936, pp. 6, 10.

847. Sallaway, Pete, "The Sports Mirror," Victoria (British
      Columbia) Daily Times, June 19, 1936.

848. Salsinger, H. G., "Brescia Annoys Louis, So Bout Ends
      in Third," Detroit News, October 10, 1936.

849. _____, "Max Unlike Other Foes," Detroit News,
      June 16, 1936.

850. _____, "Pluck Makes Ettore Easy Victim for Louis,"
      Detroit News, September 23, 1936.

851. "Schmeling Begins Sparring Sessions: German Heavyweight
      Opens Campaign of Hard Training for Fight with Louis,"
      New York Times, May 16, 1936, p. 20.

852. "Schmeling Elated Over Victory, Praises Gameness of
      Detroiter," New York Times, June 21, 1936, p. 11.

853. "Schmeling's Handlers to Work on Ex-Champ's Legs,"
      Chicago Defender, May 16, 1936.

854. "Schmeling Not Interested in Return with Joe Louis,"
      New York Amsterdam News, July 25, 1936.

855. "Schmeling May Aid Louis," New York Amsterdam News,
      December 5, 1936.

856. "Schmeling Thinks Louis Should Have Waited," New York
      Sun, August 11, 1936.

857. "Schmeling Will Train for Fight at Naponoch," Fresno Bee
      (Calif.), April 28, 1936.

858. Scotter, G. St. C., "Joe Louis' Prospects," Jamaica
      (B.W.I.) Daily Gleaner, October 14, 1936.

859. Scott, Lester, "Joe Sags in Defeat Room Where He Once
      Rejoiced," New York World-Telegram, June 20, 1936.

860. _____, "Physical Condition Seen Schmeling's
      Only Asset in Battle with Tan Bomber," New York World-
      Telegram, June 17, 1936.

861. _____, "Schmeling Remains Calm," New York World-
      Telegram, June 16, 1936.

862. "See Max Schmeling as Joe Louis' Next Opponent,"
      Chicago Defender, August 22, 1936.

863. Shave, Ed L., "Schmeling Looks Aged as He Weighs In;
      Adds 10 Pounds," St. Paul Daily News, June 19, 1936.

864. Shevlin, Maurice O., "The Sporting Mill," Nashville
      Tennessean, January 7, 1936.

865. "Shootings Mark Louis' Victory," New York World-
      Telegram, August 19, 1936.

866. "$60,000 Richer, Louis Rests," New York Amsterdam News,
      September 26, 1936, pp. 1, 15.

867. Smith, Harry B., "Louis Must Be the Top," San Francisco
      Chronicle, January 18, 1936.

868. _____, "Louis' Rival of Tomorrow Rated Tough,"
      San Francisco Chronicle, January 16, 1936.

869. "Sparmates of Joe Headline Boxing Show," Chicago
      Defender, June 6, 1936.

870. Spencer, W. I., "Post Mortems in Sports: Suppose He
      Does Tag Him?" Baton Rouge (La.) Morning Advocate,
      January 17, 1936.

871. Stewart, Walter, "Early Rush Joe's Plan to End Bout,"
      New York World-Telegram, June 16, 1936.

872. _____, "First-Round Kayo Is Seen if Max
      Opens," New York World-Telegram, June 17, 1936.

873. _____, "First Round May Be Vital," New York
      World-Telegram, August 11, 1936.

874. _____, "Joe's Future in Own Hands," New York
      World-Telegram, June 22, 1936.

875. _____, "Jolt Into 10 Dollar Clash May Prove
      Help to Louis," New York World-Telegram, May, 1936.

876.   _____, "Joe Longs to Box Max Again," <u>New York World-Telegram</u>, August 6, 1936.

877.   _____, "Louis Called Erratic Despite Knockout of Al Ettore," <u>New York World-Telegram</u>, September 23, 1936.

878.   _____, "Louis Guards Chin Now," <u>New York World-Telegram</u>, August 14, 1936.

879.   _____, "Louis Picked Early Victor Over Simms," <u>New York World-Telegram</u>, December 14, 1936.

880.   _____, "Louis Rallies Legal Goblins to Scare Max," <u>New York World-Telegram</u>, September 17, 1936.

881.   _____, "Louis Shows Destructive Ring Rhythm," <u>New York World-Telegram</u>, September 14, 1936.

882.   Sullivan, Ed, "Broadway: Dawn Patrol," <u>New York Daily News</u>, May 29, 1936.

883.   Super, Henry, "Champion Jimmy Braddock Elected Most Startling Performer During 1935; Max Baer Is Called 'Yellow Palooka'," <u>Baton Rouge (La.) State Times</u>, January 6, 1936.

884.   "Sure, I'm on a Spot, But I Like It: Retzlaff: Charlie Sure He'll Beat Louis on Jan. 17," <u>Chicago Daily Tribune</u>, January 8, 1936.

885.   "'Take' for Chicago Scrap Is Heavy," <u>Grand Rapids (Mich.) Press</u>, January 17, 1936.

886.   "The End of a Myth, Louis Knocked Out by Max," <u>Detroit Evening Times</u>, June 20, 1936.

887.   "'There's My Man,' Max Repeats About Louis," <u>Detroit Free Press</u>, April 22, 1936.

889.   "Three-Round Knockout Win Seen for Louis: Retzlaff Conceded Little Chance to Go Limit with Bomber," <u>Baltimore Evening Sun</u>, January 15, 1936.

890.   "Today's Chat with C.E.," <u>New York Post</u>, July 1, 1936.

891.   "Trip Abroad (in London) for Joe Louis Planned," <u>Pittsburgh Courier</u>, November 14, 1936.

892.   "20,000 to See Battle in Chicago," <u>Albuquerque (N.Mex.) Journal</u>, January 17, 1936.

893.   "20,000 to See Louis Go after 23rd K.O.: Fight Experts Rate Retzlaff 1-10 Underdog," <u>Philadelphia Record</u>, January 16, 1936, p. 1.

894. "Urge Retzlaff to Slug with Brown Bomber," Leavenworth (Kansas) Times, January 16, 1936.

895. Van Every, Edward, "Bomber Weathers Stiff Right," New York Sun, October 10, 1936.

896. _____, "Fans Got Money's Worth," New York Sun, June 22, 1936.

897. _____, "Haynes Picks on Bomber's Victims," New York Sun, April 17, 1936.

898. _____, "Joe Louis Passes Up Series," New York Sun, October 2, 1936.

899. _____, "Joe Louis Wins Tape Argument," New York Sun, October 7, 1936.

900. _____, "Louis Thinks He Is Better," New York Sun, August 5, 1936.

901. _____, "Schmeling Amused at Fight Experts," New York Sun, June 17, 1936.

902. _____, "Uhlan's Nerve Impresses Joe," New York Sun, June 17, 1936.

903. Van Ness, Fred, and Joseph C. Nichols, "Louis to Try for Quick Knockout; Is Warned Against Carelessness," New York Times, June 16, 1936, p. 35.

904. _____, "Peak of Condition Reached by Louis," New York Times, June 14, 1936, p. 6.

905. Wallace, Francis, "Public Knows It'll Be No Match, But Joe Louis Draws the Mob," New York World-Telegram, June 17, 1936.

906. Walsh, Davis J., "Louis Supposed to Be Nervous," Dubuque (Iowa) Telegraph-Herald, June 19, 1936.

907. _____, "Louis to Face Jorge Brescia," Clinton (Iowa) Herald, October 8, 1936.

908. _____, "Maxie Schmeling Seems Unafraid of Dusky Bomber," Beaumont (Tex.) Journal, May 14, 1936.

909. _____, "Schmeling May Pass," Akron (Ohio) Beacon Journal, January 2, 1936.

910. Washington, Chester L., "How Louis Will Lick Schmeling," Pittsburgh Courier, June 20, 1936.

911. Webber, Harry B., "One Tale Had Louis Stricken in Hospital," Journal and Guide, June 27, 1936, pp. 1, 10.

912. Webster, John, "Ettore Real Tester in Stadium Combat,"
      Philadelphia Inquirer, August 30, 1936.

913. Weekes, William, "Bomber Promises Speedy Knockout:
      Retzlaff Believes that His Hard Right Hand Can Batter
      Louis Down for Count," *Lockport (N.Y.) Union Sun and
      Journal*, January 16, 1936.

914. _____, "C. Retzlaff to Start Fast," *San Jose
      (Calif.) News*, January 16, 1936.

915. _____, "Joe Louis Is Picked to Win,"
      Charleston (S.C.) News and Courier, January 16, 1936.

916. _____, "Louis and Retzlaff Are Confident of
      Victory," *Worcester (Mass.) Evening Post*, January 16,
      1936.

917. _____, "Louis Taking Life Easy as Match Nears,"
      Johnson City (Tenn.) Press, January 16, 1936.

918. _____, "My Right to His Jaw Will Beat Joe
      Louis--Retzlaff," *San Antonio (Tex.) Evening News*,
      January 16, 1936.

919. _____, "North Dakota Farmer Plans Slugging
      Duel," *Bridgeport (Conn.) Post*, January 16, 1936.

920. _____, "Retzlaff Set to Toss Arms at Bomber,"
      Portland (Oregon) Daily Journal, January 17, 1936.

921. _____, "Right to Jaw Will Win, Says White Lad,"
      San Francisco Chronicle, January 17, 1936.

922. _____, "Sock to Decide Retzlaff's Fate,"
      Daily Independent (St. Petersburg, Fla.), January 16,
      1936.

923. "Will Capture Crown of Heavy Ranks, Joe Says, Ready to
      Rest," *New York Amsterdam News*, June 27, 1936.

924. "Will Montana's Left Hook Worry Lynch in Title Fight?"
      Reynolds (London) News, December 27, 1936.

925. Williams, Joe, "British Louis Bid Serious; Eager to
      See Joe Abroad and Willing to Foot Bill," *New York
      World-Telegram*, August 22, 1936.

926. _____, "Condemned Man's Schmeling Startles
      Ring World by Electrocuting Warden," *Salt Lake City
      (Utah) Telegram*, June 20, 1936.

927. _____, "Did Schmeling Ruin Joe?; Dempsey's
      Vote Is 'Yes'; Johnston Says He Quit," *New York World-
      Telegram*, June 20, 1936.

928. _____, "Don't Call It an Upset! The Experts Were Wrong; Visitor Figured to Win," New York World-Telegram, June 20, 1936.

929. _____, "How Long Will It Last? This Depends on German Quick K.O. If He Rushes," New York World-Telegram, June 17, 1936.

930. _____, "If Braddock Meets Louis Outlook Dark for Champ How Dempsey Looks at It," New York World-Telegram, December 1, 1936.

931. _____, "Louis Not One of Greatest Schmeling Kayo Lingers on Ettore Was Made to Order," New York World-Telegram, September 23, 1936.

932. _____, "Rowing Experts Are Wise; They Pick Three Winners; Louis Dazed or Stupid?" New York World-Telegram, June 22, 1936.

933. _____, "The 'Who'd He Lick?' Cry It's Aimed at All Boxers Now Fired at Joe Louis," New York World-Telegram, June 10, 1936.

934. Wilson, W. R., "Grim, Determined Joe Louis Drills at Pompton," Pittsburgh Courier, August 15, 1936.

935. "Winner of Louis-Schmeling Bout Will Be Contender for Title of J.J. Braddock," New York Times, May 20, 1936, p. 31.

936. "Win or Lose Charlie Retzlaff to Get $15,000 for Louis Bout," Independence (Kansas) Daily Reporter, January 17, 1936.

937. "Wins Shortest Bout of Career," Jackson (Michigan) Citizen Patriot, January 18, 1936, p. 1.

938. Wood, Wilbur, "Answering Some Questions: Louis Merely Had One of Those Bad Nights They All Experience Sooner or Later," New York Sun, June 22, 1936.

939. _____, "Crowd Is Wild as Max Wins," New York Sun, June 20, 1936.

940. _____, "Louis Passed Up His Best Bet," New York Sun, June 23, 1936.

941. _____, "Showers Delay Louis-Schmeling Bout Until Tomorrow Night: Bomber Top-Heavy Favorite," New York Sun, June 18, 1936.

942. Woodruff, Harvey, "Schmeling Is Glad Louis Is Favorite," Chicago Daily Tribune, June 17, 1936.

943. Young, Dave, "Primo's New Nemesis Has Set of Plans:
      And They Don't Include Fight with Bomber from Detroit,"
      Chicago Defender, March 28, 1936, p. 1.

944. Ziff, Sid, "The Inside Track," Los Angeles Evening
      Herald and Express, January 16, 1936.

                       B.   FAMILY

945. "Louis Doped, Sister Charges," Pittsburgh Courier,
      July 18, 1936.

946. "Louis In Guef at Bedsie of Devoted 'Dad'," New York
      Amsterdam News, July 11, 1936, p. 1.

947. "Louis' Stepfather Not Told of Result," New York Times,
      June 20, 1936, p. 11.

948. "Mrs. Joe Louis to Help Kiddies: Will Sell Tickets
      for Summer Camp Fund," New York Amsterdam News,
      June 6, 1936.

                       C.   FOLK HERO

949. Adams, Caswell, "Louis Adding a New Chapter to Ring
      History of His Race," New York Herald, September 25,
      1936.

950. Atkinson, Le Roy, "Near Riot in Philadelphia as Louis
      Kayoes Al Ettore: Negroes Go on Rampage as Bomber Wins
      Scrap," Boston Traveler, September 23, 1936.

951. Cooke, Marvel, "Death and Sadness Mark Louis Defeat;
      Shock Fatal to 12, and Harlem Mourns," New York
      Amsterdam News, June 27, 1936.

952. _____, "That Old Circus Stuff Has Been Put
      Aside; Louis Is Mad and Plans to Show the World,"
      New York Amsterdam News, August 15, 1936.

953. "Detroit Harlem in Gloom as Idol Collapses," Detroit
      Evening Times, June 20, 1936.

954. "Fan Praise Defender's Stand on Louis and Max Schmeling
      Fight with Letters," Chicago Defender, July 18, 1936.

955. "Harlem Attends Wake En Masse; Joe Louis Flees," Chica-
      go Defender, June 27, 1936.

956. "Harlem Disorders Mark Louis Defeat," New York Times,
      June 20, 1936, p. 34.

957. "Harlem Noisy as Louis Wins," New York Amsterdam News,
      August 22, 1936.

958. Harrington, Ollie, "Yea, (Joe Louis) Brotherly Love," New York Amsterdam News, September 26, 1936, p. 15.

959. "He Wasn't Himself, Says Harlem, Sadly Paying Bets on Joe Louis," New York World-Telegram, June 20, 1936.

960. Holst, Doc, "Joe Louis Can't Lose Fight--He Told His Mother So: Meanwhile 'Little Harlem' (Detroit), Short of Cash But Long on Hope, Sticks, to Bomber," Detroit Free Press, August 18, 1936.

961. Kieran, John, "Sports of the Times: New Jersey Goes Wild," New York Times, June 16, 1936, p. 35.

962. "Lifting Young Hearts," New York Amsterdam News, January 18, 1936.

963. "Louis Adding a New Chapter to Ring History of His Race," New York Herald, September 25, 1936.

964. "Louis No Dirty Ring Man, Roxborough Answers Max," New York Amsterdam News, September 5, 1936.

965. MacNamara, Harry, "Negro Sensation Came Along When Boxers Were Few: Good Men Scarce, He Declares," Chicago Herald and Examiner, January 16, 1936.

966. _____, "The Real Joe Louis," Boston Daily Record, January 16, 1936.

967. McClain, John, "Joe Louis Is Example," New York Amsterdam News, January 11, 1936.

968. McMillan, Allan, "Brown Bomber Redeemed Self," Chicago Defender, August 29, 1936.

969. Murray, Charles D., "Joe Louis, We Are with You," Louisville (Ky.) Defender, June 27, 1936.

970. "One Killed, Four Wounded as Harlem Celebrates Louis' Return to Fistic Glory," Chicago Defender, August 29, 1936.

971. Ottley, Roi, "Hectic Harlem: Moanin's Law (After Louis Lost to Schmeling)," New York Amsterdam News, June 27, 1936.

972. _____, "Trumpets Are for Idols," New York Amsterdam News, August 22, 1936.

973. "Slight on Joe Louis' Race Laid to Dempsey in South," New York Amsterdam News, July 18, 1936, p. 4.

974. "What Joe Louis' Success Means," The Barbados Herald, January 11, 1936.

975.   "'White Hope' (Bob Pastor) Claims His Color Keeps Him from Getting Crack at Louis," Nashville (Tenn.) Globe and Independent, November 6, 1936.

D.   PERSONAL LIFE

976.   "Bomber Ardent Member of Fish and Rod Club," New York Evening Journal, June 1, 1936.

977.   Boozer, Thelma Berlack, "Joe's Always to Be Boss of the Family," New York Amsterdam News, June 20, 1936.

978.   Cowans, Russell J., "Backwoods Kin of Joe Louis Offer a Prayer Every Time He Fights," Afro-American, April 25, 1936.

979.   _____, "Louis Asked to Buy Ball Club in Detroit or Chicago," Chicago Defender, January 1936, p. 1.

980.   Davis, Frank M., "Louis and Marva Deny Love Row Caused K.O. by German," New York Amsterdam News, July 4, 1936.

981.   "Diamond League to Meet Friday: Joe Louis May Enter Team in Circuit," New York Amsterdam News, January 4, 1936.

982.   "Gross Earnings of Louis Estimated at $1,800,000," Pittsburgh Courier, November 14, 1936.

983.   Igoe, Hype, "Joe Louis' Future," The Ring, November, 1936.

984.   "It'll Buy a Lot of Fried Chicken," Lethebridge (Alberta) Herald, June 19, 1936.

985.   "Joe Louis Breaks 100 after 12 Rounds of Golf," New York Sun, May 9, 1936.

986.   "Joe Louis' Case Muddled: Tsk! Tsk! Who's First in Joe Louis Suit Filings?" Chicago Defender, July 25, 1936.

987.   "Joe Louis Denies Story of Doping: Tells of Gang Pressure on Marriage License," New York Sun, July 16, 1936.

988.   "Joe Louis Doped, Gen. Phelan Told: Detective Declares He Got the Story from Sister," New York Sun, July 14, 1936.

989.   "Joe Louis of the Dead Pan, Marvel of the Prize Ring," Literary Digest, June 13, 1936, p. 36.

990.   "Joe Louis Plans Own Gymnasium" Chicago Defender, January 11, 1936.

991. "Joe Louis Stumps for Roosevelt, But Forgets to Mention His Name," New York World-Telegram, September 30, 1936.

992. Kahn, James M., "Bomber Still a Sepia Sphinx: Reveals No Jubilation or Emotion After Triumph Over Sharkey in Stadium," New York Sun, August 19, 1936.

993. Lane, French, "X=How Long Fight Will Go, But What = X?: Louis' Backers Turn to Algebra," Chicago Daily Tribune, January 15, 1936.

994. "Louis and Marva Deny Love Row Caused K.O. by German," New York Amsterdam News, July 4, 1936, p.1, 2.

995. "Louis Cancels Detroit Battle for Honeymoon," Detroit Free Press, January 18, 1936.

996. "Louis Carefully Investing His Money; Had $150,000 before Schmeling Battle," New York Amsterdam News, July 4, 1936.

997. "Louis Meant Well, But Forgot F.D.R.," New York Amsterdam News, October 3, 1936, p. 1.

998. "Louis to Referee Amateur Bouts (in Detroit)," Saginaw (Mich.) News, September 27, 1936.

999. Mac Namara, Harry, "Joe Louis Wanted (as a boy) to Be a Trumpet Player in Band, He Reveals," New York American, January 20, 1936.

1000. _____, "Louis Credits Luck with Fistic Success," Miami (Fla.) Herald, January 17, 1936.

1001. _____, "Luck, Says Joe Louis, Played a Major Part in His Career," Chicago Herald and Examiner, January 16, 1936.

1002. "Philadelphia Has Idea Joe Is Political," Chicago Defender, February 8, 1936.

1003. "Retzlaff Out, Louis Will Go on Honeymoon," New York Amsterdam News, January 25, 1936, p. 1.

1004. Rockwell, Tod, "Joe Louis Makes It a Highly Secretive Homecoming," Detroit Free Press, June 22, 1936.

1005. Roe, Dorothy, "Joe Louis Wants Filling Station," San Francisco Examiner, June 19, 1936.

1006. "Southside Happy!: Joe's Neighbors Are Jubilant," Detroit Evening Times, August 19, 1936.

1007. Waxner, Lodi, "Louis Plan to Fight in Dixie Causes Stir," New York Amsterdam News, November 7, 1936.

1008. Wood, Wilbur, "Boxer's Morale Is Unaffected," New York Sun, June 17, 1936.

3.   1937

A.   BOXER

1009. Adams, Caswell, "Louis Stops Braddock in 8th for World Title," New York Herald Tribune, June 23, 1937.

1010. Avery, Leslie, "Joe Spills Three to Wind Up Drill," Miami Tribune, August 25, 1937.

1011. _____, "Pastor Probably Will Get Return Bout with Louis," Washington Daily News, January 30, 1937, p. 12.

1012. "Back-Pedaling Pastor Makes Victorious Joe Louis Look Bad," Detroit News, January 30, 1937.

1013. "Beefin' Bob Will Prove Louis Meat," New York Amsterdam News, January 23, 1937.

1014. Blake, Morgan, "Sportanic Erruptions: Waiting for Max to Get Rusty," Atlanta Journal, August 24, 1937.

1015. "Bob Pastor in Bid for Quick Fame Tonight," Hollywood (Calif.) Citizen-News, January 29, 1937.

1016. "Bomber-Farr Fight Noitce Causes Suit," New York Amsterdam News, July 17, 1937.

1017. "Bomber Goes to the Post 7-1 Favorite," New York Amsterdam News, January 30, 1937.

1018. "Bomber Signs New Contract," Peoria (Ill.) Journal-Transcript, June 23, 1937.

1019. "Bomber Ticket Bill Is Killed," New York Amsterdam News, April 3, 1937.

1020. "Both Fighters Are Calm on Eve of Title Scrap," Wyoming State Tribune-Cheyenne State Leader, June 21, 1937.

1021. "Both Fighters Claim Victory," Miami Daily News, June 22, 1937.

1022. Bourne, St. Clair, "Fans Pulling for Bomber (Louis vs. Braddock)," New York Amsterdam News, June 19, 1937, pp. 1, 16.

1023. _____, "Louis in Shape, Training Lightly," New York Amsterdam News, August 7, 1937.

1024.   _____, "No Advice (to Joe Louis)," New Amsterdam News, July 3, 1937, p. 16.

1025.   _____, "Title Bout with Braddock Marks Peak of Joe Louis' Climb to Fame," New York Amsterdam News, June 26, 1937.

1026.   "Boxing Fans of Enid Will Get Glimpse of Joe Louis in Exhibition Bout Tonight," Enid (Oklahoma) Morning News, March 17, 1937.

1027.   "Boxing: The Defeat of Braddock," London Times, June 24, 1937.

1028.   Braddock, James J., "How I Shall Knock Out Joe Louis," Liberty, June 26, 1937.

1029.   "Braddock-Louis Title Bout Proposed," New York Times, February 1, 1937, p. 23.

1030.   "Braddock and Louis to Sign," New York Times, February 5, 1937, p. 24.

1031.   "Braddock and Louis Train," New York Times, June 6, 1937, p. 12, sec. 5.

1032.   "Braddock Off to Train for Louis," New York Amsterdam News, April 10, 1937.

1033.   Bradley, Hugh, "Farr'll Get Lumps But One in Pocket May Annoy Solons," New York Post, August 30, 1937.

1034.   _____, "Warning for Louis Noted in Pastor's Refusal of Steaks," New York Post, January 19, 1937.

1035.   Braucher, Bill, "Tommy Farr May Be Just Another British Heavy Pug," The Star-Tribune (Providence, R.I.), July 14, 1937.

1036.   Brietz, Eddie, "Jim Was One Game Fighter," Decatur (Ala.) Daily, June 23, 1937.

1037.   _____, "Louis' Downfall Booms Interest," Washington (D.C.) Sunday Star, December 27, 1937.

1038.   _____, "Mike Jacobs Promises to Show Louis in England Against Either Harvey or Doyle," Pueblo Star-Journal (Colorado), July 14, 1937.

1039.   _____, "Schmeling and Louis May Not Be Signed This Year," Raleigh Times (N.C.), July 14, 1937.

1040.   _____, "Why Louis Won't Fight Max," Detroit News, July 14, 1937.

1041. Bromberg, Lester, "Louis Needs Footwork Lessons, Say Veterans," New York World-Telegram, September 1, 1937.

1042. Broun, Heywood, "Joe Louis at Pompton Lakes, N.J.," Washington Daily News, January 30, 1937, p.17.

1043. Brown, Harry F., "Jack Johnson Says 'Louis Is a Puncher'--Will Never Be a Great Fighter," The Boxing News, July, 1937.

1044. Brown, Warren, "Braddock-Louis Bout to Bring City (Chicago) Millions," Chicago Herald and Examiner, June 21, 1937.

1045. "Brown Expects to Stay with Louis," Atchison (Kansas) Daily Globe, February 16, 1937.

1046. "Brown Is Not Concerned Over Second Louis Bout," Kansas City (Mo.) Journal-Post, February 15, 1937.

1047. Buck, Al, "Physically Tops for Louis Brawl," New York Post, June 12, 1937.

1048. _____, "Schmeling Haunts Louis," New York Post, August 31, 1937, p. 18.

1049. _____, "Twelve to One Figure Likely Before Champ Enters Ring," New York Post, August 30, 1937.

1050. Burchard, James A., "Any Good Heavyweight Can Take Louis-Tunney," New York World-Telegram, October 28, 1937.

1051. Butts, Sam, "Ifs, Ands, and Buts," Florida Times-Union (Jacksonville), June 22, 1937.

1052. "J.P. Carmichael--Chi Daily News (Over Joe Louis' Fight with Jimmy Braddock)," Pittsburgh Courier, July 3, 1937, p. 18.

1053. Carroll, Parke, "Ex-Champion May Appear in London Fight," Kansas City (Mo.) Journal-Post, June 23, 1937.

1054. _____, "Joe Louis Favored to Win by Knockout Over Natie Brown in Early Round," Kansas City (Mo.) Journal-Post, February 17, 1937.

1055. "Celebrities Rush to Chicago Scrap," News and Courier (Charleston, S.C.), June 22, 1937.

1056. "Champ Falls in 8th to be Counted Out," Johnson City (Tenn.) Chronicle, June 23, 1937.

1057. "Champion Ribs Challenger at Weighing In," Richmond (Va.) News Leader, June 22, 1937.

1058.   Clarke, John Louis, "De Winnah! Big Bill Watson,"
        New York Amsterdam News, May 29, 1937.

1059.   Cochrane, Edward W., "'Cinderella Man' Yields Crown,
        Retaining Golden Slippers," Chicago American, June 23,
        1937.

1060.   Considine, Bob, "Terrific Right in Eighth Round Wins
        Title for Louis," New York American, June 23, 1937.

1061.   "Courts Clear Way for Fights; Braddock and Louis All
        Set," Daily (Vancouver, B.C.) Province, May 15, 1937.

1062.   "Crown Settles on Joe's Head: Crown Opens Way to
        Extreme Riches for Negro Champion," New York Daily
        News, June 23, 1937.

1063.   "Crown Settles on Joe's Head: Crown Opens Way to
        Extreme Riches for Negro Champion," New York News,
        June 23, 1937, pp. 26, 27.

1064.   "Crown Settles on Joe's Head," New York Amsterdam News,
        July 3, 1937, p. 16.

1065.   Cuddy, Jack, "Double Cross Is Feature of Today's Box
        Fighting," Savannah Morning News, June 29, 1937.

1066.   _____, "Wanted--A Heavyweight," Honolulu Adver-
        tiser, August 30, 1937.

1067.   Dartnell, Fred, "Why Farr-Louis Fight Is Postponed--
        The Truth: Poor Gate--Not Rain--The Cause: Jacobs
        Wants Saratoga Crowd," News Chronicle (London, England),
        August 27, 1937.

1068.   Dawson, James P., "Farr Seen Doomed to Quick Knockout,"
        New York Times, August 22, 1937, p. 8.

1069.   _____, "Louis Favored as High as 1-10 in
        Encounter with Farr Tonight," New York Times, August
        30, 1937, p. 17.

1070.   _____, "60,000 See Louis Knock Out Braddock in
        Eighth Round and Win World Title," New York Times,
        June 23, 1937, p. 1.

1071.   Dempsey, Jack, "Louis Improved Fighter Gains by Ex-
        perience," Ottawa Journal, August 24, 1937.

1072.   Dunkley, Charles, "Braddock Discarded all Caution and
        Showed Stout Heart in Loss of Heavyweight Title to
        Louis," Savannah Evening Press, June 23, 1937.

1073.   _____, "Braddock Now on Short End of 5-2
        Wagers," Las Vegas (N. Mex.) Daily Optic, June 22,
        1937.

1074. _____, "Challenger Is Favorite for First
Time in History," New Orleans States, June 22, 1937.

1075. _____, "Louis Dethrones Jim Braddock as
World's Champion," Reno (Nev.) Evening Gazette, June
23, 1937.

1076. _____, "Ring Experts See Knockout Win for
Louis," Norfolk Ledger-Dispatch, June 22, 1937.

1077. _____, "Title Fight Success Assured,"
Montreal (Canada) Daily Herald, June 21, 1937.

1078. Edgar, W. W., "Dozen Cities Anxious for September
Battle," Detroit Free Press, June 24, 1937.

1079. _____, "Louis Still Shy of Right Hand,"
Detroit Free Press, June 20, 1937.

1080. _____, "Louis Wins Title," Detroit Free Press,
June 23, 1937.

1081. _____, "The Second Guess," Detroit Free Press,
June 25, 1937.

1082. "Experts Doubt that Louis' Fight with Schmeling Will
Be Put off until Next Year," Dallas (Tex.) Journal,
August 24, 1937.

1083. "Farr Actually Finds Someone Supporting Him; Fight
Delayed for Saratoga Money," Burlington (N.C.) Daily
Times-News, August 27, 1937.

1084. "Farr and Louis Meet at Signing for Bout," New York
Times, July 28, 1937, p. 26.

1085. "Farr Is Leading by Wide Margin," Regina (Saskatchewan)
Daily Star, August 25, 1937.

1086. "Federal Court Ruling Favors Braddock-Louis Fight in
Chicago," Winnipeg (Canada) Free Press, May 15, 1937.

1087. Fogarty, Billy, "Charge Gambling Coup Scored on Louis
Fights," New York Enquirer, January 31, 1937.

1088. Gallagher, P. R. (Reddy), "Joe Louis Appears Here
Thursday Against Seal Harris," Denver Post, March 11,
1937.

1089. Garrett, Norb, "Rest for Louis Who Is Ill with Slight
Cold," Kansas City (Mo.) Journal-Post, February 17,
1937.

1090. Gould, Alan, "Challenger Favored, First Time in History,"
Portland Press Herald (Maine), June 22, 1937.

1091. _____, "Fight Crowds Fail to Show Any Interest,"
       Halifax (Nova Scotia) Chronicle, August 25, 1937.

1092. _____, "Louis Made Favorite Over Champion in
       Title Fight: Bout Begins in Chicago Arena About
       8:30 P.M.," Birmingham Age-Herald (Alabama), June 22,
       1937.

1093. _____, "Louis' Prestige Dealt Blow as He
       Barely Outpoints Pastor," Detroit Free Press, January
       30, 1937.

1094. _____, "Louis to Be Fighting Champ; Signs
       New Pact with Jacobs," The Constitution (Atlanta, Ga.),
       June 24, 1937.

1095. _____, "Small Chance for 75,000 Sellout Seen,"
       Courier-Journal (Louisville, Ky.), June 22, 1937.

1096. _____, "Terrific Smash by Brown Bomber Floors
       Champion," The Constitution (Atlanta, Ga.), June 23,
       1937.

1097. _____, "$350,000 Gate Due Thursday: Schmeling
       Fight Now Slated for June," Detroit Free Press,
       August 22, 1937.

1098. Graham, Frank, "Setting the Pace: A Long Shot at a
       Million Dollars," New York Sun, August 26, 1937.

1099. _____, "Setting the Pace: An Idea--But Joe
       Wouldn't Dicker," New York Sun, August 27, 1937.

1100. _____, "Setting the Pace: Jim Braddock Seems
       Happier Now, " New York Sun, August 9, 1937.

1101. _____, "Setting the Pace: Louis vs. Braddock,"
       New York Sun, June 23, 1937.

1102. Grayson, Harry, "Bomber Ready Now to Start Training
       for Title Defense," Ogden (Utah) Standard Examiner,
       July 15, 1937.

1103. _____, "Schmeling Fight Put Joe at Top,"
       New York World-Telegram, June 23, 1937.

1104. _____, "Victory Over Max Baer Brought Big
       Chance for Tom Farr," Mobile Times, June 29, 1937.

1105. Harrington, Lonnie, "Joe 'Quicker on the Draw' Than
       Jimmy, Says Harrington; Picks Louis by K.O.,"
       Pittsburgh Courier, June 19, 1937, p. 18.

1106. _____, "Harrington Weighs Foes Joe Will Have
       to Face: Lewis, Brescia, Thomas," Pittsburgh Courier,
       June 26, 1937, p. 18.

1107.   _____, "Along the Fistic Front," Pittsburgh Courier, March 13, 1937.

1108.   _____, "Joe Louis Will Cop Heavyweight Title But Must Beat a Great 'Money Fighter' to Win," Pittsburgh Courier, June 12, 1937, p. 18.

1109.   Harrington, O. L., "Bootsie Visits Louis' Camp," New York Amsterdam News, August 21, 1937.

1110.   Hayes, Jere R., "Dallas Fans See Joe Louis' Wallops," Dallas Time Herald, March 23, 1937.

1111.   Hilligan, Earl, "Chicago Mercahnts Get Benefit of Fight Crowd," Tampa (Fla.) Daily Times, June 22,1937.

1112.   _____, "Ex-Champ Is Voted Gamest," Montreal Daily Herald, June 23, 1937.

1113.   _____, "Now Champion Asks for, Will Get Lots of Work," New Orleans States, June 24, 1937.

1114.   Holland, S. T., "10,000 Detroit Fight Fans Witness Louis-Braddock Fight," Pittsburgh Courier, June 26, 1937, p. 1.

1115.   "I Will Be the Next Champion," Says Joe," Boston Traveler, June 21, 1937.

1116.   "Jacobs' Control of Boxing Talent Being Questioned," Shreveport (La.) Times, July 15, 1937.

1117.   "Jacobs-Louis Split Hinted," New York Amsterdam News, January 6, 1937.

1118.   "Jim Braddock Stakes Championship Tonight: Stage Is Set for Title Bout in Chicago Stadium," Beckley Post-Herald (W. Virginia), June 22, 1937.

1119.   "Jim, Joe Train, Court Tiff Drags," New York Amsterdam News, April 24, 1927.

1120.   "Joe Challenges: Schmeling Avoids Bout with Louis," Kansas City Journal-Post, June 24, 1937.

1121.   "Joe Drills in Kenosha Champ; Seek Sparmates," Pittsburgh Courier, May 22, 1937, p. 17.

1122.   "Joe Gives Braddock the Beating of His Life," Pittsburgh Courier, June 26, 1937, p. 12.

1123.   "Joe in Top Shape Despite Stories," New York Daily Worker, Juen 17, 1937.

1124.   "Joe Louis," Pic, May, 1937, pp. 1-4.

1125.   "Joe Louis and Farr Swing into Heavy Drills: 800 See
        Champ in Workout," Pittsburgh Courier, August 14, 19-
        37, p. 16.

1126.   "Joe Louis at Wichita," Dodge City (Kansas) Daily
        Globe, February 16, 1937.

1127.   "Joe Louis Coming, But Has Not Yet Signed," Daily
        (London) Sketch, April 22, 1937.

1128.   "Joe Louis Has Ended the Career of Many Fighters,"
        Bangor (Maine) Daily Commercial, January 18, 1937.

1129.   "Joe Louis Hits Canvas in Bout with Sparring Partner,"
        Detroit Free Press, January 28, 1937.

1130.   "Joe Louis in Local Exhibition Bout (in San Diego)
        Tonight," San Diego Union, April 2, 1937.

1131.   "Joe Louis in Two Exhibition Bouts Here (Tulsa,
        Oklahoma) Tonight," Tulsa Daily World, March 18,
        1937.

1132.   "Joe Louis Made $281,930 in Ring During (1936) Year,"
        Pittsburgh Courier, January 2, 1937, p. 1.

1133.   "Joe Louis 'Not Worth a Damn'--in Florida (States
        Florida Governor Fred P. Cone)," New York Amsterdam
        News, February 13, 1937.

1134.   "Joe Louis' Pilots Are Confident," Victoria (B.C.)
        Daily Times, August 25, 1937.

1135.   "Joe Louis Shows He Still Packs Wallop," Detroit
        Evening Times, June 16, 1937.

1136.   "Joe Louis Signed (with Mike Jacobs) for Five More
        Years," New York Telegram, June 24, 1937.

1137.   "Joe Louis, 23 Today, Has Earned $758,000 in 3 Years,"
        Detroit News, May 13, 1937.

1138.   "Joe Louis Wins by Knockout," Arizona Republic
        (Phoenix), June 23, 1937.

1139.   "Joe 15th Champ Since Late John L.," New York
        Amsterdam News, August 28, 1937.

1140.   "Joe Ordered to Face Max in 6 Months," New York
        Amsterdam News, July 31, 1937.

1141.   "Joe Scores 5 Knockdowns," Pittsburgh Courier, June 12,
        1937, p. 16.

1142.   "Joe Tells Joe About Hitting," Detroit Free Press,
        August 17, 1937.

1143.   Jones, Jersey, "Louis, in Challenger Role, Is Providing Biggest Question Mark in 'Heavy' Annals," Kenosha (Wis.) Evening News, June 14, 1937.

1144.   "June Bout with Louis Planned," New York Times, September 4, 1937, p. 7.

1145.   Kahn, James M., "Louis Finally Gets Evidence He's Champion," New York Sun, August 19, 1937.

1146.   Kelly, Clair, "Joe Louis Seems to Have Lost His Instinct to Fight," Detroit Sunday Times, June 13, 1937.

1147.   Kessler, Gene, "Louis, Schmeling War Flares," Chicago Daily Times, June 24, 1937.

1148.   _____, "70,000 to See Battle; Louis Is 11-5 Choice," Chicago Daily Times, June 22, 1937.

1149.   Kieran, John, "Sports of the Times: A Heavy and Hilarious Color Line," New York Times, February 8, 1937, p. 42.

1150.   Lane, French, "Broadway Hot and Bothered But Not Over Louis and Farr," Chicago Sunday Tribune, August 22, 1937.

1151.   Lardner, John, "Bomber Hindered by Sluggish Brain: Appears to Have 'Making' of Real Fighter, But No Ring Imagination," Washington (D.C.) Evening Star, February 1, 1937.

1152.   _____, "Louis Ranks with Greatest Hitters," Cleveland (Ohio) Plain Dealer, June 23, 1937.

1153.   _____, "Schmeling in Fall Is Louis' Plan," Lexington (Ky.) Herald, June 24, 1937.

1154.   Left, Straight, "Joe Louis' Record Holds Its Own with Those of the 'Great' Boxers," Jamaica (B.W.I.) Daily Gleaner, September 6, 1937.

1155.   "Leonard Dixon Is Added to Joe's Camp," Pittsburgh Courier, June 5, 1937, p. 17.

1156.   Lewin, Murray, "Joe Lauds Jim's Courage," New York Daily Mirror, June 23, 1937.

1157.   "Louis and Braddock to Sign," New York Times, February 18, 1937, p. 25.

1158.   "Louis and Braddock Sign, Madison Square Garden Corp Threatens Action," New York Times, February 20, 1937, p. 11.

1159. "Louis and Farr Training," New York Times, August 8, 1937, p. 6.

1160. "Louis and Schmeling Plan Other Bouts Before Title Fights," New York Times, December 16, 1937, p. 41.

1161. "Louis Asked to Fight Nagurski in Detroit," Detroit Evening Times, July 14, 1937.

1162. "Louis 'Carried' Farr for Radio $$$," National Police Gazette, Vol. 144, No. 9, October, 1937, p. 2.

1163. "Louis' Condition," New York Times, June 11, 1937, p. 28.

1164. "Louis Drops Natie Brown for Count of Ten (Before 12,000)," New York Times, February 18, 1937, p. 25.

1165. "Louis-Farr Match: Postponement Until Monday," The Scotsman (Edinburgh, Scotland), August 27, 1937.

1166. "Louis-Farr Result Voted Biggest Surprise of Year in A P Poll," New York Times, December 18,1937, p. 14.

1167. "Louis Fights Two Exhibition Foes Here (Oklahoma City) Tonight," Daily Oklahoman, March 16, 1937.

1168. "Louis First Negro in Heavy Title Bout Since (Jack) Johnson's Defeat," Boston Herald, June 22, 1937.

1169. "Louis Floored by Sparmate in Bout: 'Just Slipped' Laughs Joe," Washington Post, January 28, 1937.

1170. "Louis in First Trip Here Since Winning Title: Champion Slated to Get License to Meet Tommy Farr," New York World-Telegram, July 27, 1937.

1171. "Louis Knocks Out Pair in Local (Tucson, Ariz.) Arena," Tucson Daily Citizen, March 31, 1937.

1172. "Louis Leads in Ring Magazine Rankings," New York Times, December 27, 1937, p. 18.

1173. "Louis May Defend Title in London Bout with J. Doyle or L. Harvey," New York Times, June 25, 1937, p. 28.

1174. "Louis Preparing Axe for Brown's Beef as Title Fight Simmers," New York Amsterdam News, February 13,1937.

1175. "Louis Pronounced in Fine Condition," New York Times, June 11, 1937, p. 28.

1176. "Louis Ready to Fight Any Challenger," Chicago Sun, June 24, 1937.

1177.   "Louis Relates Training Here," Kenosha Evening News
        (Wisconsin), June 25, 1937.

1178.   "Louis Says He Adopted Tunney's Training Methods:
        Real Preparation for Scrap Went on Behind Scenes,"
        New Orleans States, June 25, 1937.

1179.   "Louis Sets up Kenosha, Wis. Training Camp," New York
        Amsterdam News, May 15, 1937.

1180.   "Louis Signs with Jacobs for 5 Years," Louisville
        Times, June 23, 1937.

1181.   "Louis to Battle Sparring Mates Here (Springfield,
        Mo.) Tonight," Springfield (Mo.) Daily News, March 19,
        1937.

1182.   "Louis Wins," New York Times, June 23, 1937, p. 1.

1183.   "Louis Wins by Decision," New York Times, August 31,
        1937, p. 1.

1184.   "Louis to Rest for 2 to 6 Months," New York Times,
        September 2, 1937, p. 28.

1185.   Lytle, Andy, "Behind the Sport Cue," Toronto (Canada)
        Daily Star, May 26, 1937.

1186.   McCann, Richard, "No Peace for Farr; Trouble Sprouts
        in Challenger's Camp," Capital News (Boise, Idaho),
        August 27, 1937.

1187.   McIntyre, Ronald, "1,500 Welcome Joe Louis at Kenosha
        Camp," Milwaukee Sentinel, May 21, 1937.

1188.   McLemore, Henry, "Challenger Favored to Defeat Cham-
        pion," Albany (Ga.) Herald, June 22, 1937.

1189.   _____, "Favor Louis to Win Over Braddock:
        Champion Underdog in Battle," Daily Citizen (Beaver
        Dam, Wisconsin), Juen 22, 1937.

1190.   _____, "Jim Braddock's Judgment Questioned
        by M'Lemore," Toronto Daily Star, June 23, 1937.

1191.   MacNamara, Harry, "Jacobs Signs Louis to Five-Year
        Term: Joe Assured Four Fights a Year, Chicago Herald
        and Examiner, June 24, 1937.

1192.   Martin, Whitney, "'Brown Bomber' Doesn't Mean a Thing
        to Natie Brown But Fans Wonder a Little," Coffeyville
        (Kansas) Daily Journal, February 16, 1937.

1193.   _____, "Joe Louis Scores Knockout Over Natie
        Brown in Fourth," Winnipeg (Canada) Free Press,
        February 18, 1937.

1194.   Martinez, Harry, "Brown Bomber Now Wants to Take on Max Schmeling," New Orleans States, June 23, 1937.

1195.   McNeely, Louis P., "State's Fans Led to Fight by Chandler," Louisville (Ky.) Times, June 22, 1937.

1196.   Mercer, Sid, "Ired Louis Says 'Moxie' Fears Him," New York Journal and American, December 13, 1937.

1197.   Mickelson, Paul, "Conseil De Braddock A Tommy Farr," Le Soleil (Quebec), August 28, 1937.

1198.   _____, "Pastor Ballyhoo Puts Louis in Angry Mood," Detroit Free Press, January 29, 1937.

1199.   _____, "Scribes Have Their Fun in Tagging Tommy Farr," Knoxville (Tenn.) Journal, August 24, 1937.

1200.   _____, "Whip Is Held By Schmeling," Detroit Free Press, June 24, 1937.

1201.   "Mighty Brown Bomber Crushes Foes on March to Title," Pittsburgh Courier, June 26, 1937, p. 13.

1202.   Miley, Jack, "Joe Louis Hangs Up New Record Earns $700 Per Second in Last Fight," Boxing News, January, 1937.

1203.   Miller, "Buster", "Joe Louis: New King of Fistiana," Long Island (N.Y.) Review, July 1, 1937, p. 10.

1204.   Moss, Morton, "Tonypandy Tommy's Joke (Joe Louis vs. Tommy Farr)," New York Post, August 31, 1937.

1205.   "Moxie Pleads for Shot at Louis," Detroit Evening Times, July 14, 1937.

1206.   Murphy, Bob, "'He Can't Punch' Makes Farr's Chances Slim," Detroit Sunday Times, August 22, 1937.

1207.   _____, "'I'll Quit If I Don't Win'---Louis," Detroit Evening Times, June 22, 1937.

1208.   _____, "Joe Too Good for Champ Braddock," Detroit Evening Times, June 21, 1937.

1209.   _____, "Louis Is Thrilled Over His Victory: New Champ All Smiles After Bout," Detroit Evening Times, June 23, 1937.

1210.   _____, "Louis' Workouts Stress Defense," Detroit Evening Times, June 17, 1937.

1211.   _____, "Making a Champ: Defeat of Carnera Made Loius Think of Becoming Titleholder," Detroit Evening Times, July 7, 1937.

1212. "Natives Oppose Joe's Camp Site," New York Amsterdam News, May 8, 1937.

1213. "NBA Grudgingly Places Louis at Head of Rankings," New York Times, September 14, 1937, p. 28.

1214. "Negotiate London Fight in August: Crown Settles on Joe's Head," New York Amsterdam News, July 3, 1937.

1215. Nichols, Joseph C., "Louis Near Peak Against Partners," New York Times, August 22, 1937, p. 8, Section 5.

1216. "Nunn Visits Both Camps, Picks Joe to Win," Pittsburgh Courier, June 19, 1937, p. 17.

1217. Nunn, William G., "Louis-Braddock Await Bell: Both Men in Superb Form for Big Bout," Pittsburgh Courier, June 19, 1937, pp. 1, 17.

1218. _____, "Louis Has Right Mental Attitude, Nunn Finds on Visit to Joe's Kenosha Camp," Pittsburgh Courier, May 29, 1937, p. 17.

1219. "Offer Made for Title Bout Between Louis and Winner of Gastanga-Thomas Fight," New York Times, July 12, 1937, p. 24.

1220. Ottley, Roi, "Louis Hope Rises; Braddock to Balk If Boycott Grows," New York Amsterdam News, January 16, 1937.

1221. _____, "Reversed English," New York Amsterdam News, February 13, 1937.

1222. "Pastor May Quit Ring Career If Joe Wins Friday," Long Island Daily Press, January 25, 1937.

1223. "Plans for Louis-Schmeling and Schmeling-Farr Bouts May Be Dropped in Favor of NYC Louis-Farr," New York Times, July 2, 1937, p. 14.

1224. "Plans Stalled by Proposal to Move Bout from Soldier Field to Comiskey Park," New York Times, February 6, 1937, p. 21.

1225. "Poll of Sports Writers Picks Louis to Take Title," Chicago Sunday Tribune, June 20, 1937.

1226. Powers, Francis J., "Farr Will Be Easy for Joe Says Writer," Beaumont (Tex.) Enterprise, July 14, 1937.

1227. Prattis, P. L.,"'Louis Doesn't Have to Whip Braddock,' Says P. L. Prattis," Pittsburgh Courier, June 12, 1937, p. 18.

1228.   "Prices for Braddock-Louis Fight Set," New York Times, February 25, 1937, p. 27; February 27, 1937, p. 13.

1229.   "Protest Louis Training Camp in Lake Geneva," Chicago Daily Tribune, May 1, 1937.

1230.   Purser, Howard, "Sports: Both Men in Good Shape," Wisconsin (Milwaukee) News, June 22, 1937.

1231.   Rabuin, Hank, "Joe Louis Heads Coliseum Fight Program Tonight (in Fort Worth)," Fort Worth (Texas) Press, March 23, 1937.

1232.   Rice, Grantland, "Louis Has Too Many Big Guns," New Orleans Item, June 22, 1937.

1233.   _____, "The Sportlight--On Finding a Punch," Detroit Free Press, August 16, 1937.

1234.   Richardson, Martin D., "The Periscope: Joe Louis," Boston Chronicle, December 25, 1937.

1235.   Roden, M. J., "On the Highways of Sport," Globe and Mail (Toronto, Canada), June 22, 1937.

1236.   Rouzeau, Edgar T., "Schmeling Bout Looms If Joe Beats Braddock: Max Agrees to Meet Louis If Bomber Wins," Pittsburgh Courier, June 12, 1937, p. 18.

1237.   "Roxborough Wants Fight in Detroit," Honolulu Advertiser, February 9, 1937.

1238.   Runyon, Damon, "The Brighter Side," Detroit Evening News, August 24, 1937.

1239.   Salsinger, H.G.,   "Joe's Task: To Win Spectacularly, Quickly, Decisively," Detroit News, June 22, 1937.

1240.   _____, "Louis Takes Heavy Crown," Detroit News, June 23, 1937.

1241.   _____, "The Umpire: Rights and Rights," Detroit News, June 24, 1937.

1242.   _____, "Why Braddock Picked Louis First Is Told," Detroit News, June 21, 1937.

1243.   "Schmeling Could Learn From Wily Londos," Detroit Free Press, August 21, 1937.

1244.   "Schmeling--Joe in June--Maybe," New York Amsterdam News, August 28, 1937.

1245.   "Schmeling Noch Immer Auf Der Fahrte Wach Einem Titel--Kampf Mit Joe Louis," N. Y. Staats--Zeitung Und Herald (Donnerstag, Germany), August 19, 1937.

1246. Scott, Lester, "Farr Dominates Weighing Ceremonies; Louis Displays Trance of Nervousness," New York World-Telegram, August 20, 1937, p. 1.

1247. Sentner, David P., "Schmeling Will Not Seek Battle with Bomber Joe," Wichita Beacon (Kansas), June 23, 1937.

1248. "Set Plans for London Bout for Louis in August: New Champ to Box Len Harvey, Foord or Doyle," Pittsburgh Courier, July 3, 1937, p. 16.

1249. Shaver, Bud, "City as Fight Site: Joe May Meet Max Here," Detroit Evening News, June 23, 1937.

1250. _____, "Der Max Holds Key: Animosity Sways Schmeling," Detroit Evening Times, June 24, 1937.

1251. _____, "Logic Favors Louis: Sentiment on Braddock's Side," Detroit Sunday Times, June 13, 1937.

1252. _____, "Louis Wins Fight Decision, Farr Wins Cheers," Detroit Evening Times, August 31, 1937.

1253. Siegel, Arthur, "Braddock Battle Plan Was Built on Gamble," Boston Traveler, June 24, 1937.

1254. "Wife (Marva Louis) Given Divorce From Joe Louis," Washington Times-Herald, March 28, 1937.

1255. "Spokane Ring Enthusiasts Favor Braddock in Battle," Spokane Daily Chronicle (Wash.), June 22, 1937.

1256. "Sports Experts Praise Joe's Victory Over Champ (James Braddock)," Pittsburgh Courier, July 3, 1937, p. 16.

1257. Stewart, Walter, "Ol' Melonjaws Louis Is 'Not Quite Human,'" Rocky Mountain (Denver, Colo.) News, January 10, 1937.

1258. Super, Henry, "Joe Louis to Stop in El Paso Monday," El Paso (Texas) Times, March 28, 1937.

1259. Sutton, Frank, "Champ at Peak, Joe Must Reach It to Win, Sutton Finds on Trip," Pittsburgh Courier, June 19, 1937.

1260. Talbot, Gayle, "Brown Bomber Just Dud to Welshman," Independent (St. Petersburg, Fla.), August 31, 1937.

1261. _____, "Champ (Louis) Acts Up to Role Before Ring-Crazy Mob," Washington Star, January 20, 1937.

1262. Taub, Billy, "Braddock-Louis: Here's the Lowdown," New York Amsterdam News, June 19,1937, p. 17.

1263. "The Three Heavyweights," Sunset (Bluefield, W. Va.)
      News, April 13, 1937.

1264. "Title Battle Enriches 'Jolting Joe's' Drawing Power
      Over a Million," Pittsburgh Courier, June 26, 1937,
      p. 18.

1265. "260 lb. Sparmate Floored by Joe with Lethal Left,"
      Pittsburgh Courier, May 29, 1937, p. 17.

1266. "Twenty Thousand Negroes See Title Go (to Joe Louis),"
      New York Amsterdam News, June 26, 1937, p. 17.

1267. "Two Sparring Partners Kayoed by Joe Louis in
      Exhibition Bouts (in St. Joseph, Missouri)," St.
      Joseph Gazette, March 13, 1937.

1268. "Uzcudan Stops on Battlefield to Pick Louis," Detroit
      Free Press, August 22, 1937.

1269. Van Every, Edward, "Injured Hands Hamper Negro,"
      New York Sun, August 31, 1937, p. 26.

1270. _____, "Joe Louis: Superman and Super-Fighter,"
      National Police Gazette, Vol. 143, Nos. 1-8, January-
      November, 1937.

1271. _____, "Louis Is Lauded by Handlers," New York
      World Telegraph, June 23, 1937.

1272. _____, "Louis Is Not Yet at His Peak: Brown
      Bomber Became Champion Two Years Too Soon, Contends
      Johnny Attell," New York Sun, August 17, 1937, p. 33.

1273. _____, "Louis to Weigh Under 200," New York
      Sun, July 28, 1937.

1274. "Victory by Kayo Seen for Louis," New York Amsterdam
      News, August 28, 1937.

1275. "Voice of the People: Joe Louis vs. Tommy Farr,"
      New York Daily News, September 2, 1937.

1276. Walsh, Davis J., "Carries His Left Low But Farr Is
      Cute," Detroit Evening Times, July 31, 1937.

1277. _____, "Everybody Seems to Be Conspiring to
      Make Joe Look Like Bum," Cincinnati Time-Star, June 21,
      1937.

1278. _____, "Louis Fine Fighter," Mobile (Ala.)
      Times, June 23, 1937.

1279. Ward, Arch, "Louis Wins Title: Knockout--50,000 Watch
      Braddock Fall in Eighth Round," Chicago Daily Tribune,
      June 23, 1937.

1280. Washington, Chester L., "Louis World's Champ: Joe
      Flattens Braddock in Eight Savage Rounds," Pittsburgh
      Courier, June 23, 1937, p. 1.

1281. _____, "The Lion (Joe Louis) and the Lamb
      (Jim Braddock)," Pittsburgh Courier, June 26, 1937,
      p. 16.

1282. Webster, "Red", "Louis, Here (Dallas,Texas) for
      Exhibition, Confident He'll Win Crown," Dallas Dispatch,
      March 21, 1937.

1283. Wells, Robert E., "Jim Braddock vs. Joe Louis," National
      Police Gazette, Vol. 144, No. 4, May, 1937, p. 4.

1284. Williams, Joe, "Farr Is Hero in Defeat Makes Louis Look
      Dismal and Schmeling's Case O.K.," New York World-
      Telegram, August 31, 1937.

1285. _____, "Louis' Craft Is Too Much for Braddock,"
      New York World-Telegram, June 23, 1937.

1286. _____, "Louis Is Bomber of Old in Rise from
      Resin to Heavy Title," New York World-Telegram,
      June 23, 1937, p. 26.

1287. _____, "Oracle Ray Dooms Louis Too Fat and
      Speed's Gone Braddock's Chief Hazard," New York World-
      Telegram, June 10, 1937.

1288. _____, "Says Farr Can Hurt Louis . . .,"
      New York World-Telegram, August 30, 1937.

1289. _____, "Schmeling's Coming Again; Lightning
      and the Flash; Cochrane Can't Stay Out," New York
      World-Telegram, August 6, 1937.

1290. Wilson, Rollo, "Louis Wins, But Fails to Catch up with
      Pastor," Pittsburgh Courier, February 6, 1937.

1291. Wood, Wilbur, "Big Purse Braddock's Balm: Veteran
      Carried Fight to the Younger Man Until Title-Depriving
      Knockout," New York Sun, June 23, 1937.

1292. _____, "Braddock Expert in Upsets," New York
      Sun, June 9, 1937.

1293. _____, "In and Out of the Ring with Poker Face
      Louis," Boxing News, December, 1937.

1294. _____, "Louis Championship Victory Best Fight
      of Bomber's Career," New York Sun, June 23, 1937.

1295. _____, "Louis Drilling for 3 Fights," New York
      Sun, August 9, 1937.

1296. _____, "Louis Is Lucky He Faced Farr, Not Schmeling: Few Believe Bomber Could Have Won from Max on Monday Night," New York Sun, September 1, 1937.

1297. "'Worthy Champ,' Says John Henry Lewis After Seeing Joe," Pittsburgh Courier, June 26, 1937, p. 18.

1298. Young, Fay, "King Louis I: Louis Down Once But Rises to New Heights," New York Amsterdam News, June 26, 19-37, pp. 1, 4.

1299. Young, Frank, "Louis in Old Form in K.O. Over Brown," New York Amsterdam News, February 20, 1937.

B. FAMILY

1300. "Joe Louis Hears Father Is Living," New York Daily News, June 26, 1937.

1301. "Joe's Mother Has Good Word for Jim," Grand Rapids (Mich.) Herald, June 23, 1937.

1302. "Louis' Mother Takes Son's Victory (over Jim Braddock) Calmly," New York Sun, June 23, 1937.

1303. "Marva (Louis) 'Knew Joe Would Win' the Championship," Journal and Guide, July 3, 1937, p. 1.

1304. "Rumor That Joe's Dad Is Confined in Asylum," New York Amsterdam News, July 3, 1937.

C. FOLK HERO

1305. Bourne, St. Clair, "Harlem Rooting for Joe Louis," New York Amsterdam News, June 19, 1937.

1306. "Brooklyn Goes Daffy as Bomber Wins: Celebration Carries Long into the Night, Man Hits Own Head with Milk Bottle Just to Show Appreciation to Joe," New York Amsterdam News, June 26, 1937, p. 11.

1307. "Brown Bomber Lets Friends Down As He Lets Foe Stay Ten Rounds: Even Though White Lad Was Speed Demon, Joe Should Have Caught Him, Says Harlem," Nashville (Tenn.) Globe and Independent, February 5, 1937.

1308. Buck, Al, "Louis Awaits White Hopes," New York Post, June 23, 1937, p. 1.

1309. "Cheyenne Negroes Rejoice at Victory of Joe Louis," Wyoming State Tribune--Cheyenne State Leader, June 23, 1937.

1310. Cunningham, Bill, "Colored Press Did Great Job: Handled Joe Louis Victory (over Braddock) Cleverly--No Unpleasant Aftermath to Fight Crown," Boston Post, July 5, 1937.

1311.   "Detroit Hails Louis' Victory: Bomber's Alabama
         Birthplace and Chicago 'Harlem' Also Join in Celebra-
         tion," New York Sun, June 23, 1937.

1312.   Dexter, Charles E., "When Joe Is Champ: An Answer to
         Jim Crow's Radio Commentator, John Kennedy, Who Slanders
         the Famous Heavyweight and His Peiole," New York Sunday
         Worker, January 1, 1937.

1313.   Editorial. "(If Louis) Win or Lose, Let's Be Sane,"
         New York Amsterdam News, June 19, 1937, p. 1.

1314.   "Friction Is Absent as New South Hails Joe," Pittsburgh
         Courier, July 3, 1937, p. 18.

1315.   "Harlem Cool About Fight," New York Amsterdam News,
         August 21, 1937.

1316.   "Harlem Gay Over Victory," New York Amsterdam News,
         June 26, 1937.

1317.   "Harlem Holds Maddest Revel: Celebration of Joe
         Louis' Victory Is Vociferous," New York Sun, June 23,
         1937.

1318.   "Harlem Rooting for Joe Louis," New York Amsterdam
         News, June 19, 1937, p. 16.

1319.   "Howard (University) 'Prof' Predicts Louis Will Keep
         Poise as Champion: Not Expected to 'Show Off'
         Because He Is of Vagotonic Type Rather Than
         Sympathectonic--Easy Lies His Head While Wearing
         Crown," Pittsburgh Courier, July 3, 1937, p. 18.

1320.   "Louis-Pastor Go in Detroit: Fans Pack Motor City;
         Joe Favorite to Stop Bob," New York Amsterdam News,
         September 23, 1937, p. 1.

1321.   "Louis Refuses Mix-Bout Offer," Nevada State Journal,
         July 14, 1937.

1322.   "'Mild Riot' After Louis Wins Crown," New York
         Amsterdam News, July 10, 1937.

1323.   "Mile of Ivory Gleams: Detroit's Black Belt Welcome
         Louis' Rise to Peak with Big Grin-Preparations Made
         for Welcome and Dinner," New York Post, June 23, 1937.

1324.   "Negroes Here Happy as Louis Beats Farr," Toronto
         Daily Star, August 31, 1937.

1325.   "New York Goes Wild (over Joe Louis)," Pittsburgh
         Courier, July 26, 1937, p. 16.

1326. Nunn, William G., "Nunn Describes South Side (Chicago)
       As It Goes Mad After Joe Louis Victory: Howling
       Mob of Whites and Blacks Ride Backs of Autos and
       Street Cars-Racial Lines Forgotten," Pittsburgh Courier,
       June 26, 1937, p. 16.

1327. Ottley, Roi, "Is It True What They Say about Dixie?"
       New York Amsterdam News, February 27, 1937.

1328. _____, "The Bomber (Joe Louis) and the Bum
       (Bob Pastor)," New York Amsterdam News, February 6,
       1937.

1329. Shaver, Bud, "Million Dollar Gates; Negro Made Them
       Possible; Louis to Bring Them Back," Detroit Sunday
       Times, July 18, 1937.

1330. Sparling, Earl, "Harlem (N.Y.) up at Count of 10 to
       Shout, 'I Told You So!': Joe Louis' Victory Celbrated
       by Surging Mass of Humanity, Singing, Yelling and
       Dancing--Called a 'Better Sight Than One in Chic,"
       New York World-Telegram, June 23, 1937.

1331. Wilkins, Roy, "Nazis at Home and Abroad (and Joe
       Louis)," New York Amsterdam News, January 16, 1937.

1332. Williams, Joe, "Louis' Craft Is Too Much for (James)
       Braddock: Negro Is Youngest (23 years old) Champion
       in History and Second of Race to Hold Title," New
       York Daily News, June 23, 1937.

1333. "Winnipeg Fans Favor Joe Louis to Take Champion,"
       Winnipeg (Canada) Free Press, June 22, 1937.

1334. Wood, Wilbur, "Briton Appears Outclassed," New York
       Sun, August 22, 1937.

D. PERSONAL LIFE

1335. "Autos, Clothes Joe's Pet Luxuries," Daily (Vancouver,
       B.C.) Province, May 13, 1937.

1336. Bourne, St. Clair, "Joe Louis Now Leads Pugilistic
       Parade of Snappy Dressers, Says Billy Taub, Ex-Harlem-
       ite, Clothier to Champs," New York Amsterdam News,
       April 17, 1937.

1337. "Commission Medics Say Louis Is Physically Fit,"
       Pittsburgh Courier, June 19, 1937, p. 16.

1338. "Detroit Plans Fete for New Champ," Pittsburgh Courier,
       July 3, 1937, p. 18.

1339. "From the Cotton Fields to World's Ring Peak,"
       Winnipeg (Canada) Free Press, June 23, 1937.

1340. "Joe Louis Already Worth $250,000 Celebrates (23rd) Birthday," California Eagle, May 2, 1937.

1341. "Joe Louis Joins Films: Heavyweight Champion Signed to Appear in 'Spirit of Youth'," New York Times, October 6, 1937.

1342. Lake, Austen, "Wuxtree! Louis Draws Color Line Against Negro-Pugilists," Boston Evening American, February 9, 1937.

1343. "Louis Is Growing Up," New York Post, May 13, 1937.

1344. "Louis Plays Softball with His Old Gang," Twin City Sentinnel (Winston-Salem, N.C.), July 14, 1937.

1345. "Louis to Write for 'Evening Standard'," Evening Standard (London, England), August 28, 1937.

1346. "No Benefits for Ol' Joe: Plans Having $300,000 Stowed Away by 1939 in Annuities," New York Amsterdam News, January 30, 1937, p. 14.

1347. Nunn, William G., "'No Ladies Allowed,' Is Keynote of Louis' 'Hide-Away Mansion," Pittsburgh Courier, May 29, 1937, p. 18.

1348. Rainey, Joseph H. (Pennsylvania Athletic Commissioner), "Joe Displayed Power and Brains, Too," Pittsburgh Courier, June 26, 1937, p. 16.

4.   1938

A. BOXER

1349. Adams, Caswell, "Louis Knocks Out Mann in 3d Round of Heavyweight Title Bout at Garden (Before 20,000)," New York Herald Tribune, February 24, 1938.

1350. _____, "Louis Knocks Out Schmeling in 1st Round before 90,000," New York Herald Tribune, June 23, 1938.

1351. _____, "80,000 to See Louis-Schmeling Heavyweight Title Bout at Yankee Stadium Wednesday Night: Bout for Title to Be 67th in History of Class," New York Herald Tribune, June 19, 1938.

1352. _____, "Louis, Mann Meet in Title Bout Wednesday: Negro Is Rated Top Choice in Scanty Betting," New York Herald Tribune, February 20, 1938.

1353. _____, "Million-Dollar Gate Expected for 2nd Meeting," New York Herald Tribune, June 19, 1938.

1354. "All Germany Is Confident: Max Given One Choice--
       Victory," Detroit News, June 22, 1938.

1355. "Bare Nazi Death Plot on Louis: G-Men Move in to
       Guard Champ on Eve of Fight, 'Will Kill Dirty N---R'
       If He Dare Beat Our Max Schmeling, Postal Card
       Declares," New York Amsterdam News, June 25, 1938,
       pp. 1, 12.

1356. "Berlin Assures Max No Loss of Prestige," New York
       Sun, June 24, 1938.

1357. Bourne, St. Clair, "Bomber-Schmeling Battle Most
       Important Heavyweight Go in Years," New York
       Amsterdam News, June 25, 1938, p. 6, section 2.

1358. Bromberg, Lester, "Certain to Defend Crown Here in
       Winter," New York World-Telegram, June 23, 1938.

1359. _____, "K.O. by Louis Seemed Braddock End,"
       New York World-Telegram, January 24, 1938.

1360. Brown, Ned, "Joe Louis--Man of Destiny--The Real
       Reasons Schmeling Lost," National Police Gazette,
       Vol. 144, No. 17, August, 1938, pp. 7, 9.

1361. Buck, Al, "Ex-Champion Declares Age Big Handicap to
       Schmeling," New York Post, March 28, 1938.

1362. _____, "Louis Lacks Indoor Foe: Pastor, Farr
       Willing to Fight in Open Air Before Larger Crowd,"
       New York Post, September 29, 1938.

1363. _____, "Mike Jacobs Is Uncertain on Bomber's
       Next Victim," New York Post, June 24, 1938.

1364. _____, "(Promoter) Mike Jacobs Feels Long
       Layoff Will Find Joe Growing Stale," New York Post,
       July 13, 1938.

1365. _____, "Louis Seems Confused in Workouts for
       Title Battle," New York Post, June 10, 1938.

1366. Burchard, James A., "Looks Good in Kayo of Thomas,"
       New York World-Telegram, April 2, 1938.

1367. "Champion Scores K.O. in First; Avenges Defeat,"
       Call & Post, June 23, 1938, p. 1.

1368. Cuddy, Jack, "In This Corner: Joe Louis," Washington
       Post, February 26, 1938.

1369. Dawson, James P., "Louis and Mann Ready for Title
       Fight," New York Times, February 20, 1938, p. 10,
       Section 5.

1370.   _____, "Louis Defeats Schmeling by a Knockout in First; 80,000 See Title Battle," New York Times, June 23, 1938, p. 1.

1371.   Dempsey, Jack, "I Pick Schmeling (over Louis)," Weekly Magazine, June 19, 1938.

1372.   Editorial, "Joe Louis: Sport's Dead-Pan Personality," Brooklyn Eagle, June 19, 1938.

1373.   "Foul Is Claimed by German Boxer," New York Times, June 23, 1938, p. 22.

1374.   Galento, Tony, "Max Had to Meet Fire with Fire--or Else," New York World-Telegram, June 23, 1938.

1375.   Gould, Alan, "Louis K.O.'s Schmeling in First, Flooring Maxie Three Times; Fight Lasts Only 2:04 Minutes: Detroiter Avenges 1936 Knockout with Speediest Finish in Title History Before 80,000 Fans," Detroit Free Press, June 23, 1938.

1376.   Graham, Frank, "Setting the Pace: A Show They Will Never Forget," New York Sun, June 23, 1938.

1377.   _____, "Setting the Pace: Extra! Baer Knocks Out Louis," New York Sun, June 24, 1938.

1378.   _____, "Setting the Pace: Natie Asked for the Fight," New York Sun, February 25, 1938.

1379.   _____, "Setting the Pace: Not a Phantom Fight This Time," New York Sun, May 10, 1938.

1380.   _____, "Setting the Pace: The Heavyweight Champion of the World," New York Sun, May 12, 1938.

1381.   _____, "Setting the Pace: The Way a Champion Goes," New York Sun, June 3, 1938.

1382.   "(Horace) Henderson Band Features the Joe Louis Shuffle," New York Amsterdam News, July 9, 1938, pp. 6, 8, Section 2.

1383.   "'I'll Even Scores with Schmeling,' Says Joe Louis," Journal and Guide, February 5, 1938, pp. 1, 10.

1384.   "Joe Louis Bout with Winner of L. Nova-G. Barlund Bout Considered," New York Times, September 28, 1938, p. 34.

1385.   "Joe Louis-H. Thomas Preview," New York Times, April 1, 1938, p. 18.

1386.   "Joe Louis-H. Thomas Bout--Louis Wins," New York Times, April 3, 1938, p. 6, sec. 5.

1387.   "Joe Louis-H. Thomas Bout Comment," New York Times,
        April 3, 1938, p. 6, sec. 5.

1388.   Kahn, James M., "Kidney Punch Is Only Blow Max Recalls,"
        New York Sun, June 23, 1938.

1389.   "Kidney Blow Minor Foul," New York World-Telegram,
        June 23, 1938.

1390.   Kieran, John, "Sports of the Times: In the Wake of
        Schmeling's Night Out," New York Times, June 24, 1938.

1391.   _____, "Sports of the Times: Once in a
        Lifetime (Joe Louis vs. Nathan Mann)," New York Times,
        February 20, 1938, p. 10, Section 5.

1392.   _____, "Sports of the Times: Thunder on the
        Left," New York Times, February 27, 1938, p. 10, Section 5.

1393.   Lardner, John, "If Title Goes, It Stays Away: So Says
        John Lardner, Who Doesn't Trust Max," Detroit News,
        June 21, 1938.

1394.   "Letters on Louis Bout," New York Times, July 2, 1938,
        p. 9.

1395.   Lewin, Murray, "(Gene) Tunney Aids Louis in Secret
        Session," New York Daily Mirror, June 3, 1938.

1396.   "Louis Aims at Early Kayo (over Harry Thomas),"
        New York World-Telegram, March 31, 1938.

1397.   "Louis-Lewis Contract Signed," New York Times,
        December 17, 1938, p. 19.

1398.   "Louis and Thomas Practice," New York Times, March 16,
        1938, p. 30; March 27, 1938, p. 8, Sec. 5.

1399.   "Louis Comments on Future Bouts," New York Times,
        July 13, 1938, p. 25.

1400.   "Louis Delivers the Winning Punch After Battering
        Max 124 Seconds," New York World-Telegram, June 23,
        1938.

1401.   "Louis in Defense of Title Tonight," New York Times,
        April 1, 1938, p. 18.

1402.   "Louis Lunches with Braddock," Journal and Guide,
        March 5, 1938.

1403.   "Louis' Manager Sends Protest to Germany Against
        Unfair Pictures of Title Fight," New York Post, July
        27, 1938.

1404. "Louis-Schmeling Bout: Both Sign," New York Times,
       May 12, 1938, p. 31.

1405. "Louis-Schmeling Bout: Both Train," New York Times,
       May 31, 1938, p. 27.

1406. "Louis-Schmeling Bout: Louis Comment," New York Times,
       June 23, 1938, p. 14.

1407. "Louis-Schmeling Bout: Preview," New York Times,
       June 22, 1938, p. 28.

1408. "Louis-Schmeling Bout to be Held on June 22, New York
       Times, March 19, 1938, p. 18.

1409. "Louis-Schmeling Bout: Both Train," New York Times,
       May 30, 1938, p. 15.

1410. "Louis-Schmeling Bout: Louis Wins by Knockout in
       1st Round," New York Times, June 23, 1938, p. 1.

1411. "Louis-Schmeling Fight to Be Taken to Chicago by
       White Business Leaders," Black Dispatch, January 8,
       1938.

1412. "Louis Starts Hard Work for Schmeling," Sunday Worker,
       June 5, 1938.

1413. "Louis Strong Favorite in Bout with Thomas at
       Chicago Friday," New York Times, March 27, 1938, p. 8.

1414. "Louis the Winner in Fifth Round," New York World-
       Telegram, April 2, 1938.

1415. "Louis Tries Knockout Punch on Spar Mates in Final
       Drill for Title Bout with Thomas," New York Times,
       March 31, 1938, p. 16.

1416. "Louis Weighs 199 and Schmeling 193," Detroit News,
       June 22, 1938.

1417. "Louis Wins by K.O. in the 1st Round," Daily Worker,
       June 23, 1938.

1418. "Max's Doctor Finds Injury Not Serious," New York
       Times, June 24, 1938, p. 22.

1419. "Max Returns, Ready to K.O. Joe," New York Daily News,
       May 10, 1938.

1420. "Max Schmeling Denies Calling Louis 'Fouler," New
       York World-Telegram, December 10, 1938.

1421. Mitchell, Joseph, "Joe Runs True to Form, But He Was
       Right on Louis," New York World-Telegram, June 23, 19-
       38.

1422. Newman, Abe, "Left-Handed Dynamite," <u>Daily Worker</u>,
       April 3, 1938.

1423. Nunn, William G., "Louis Had Knocked Schmeling Out
       Before Referee Stopped Bout," <u>Pittsburgh Courier</u>,
       June 25, 1937, pp. 1, 2.

1424. "Offer Made to Louis for Philadelphia Bout with T.
       Galento," <u>New York Times</u>, July 6, 1938, p. 17.

1425. Phillips, Harold, "Joe Ain't Scared O' Hitter,"
       <u>Washington News</u>, June 21, 1938.

1426. "Pictures Illustrate Power and Speed of Louis as He
       Kayoes Schmeling," <u>Pittsburgh Courier</u>, June 25, 1938,
       p. 24.

1427. Powers, Francis J., "Louis Annexes Belt with Win over
       Thomas: Joe's Five-Round Knockout Clinches Ownership
       of English Trophy," <u>New York Sun</u>, April 2, 1938.

1428. "Protest on Gloves Fails at Weighing," <u>New York Sun</u>,
       June 15, 1938.

1429. "Real Blow by Blow," <u>New York World-Telegram</u>, June 23,
       1938.

1430. Rice, Grantland, "Only Joe and Max," <u>New York Sun</u>,
       March 2, 1938.

1431. _____, "The Sportlight: Only Joe and Max,"
       <u>New York Sun</u>, March 2, 1938.

1432. _____, "The Sportlight: Schmeling Gives Answer,"
       <u>New York Sun</u>, May 10, 1938.

1433. _____, "The Sportlight: The Fiercest Fusillade,"
       <u>New York Sun</u>, June 23, 1938.

1434. _____, "The Sportlight: The New Joe Louis,"
       <u>New York Sun</u>, June 24, 1938.

1435. Rodney, Lester, "The Rise of Joe Louis, A Real Ring
       Champion," <u>Washington Daily News</u>, June 21, 1938.

1436. Runyon, Damon, "Max Never Had Chance (Against Louis),"
       <u>New York Daily Mirror</u>, June 23, 1938.

1437. Salsinger, H. G., "Joe Louis' Record Tops Those of
       All Other Heavy Champions," <u>Detroit News</u>, June 24,
       1938.

1438. "Schmeling, in Hospital, Plans to Sail for Germany
       July 2, 1938," <u>New York Times</u>, June 24, 1938, p. 25.

1439. "Schmeling Win Dispute on Type of Glove," <u>Detroit
       News</u>, June 21, 1938.

1440. Scott, Lester, "Max Wants Louis Again," New York World-Telegram, June 23, 1938.

1441. Stewart, Walter, "Eddie Gets Up in a Fog After Sampling One Left," New York World-Telegram, December 15, 1938.

1442. "Topics of the Times: Straws in the Wind," New York Times, June 24, 1938.

1443. "Trouble in Cleveland: Outbreak Follows Louis Victory--Man Shot, Trolley Stoned," New York Times, June 23, 1938.

1444. Van Every, Edward, "Blackburn Confident Louis Will Win," New York Sun, May 10, 1938.

1445. _____, "Bomber Looks Beyond Mann," New York Sun, February 21, 1938.

1446. _____, "Joe Louis Finds He Must Fight Added Weight," New York Sun, February 17, 1938.

1447. _____, "Louis' Niche in Ring Annals: Fans Discuss What Joe Might--or Might Not--Have Done to Dempsey, Tunney, et al.," New York Sun, June 25, 1938.

1448. _____, "Louis Rejoices in Feeling He Is Now Real Champion," New York Sun, June 23, 1938.

1449. _____, "Louis Says Max Evaded Him," New York Sun, May 11, 1938.

1450. _____, "Max's Defeat Well Planned," New York Sun, June 24, 1938.

1451. _____, "Promoter Has Faith in Max," New York Sun, May 10, 1938.

1452. _____, "Time Works in Louis' Favor: Blackburn Presents Argument to Prove that Schmeling Is Going and Louis Coming," New York Sun, June 6, 1938.

1453. _____, "Trainer Says Louis is Ready," New York Sun, June 21, 1938.

1454. _____, "Joe Louis Can't Win in Next '38 Bout: Unless Bomber Boxes for Charity or Exercise, He Will Lose Money Through U.S. Surtaxes," New York Sun, July 7, 1938.

1455. _____, "Tunney Praises Louis' Form," New York Sun, June 15, 1938.

1456. Van Ness, Fred, "Louis Battle Here Will Have $30 Top," New York Times, April 27, 1938, p. 29.

1457. Vest, Rollo S., "Louis Earned Plenty Cash--For Uncle Sam," New York Amsterdam News, April 23, 1938, p. 15.

1458. Vidmer, Ricahrds, "Down in Front: Dollars and Sense," New York Herald Tribune, April 1, 1938.

1459. Wallace, Francis, "Joe Proved He'd Learned to Think When Max Threw Right," New York World-Telegram, June 23, 1938.

1460. Washington, Chester L., "Joe Smashes Way to Quickest Victory by K.O. in Fight History," Pittsburgh Courier, June 25, 1938.

1461. Williams, Joe, "Louis Proves His Greatness in Schmeling Kayo," New York World-Telegram, June 23, 1938.

1462. _____, "The Big Fight Will Come Here, Where It Belongs," New York World-Telegram, April 25, 1938.

1463. Wood, Wilbur, "Joe Louis Victory Sets Record," New York Sun, June 23, 1938.

1464. _____, "Louis Sets Money-Making Mark," New York Sun, June 23, 1938.

1465. "World Boxing Commission Orders Louis to Meet Schmeling or Lose Title," New York Times, April 23, 1938, p. 12.

B. FOLK HERO

1466. "All Harlem Joins in Night of Gaiety," New York Times, June 23, 1938, p. 1.

1467. Arnold, Elliott, "500,000 Hail Louis All Night As Harlem Dances in Streets: Crowd Mock Nazi Salute, Bottles Fly and Bus Is Fired," New York World-Telegram, June 23, 1938, pp. 1, 2.

1468. Buck, Al, "Louis Draws Line on Fighting Men of Own Race for Title: Jacobs (Boxing Promoter) Claims Such Matches Wouldn't Get Fans' Support," New York Post, September 30, 1938.

1469. Burley, Dan, "Harlem at Fight Time . . .," New York Amsterdam News, June 25, 1938, p. 2.

1470. "Cleveland Goes Wild as News of (Joe Louis) Victory Flashes Over Radio," Call & Post, June 23, 1938, p. 1.

1471. "Harlem Tense as Bout Nears: Bomber Holds Heavy Edge in Local Opinion," New York Amsterdam News, June 18, 1938, pp. 1, 15.

1472. McKinney, Robert, "No Color Line Is Drawn by Joe Louis: Affair with Lewis in Garden on January 27 to Be First All-Negro Heavyweight Championship Bout," New York Sun, November 3, 1938.

1473.   Malliet, A. M. Wendell, "'We Too,' West Indians
         Holler as Harlem Fans Flock to Louis," New York
         Amsterdam News, June 25, 1938, p. 11.

1474.   "Negroes Fill Streets of Harlem in Celebration of
         Louis Victory," New York Herald Tribune, June 23, 1938.

1474a.   Wood, Wilbur, "Lack of Cannon Fodder for Louis Per-
         plexes Promoters: Search for White Hope Is on,"
         New York Sun, June 24, 1938.

                    C.   PERSONAL LIFE

1475.   "Joe Glad He Proved a Worthy Champion," New York Times,
         June 23, 1938, p. 20.

1476.   "Joe Louis Demands U.S. Ambassador Protest Fight Films
         as Shown in Germany: Allege that Patched up Motion
         Picture Tells False Story Regarding Epochal Struggle,"
         Black Dispatch, August 6, 1938.

1477.   "Joe Louis Has His Big Night as Film Star (in "The
         Spirit of Youth")," Washington Post, January 21, 1938.

1478.   "Joe Louis Suing Distributor (for Wrongfully Using His
         Name) for $25,000 Damages," New York Amsterdam News,
         June 24, 1938.

1479.   "Letter on Gov. Murphy's Greeting to Louis," New York
         Times, June 24, 1938, p. 18.

1480.   "Louis Denies Reports of Retirement," New York Times,
         June 25, 1938, p. 9.

1481.   "Louis Means 'Clean Living' to His School Superin-
         tendent," New York World-Telegram, June 28, 1938.

1482.   "Negro Positive He Will Win by Knockout: Says German
         Is Going to Meet a Different Louis in June Title Bout,"
         New York Sun, May 10, 1938.

1483.   "Seek Joe Louis to Open Office of Victory Mutual Life
         Insurance Co. in Jamaica, New York," New York Amster-
         dam News, May 5, 1938.

1484.   "Sees Brother: Heavy Champ's Sister Howard v. Coed,"
         Washington, D.C. Times, January 21, 1938.

1485.   "Sift Reports that Joe Louis May Buy Hotel (Theresa),"
         New York Amsterdam News, June 11, 1938, p. 11.

5.   1939

A.   BOXER

1486.   Adams, Caswell, "Negroes' Fight (Between Joe Louis and John Henry Lewis) Likely to Draw Gate of $80,000," New York Herald Tribune, January 22, 1939.

1487.   "Anytime Joe Louis Is in Need of a Job Henry Ford Will Give Him One," Philadelphia Tribune, September 5, 1939.

1488.   Avery, Leslie, "Louis May Meet Pastor at Detroit in Fall," Washington Daily News, June 20, 1939, p. 35.

1489.   "J. Blackburn Predicts Louis Undefeated Retirement," New York Times, November 12, 1939, p. 12, sec. 5.

1490.   Bromberg, Lester, "Joe Louis 'Explains' Quick Kayoes: Just Being Kind to Aging Blackburn," New York World-Telegram, June 14, 1939.

1491.   _____, "Million for Louis-Pastor?" New York World-Telegram, September 1, 1939.

1492.   _____, "None of Current Crop Seen Match for Champ," New York World-Telegram, January 26, 1939.

1493.   Brown, Ned, "'I Can Whip Joe Louis,' Says Bob Pastor," National Police Gazette, Vol. 144, No. 29, September, 1939, pp. 7, 11.

1494.   Broun, Heywood, "It Seems to Me," Washington Daily News, September 23, 1939.

1495.   Buck, Al, "Louis Is Named Fighter of Year) by Ring Magazine)," New York Post, December 26,1939.

1496.   Butler, Jim, "Sports,-Folks and Facts," Michigan Chronicle, September 16, 1939.

1497.   "California's First Championship Fight in Three Decades Expected to Draw Big Turnout," California Eagle, April 13, 1939.

1498.   "Champion Louis Dusts Opponent in 2 Min., 20 Sec.," Philadelphia Tribune, April 20, 1939.

1499.   "Cops on Fight Duty Carry Clubs; 1917 Out," Washington Daily News, June 29, 1939, p. 22.

1500.   Cossman, Maurie, "Pastor's Kayo Leaves Fight Situation in Sorry State," Flint (Mich.) Journal, September 21, 1939.

1501.   Cuddy, Jack, "Brown Bomber Stops Lewis in 2:29 of First Round: Louis Shows no Mercy in Fifth Defense of Title," Detroit Free Press, January 26, 1939.

1502. Daniel, Daniel M., "Promoters Eye Heavies for Louis Opponents," The Ring, Vol. 17, No. 12, January, 1939, pp. 2-3, 45.

1503. Dawson, James P., "Crowd of 50,000 Sees Louis Knock Out Pastor in Eleventh Round," New York Times, September 21, 1939, p. 27.

1504. _____, "Louis, Not Surprised by Galento's Showing, Admits the Knockdown Punch Hurt," New York Times, June 29, 1939, p. 22.

1505. _____, "Louis' Savage Punches Stop (John Henry) Lewis in First Round Before 17,350 at Garden," New York Times, January 26, 1939, p. 24.

1506. Edgar, W. W., "Return of Louis-Galento Bout Is Now Planned for Detroit Next June," Detroit Free Press, September 21, 1939.

1507. Fentress, J. Cullen, "Louis 'Decapitates' Roper to Keep Crown in Title Bout Here," California Eagle, April 20, 1939.

1508. Ferguson, Harry, "Tony Within Split-Second Punch of Title: Louis Is Too Much a Craftsman for Two-Ton; Loser Asks Another Match but Isn't Likely," Washington Daily News, June 29, 1939.

1509. "Galento and Louis Train," New York Times, June 8, 1939, p. 35.

1510. "Galento Will Go Quicker, Says Louis," New York Sun, April 19, 1939.

1511. Grayson, Harry, "Louis Not Aiding Game by Signing for Roper," Washington Daily News, February 17, 1939.

1512. _____, "Louis Plans to Drive Pastor to Corner and Finish Him There," New York World-Telegram, September 16, 1939.

1513. "Joe Louis," Philadelphia Tribune, January 19, 1939.

1514. "Joe Louis is Booed; Bob Pastor Confident," Michigan Chronicle, September 16, 1939.

1515. "Joe Louis Kayoes John in First," New York Daily News, January 26, 1939, p. 52.

1516. "Joe Louis Ready for Bout with Bob Pastor," Michigan Chronicle, September 16, 1939.

1517. "Joe Louis Ready for Tony Galento Target Practice," New York Tribune, June 3, 1939.

1518. "Joe Louis: Will He Be Able to Hold Crown?" New York Herald News, January 28, 1939.

1519. Jones, "Melancholy", "Joe Louis Lacks Color Asserts Noted Scribe," Atlanta Daily World, May 22, 1939.

1520. Jordan, Ralph B., "Roper Hit Hard, Joe's Tribute to Beaten Foe," New York Journal and American, April 18, 1939.

1521. "Letter Discounting Louis Record," New York Times, June 17, 1939, p. 21.

1522. "Letters on Sports Writers Estimate of Joe Louis," New York Times, February 4, 1939, p. 9; February 11, 1939, p. 11.

1523. "Letter Praising Louis," New York Times, September 30, 1939, p. 14.

1524. Lewin, Murray, "Brown Bomber Glad Referee Stopped Bout," Daily Mirror, January 26, 1939, p. 28.

1525. "Louis-Galento Bout Planned," New York Times, February 28, 1939, p. 23.

1526. "Louis-Galento Return Bout Planned," New York Times, September 17, 1939, p. 4, sec. 5.

1527. "Louis--A. Gadoy Bout Planned," New York Times, November 14, 1939, p. 28.

1528. "Louis is Physically Fit," New York Times, September 16, 1939, p. 12.

1529. "Louis May Make Exhibition Tour," New York Times, Janaury 28, 1939, p. 9.

1530. "Louis May Meet A. Lovell," New York Times, December 13, 1939, p. 37.

1531. "Louis Naps Preparing for Roper," New York Daily Times, April 17, 1939, p. 21.

1532. "Louis Now 10-1 to Beat Roper in Fight on Coast," New York Herald, April 16, 1939.

1533. "Louis-Pastor Bout--Louis Retains Title," New York Times, September 21, 1939, p. 27.

1534. "Louis-Pastor Bout: Preview," New York Times, September 20, 1939, p. 35.

1535. "Louis-Pastor Bout: Training," New York Times, September 14, 1939, p. 29.

1536. "Louis-J. Roper Bout Planned," New York Times, February 8, 1939, p. 26.

1537. "Louis-Roper Bout Plans," New York Times, April 16, 1939, p. 10, sec. 5.

1538. "Louis-Roper Bout Preview," New York Times, April 17, 1939, p. 21.

1539. "Louis-Roper Bout-Louis Retain Title," New York Times, April 18, 1939, p. 30.

1540. "Louis Victory Provides Thrill for D.C. Fans," Washington Tribune, July 1, 1939.

1541. "Louis Will Strive to End Bout Early," New York Tribune, December 12, 1939.

1542. "Louis Trains for Proper Bout," New York Times, March 29, 1939, p. 27.

1543. "Louis Wins," New York Times, January 26, 1939, p. 24.

1544. Miley, Jack, "U.S. Pugilistic Market Should Satisfy Bomber: Why Go to Chile for Arturo Godoy When He Can Find Enough Chumps Here?" New York Post, October 12, 1939.

1545. Monroe, Al, "Black Says Bomber Walked into Punch that Floored Him," Chicago Defender, July 8, 1939.

1546. "New York State Athletic Commission Approves Louis-Gallato Bout," New York Times, April 1, 1939, p. 13.

1547. "Now Joe Says Tony's (Galento) a Bum," New York Post, October 28, 1939.

1548. "Odds on Bomber Defeat Lewis Skyrocket to 10 to 1: Joe to Draw $100,000," Detroit Free Press, January 25, 1939.

1549. "150 Detroit Get Free Trip to Champ's Camp," Michigan Chronicle, September 16, 1939.

1550. Parker, Dan, "Louis Kayos Jim in Eighth Round: Right Cross to Jaw Gives Joe Henry Title," New York Daily News, June 23, 1939.

1551. _____, "Louis K.O.'s Lewis in 1st: Drops Frightened Rival 3 Times, Referee Donovan Stopping 'Battle' in 2:29," Daily Mirror, January 26, 1939, p. 28.

1552. Pastor, Bob, "I Know How to Beat Joe Louis," Detroit News, September 17, 1939.

1553.   Powers, Jimmy, "The Power House," New York Daily News,
        June 24, 1939, p. 29.

1554.   _____, "The Power House," New York Daily News,
        June 26, 1939, p. 39.

1555.   "Retains Heavyweight Crown," Detroit Tribune, July 1,
        1939.

1556.   Rice, Grantland, "A New Style Louis," New York Sun,
        February 17, 1939, p. 34.

1557.   _____, "As in Another Time: Joe Has No Shadow,"
        New York Sun, January 24, 1939.

1558.   _____, "Joe Louis: The Fastest Heavyweight,"
        New York Sun, June 27, 1939.

1559.   Roberts, Ric, "Roberts Believes Titanic Battle to
        Feature Tilt: Experts Write of Possible Upset;
        Opinion Varies as to Round of Louis Kayo,"
        Atlanta Daily World, June 28, 1939.

1560.   Runyon, Damon, "Donovan's Act Merciful in Halting
        One-Sided Bout," Daily Mirror, January 26, 1939.

1561.   _____, "Jim a Sad Case When Legs Went,"
        New York Daily News, June 23, 1939.

1562.   Scott, Lester, "If Louis Doesn't Retire There Won't
        Be Any Heavyweights," Daily News, January 26, 1939.

1563.   _____, "There Should Be a Law Against
        Putting Men in Ring with Louis," New York World-
        Telegram, January 26, 1939.

1564.   "'So Sorry,' Says Joe Louis as He Drops Georgie,"
        Washington Afro-American, September 9, 1939.

1565.   Van Every, Edward, "Blackburn Defends Joe Louis:
        Fails to See Career of Any Former Ring Champion
        Excelling Current Titleholder's," New York Sun,
        June 19, 1939.

1566.   _____, "Braddock Picks Louis to Defeat Lewis
        in Six Rounds: Rates Joe as Greatest Ever, Former
        Champion, Who Fought Both Men, Says Bomber, Hits
        too Fast for Foe," New York Sun, January 24, 1939.

1567.   _____, "Joe Found Foe (Tony Galento) Pretty
        Tough," New York Sun, June 29, 1939.

1568.   _____, "Louis Acclaim Breeds Myth: Ring
        Followers of Distant Future May Picture Joe as a
        Superman," New York Sun, January 28, 1939.

1569.   _____, "Louis Out to Get 'Em Early: Bomber Promises Hereafter to Try to Finish His Opponents in First Round," New York Sun, January 26, 1939.

1570.   _____, "Louis' Star Reaches Zenith: Ring Veterans Now Acclaim Bomber as Greatest Heavyweight of All time," New York Sun, January 27, 1939.

1571.   Vidmer, Richard, "Silent Fight: Between Louis and Jack Roper," New York Herald Tribune, April 16, 1939.

1572.   Washington, Forrester B., "There Would Be No Joe Louis Without John Roxborough Asserts Forrester B. Washington in Today's Guest Column," Atlanta Daily World, July 23, 1939.

1573.   White, Frank, "Louis Calm, Dissects Bout: Joe Takes Victory in Stride--Says Tony's Not too Tough," New York Post, June 29, 1939.

1574.   Williams, Joe, "If Galento Wants His Ears Pinned Back That's His Business," New York World-Telegram, March 2, 1939.

1575.   _____, "Jack Dempsey Never Held On," Washington Daily News, June 30, 1939.

1576.   _____, "Lack of Opponents May Force Louis to Retire," New York World-Telegram, December 7, 1939.

1577.   _____, "Louis is Champ What Does that Make Schmeling?" New York News, June 25, 1939.

1578.   Wood, Wilbur, "Says Louis Had Metal in Glove; Joe Jacobs Charges Champion Used a Gadget Night He Beat Schmeling," New York Sun, June 14, 1939.

1579.   Young, Frank A., "Is Joe Louis the Greatest Figher of All Time?: Louis Knocks Out the Braddock for Title," Chicago Defender, February 4, 1939.

B. FAMILY

1580.   Berlack-Boozer, Thelma, "Mother Wants Brown Bomber to Quit Ring Immediately," New York Amsterdam News, July 8, 1939.

1581.   Burley, Dan, "Louis May Quit to Suit Mother," New York Amsterdam News, July 1, 1939.

1582.   "Mother Sees Louis Blast Spar Mates in Best Drill," Bronx Home News, June 26, 1939.

C.   FOLK HERO

1583.   "Joe Louis Called Best in the World," New York World-Telegram, June 16, 1939.

1584.   Post, Ted, "There's Treason in Harlem Over Tonight's Brawl: Cops Hear a Few Are Betting on Galento, So 2,000 Will Go Up," New York Post, June 28, 1939.

1585.   _____, "Harlem Wants an Encore to Louis' Mayhem Act," New York Post, June 29, 1939.

6.   1940

A.   BOXER

1586.   Adams, Caswell, "Louis Knocks Out Paycheck in 2d Round at Garden in Tenth Defense of Heavyweight Title (Before 11,620)," New York Herald Tribune, March 30, 1940.

1587.   _____, "Louis Knocks Out Godoy in 8th Round at Yankee Stadium in 11th Defense of World Title (Before 27,786)," New York Herald Tribune, June 21, 1940.

1588.   Bromberg, Lester, "Godoy Advises Paycheck on How to Fight Louis," New York World-Telegram, March 28, 1940.

1589.   _____, "Louis Mental Quirks: Newly-Found Imagination May Work Against Joe in Paycheck Battle," New York World-Telegram, March 27, 1940.

1590.   Buck, Al, "Louis Gets $100,000 Offer: Philly Group Will Back Title Bout (Between Joe Louis and Henry Taylor)," New York Post, March 14, 1940.

1591.   _____, "Louis Must Kayo Foe (Arturo Godoy) or Lose Prestige," New York Post, June 19, 1940.

1592.   _____, "Louis Needs Proven Foe: Paycheck No Match for Champ," New York Post, March 30, 1940.

1593.   _____, "(Johnny) Paycheck Just Another Foe to Louis," New York Post, March 27, 1940.

1594.   "Conn Not Ready for Joe Louis Says (Jack) Dempsey," New York World-Telegram, January 13, 1940.

1595.   Cuddly, Jack, "Louis TKO's Godoy in Eighth to 'Retain' Crown: Chilean Hits Deck Thrice Near End of Bloody Battle," Washington Post, June 21, 1940, p. 21.

1596.   _____, "Godoy Says Referee Donovan Has Not Treat-
ed Him Fairly," Washington Daily News, June 18, 1940.

1597.   Daniel, Daniel M., "Joe's Second Godoy Test a Challenge,"
The Ring, Vol. 19, No. 6, July 1940, pp. 6-7, 34.

1598.   Dawson, James P., "Louis Wins, Keeps Title; Godoy
Avoids a Knockout: Boxing World Surprised as Bout
Lasts Fifteen Rounds--One Judge Votes for Chilean--
Heavyweight King Booed at Garden," New York Times,
February 10, 1940, p. 10.

1599.   "(Jack) Dempsey Blasts Boxing Monopoly . . ." Ex-
Champion Says Inability to Withstand Punch Keeps Bomber
From Higher Rank," New York Times, March 19, 1940, p. 32.

1600.   "Dempsey Hits Louis--Vocally," New York Daily News,
November 2, 1940.

1601.   "Godoy Earns Rematch by Staying 15: Arturo Came up
Too High for This One," Sunday Worker, February 11,
1940.

1602.   Jenkins, Burris, Jr., "'Next' Champ," Detroit Evening
Times, March 28, 1940.

1603.   "Jesse Owens, Joe Louis, 'Sportsmen of the Decade,'"
Journal and Guide, January 20, 1940, p. 18.

1604.   "Joe Louis Makes History Stiffening Nicholson:
Sparmate Kayoed for First Time," New York World-Telegram, May 29, 1940.

1605.   "Joe Louis Trophies at Chicago Exhibition Draw Huge
Throngs," Daily Worker, July 18, 1940, p. 9.

1606.   Kurman, Stan, "Joe Set to Quit After Two More Fights
This Year," Daily Worker, April 2, 1940.

1607.   _____, "Joe Winds Up Training Sees K.O.:
Paycheck Rated Tough," Daily Worker, March 28, 1940.

1608.   _____, "Louis a Prohibitive Favorite Tonight:
Champ's 10th Title Defense Finds Odds Long as Usual,"
Daily Worker, March 29, 1940.

1609.   _____, "Louis Big Favorite to K.O. Godoy:
Champ Sees Hard Title Fight Tonight; Out to Win,
Says Rugged Chilean," Daily Worker, February 9, 1940,
p. 8.

1610.   _____, "Not Joe's Best, But Easy Win (Over
Arturo Godoy)," Daily Worker, February 11, 1940,
Section 2, p. 8.

1611.   _____, "Underrated Godoy Will Be Far From
         Pushover for Louis Friday Night: Chilean Challenger
         Impresses in Workouts," Daily Worker, February 6,
         1940, p. 8.

1612.   _____, "Why Louis Is Greatest of 'Em All,"
         Daily Worker, March 27, 1940.

1613.   "Louis Disappointed at 'Poor' Showing: Champion Asserts
         He Coasted Near End to Save His Hands--Rival's Antics
         Puzzling," New York Sun, February 20, 1940.

1614.   "Louis-Godoy Return in Year's Big Spot: Joe Anxious
         for Another Try at Arturo--Paycheck, Savold, Galento
         All Seeking Big Scrap But Chilean Has It Cinched,"
         Daily Worker, February 13, 1940, p. 8.

1615.   "Maybe Paycheck Is Playing Possum: Seems to Be Hiding
         His Skill in Training for Louis--Praised by Former
         Opponents," Daily Worker, April 12, 1940.

1616.   Miley, Jack, "Arturo's Fatal Error Was Making Joe
         Mad," New York Post, Juen 21, 1940, p. 6.

1617.   _____, "Louis Looks Like Perpetual Motion,"
         New York Post, March 29, 1940.

1618.   Moss, Morton, "Louis Kayoes Paycheck Early in Second
         Round," Detroit Evening Times, March 30, 1940.

1619.   Murphy, Bob, "'Mot Unafraid Man I Ever Fought'--
         Louis: Wanted to Fight," Detroit Evening Times,
         June 21, 1940.

1620.   Newman, Abe, "On the Score Board: Joe Louis,"
         Daily Worker, February 10, 1940.

1621.   _____, "Pastor and Conn, Max and Pat--Where
         Does Joe Louis Come In?" Daily Worker, September 2,
         1940.

1622.   "No More 'Unknown' Fighters in Title Matches (Against
         Louis) Here--Jacobs," Daily Worker, April 1, 1940.

1623.   "Pittsburgh Wants Conn-Louis Fight," Detroit News,
         December 18, 1940.

1624.   "Record of Heavyweight Title Defenses Shows Louis
         Far Ahead of Field with 9," Daily Worker, February 8,
         1940, p. 8.

1625.   Rice, Grantland, "Louis and Paycheck," New York Sun,
         March 29, 1940.

1626.   _____, "Pilot Needs Help of Front Office,"
         Detroit Free Press, June 19, 1940.

1627.   _____, "Type to Beat Joe Louis," New York Post, March 28, 1940.

1628.   Rodney, Lester, "Louis Hit New High in Godoy Win: Adapted Style in KOing Rugged, Game Challenger," Daily Worker, June 22, 1940.

1629.   Salsinger, H. G., "'It Was My Worst Fight in 3 Years,' Says Joe Louis," Detroit News, February 10, 1940.

1630.   _____, "The Umpire," Detroit News, December 18, 1940.

1631.   "Scribes and Fans A-Plenty Disagree with Igoe's Rating of Dempsey Over Louis," Pittsburgh Courier, September 21, 1940.

1632.   Sullivan, Alex, "Averages Prove Joe Louis Best Champ to Date," National Police Gazette, Vol. 144, No. 33, January 1940, pp. 10, 12.

1633.   Van Every, Edward, "Godoy Is a Difficult Target: Louis Admits Hitting Just One Clean Blow--Has Only Praise for Foe," New York Sun, February 10, 1940.

1634.   _____, "Joe's Defect Under Scrutiny," New York Sun, March 29, 1940.

1635.   _____, "Louis Lets Loose Deadliest Punch to Cancel Paycheck: Johnny Offers No Opposition," New York Sun, March 30, 1940.

1636.   _____, "Louis Ignores Bearish Tales About Paycheck," New York Sun, March 22, 1940.

1637.   _____, "Louis Stands Alone As King: Bomber Only Heavyweight Champion Not to Pick His Challengers," New York Sun, March 25, 1940.

1638.   _____, "Why Godoy Expects to Win: Arturo Thinks He Is the Smarter and Can Take Punch Better Than Louis," New York Sun, June 18, 1940.

1639.   Vidmer, Richards, "Master Craftsmen: Joe Louis," New York Herald Tribune, February 9, 1940.

1640.   Wade, Eddie, "Encores Out with Joe: One Dance, Then Bomber Pitches," New York Post, June 20, 1940.

1641.   Williams, Joe, "An Angry Louis Figures to Belt Godoy Out Early," New York World-Telegram, June 20, 1940.

1642.   Wood, Wilbur, "Louis Education Completed: Anniliation of Godoy Is Final Lesson--Conn May Yet Land September Bout," New York Sun, June 22, 1940.

1643.   _____, "Louis to Defend Title Against Godoy Again in June," New York Sun, February 10, 1940.

B. FOLK HERO

1644.   Bromberg, Lester, "Joe Louis Turns Harlem's (New York) Voters Toward Wilkie," New York World-Telegram, November 1, 1940.

C. JOE LOUIS AND POLITICS

1645.   Darnton, Byron, "Joe Louis Tours (New York) City for Willkie," New York Times, November 1, 1940, p. 34.

1646.   "Joe Louis As a Vote-Getter (For Wendell L. Willkie)," New York Post, November 1, 1940.

1647.   "Joe Louis Explains: GOP 'Promises My People More,'" New York Post, October 31, 1940.

1648.   "Joe Louis Says Roosevelt Has Made 'My People' Lazy: Bomber Says That's Why He's for Willkie; Calls Appointment of Negro General," New York World-Telegram, October 31, 1940.

1649.   "Joe Louis to Hit Hard for (Wendell L.) Willkie for President of U.S.: May Make 7 Speeches--Negro Elks Come Out Too," New York Sun, October 28, 1940.

1650.   Miley, Jack, "Louis Is Stooge for GOP Boys," New York Post, October 30, 1940.

1651.   Williams, Joe, "Farley Slight Makes Joe Louis Go for (Wendell L.) Willkie for President of U.S.," New York World-Telegram, October 29, 1940.

D. PERSONAL

1652.   "Honor 1st Lady, Joe Louis for Aiding Negroes," Cincinnati (Ohio) Post, February 14, 1940.

1653.   "Joe Louis Opens Cancer Drive," People's Voice, February 21, 1940, p. 11.

1654.   "Life Magazine Apologizes for Louis Article," Washington Tribune, June 29, 1940.

1655.   "Louis Honored for Helping to Improve Relations of Race," Shreveport (La.) Times, February 15, 1940.

1656.   "Louis Preserves Home for Whites Whose Ancestors Helped Slaves Win Freedom," Pittsburgh Courier, February 24, 1940.

1657.   "Mrs. Roosevelt, Joe Louis Honored," Columbus (Ohio) Citizen, February 14, 1940.

1658.   Newton, Bill, "Life (Magazine) Still Trying to Peddle Old Fish About Joe Louis: And Answers Refutation of Insulting Article by Quoting Joe Williams' Approval of it!" Daily Worker, July 9, 1940.

1659.   Wedge, Will, "Joe Louis' Teeth Tell Story: Dr. Walter Jacobs, Maker of Fistic Casts, Thinks Champion Is Throw-Back," New York Sun, January 6, 1940.

7.   1941

A.   BOXER

1660.   "Bomber, Bobcat in Big Battles: To Head Benefit Shows," Philadelphia Tribune, November 29, 1941.

1661.   Boyack, James Edmund, "Gene Tunney Suggests Champ 'Join up with Colores'," Pittsburgh Courier, July 19, 1941, p. 1.

1662.   _____, "Louis Has Earned Right to Retire"-- Dempsey," Pittsburgh Courier, July 26, 1941, p. 1.

1663.   Bromberg, Lester, "Louis Selects Conn's Foes: Afraid to Lose Him for June," New York World-Telegram, March 3, 1941.

1664.   _____, "Punch That Stopped Nova Seen Hardest of Career," New York World-Telegram, September 30, 1941.

1665.   Buck, Al, "Jacobs Says Godoy Is Sensible Ignoring Louis for Movies!!" New York Post, February 20, 1941.

1666.   _____, "Joe Louis First to Win 2 Awards: Honored as "Fighter of Year" for Fourth Time (Won Award in 1936, 1938 and 1939)," New York Post, December 29, 1941.

1667.   _____, "Punch That Kayoed Burman His Hardest, Says Louis," New York Post, February 1, 1941, p. 1.

1668.   _____, "'Shouldn't Have Stopped It,' Says Dorazio of Louis Kayo," New York Post, February 18, 1941.

1669.   Dawson, James P., "56,549 See Louis Stop Nova in 6th and Retain Title," New York Times, September 30, 1941, p. 29.

1670.   "Editorial on Louis," New York Times, October 1, 1941.

1671.   "Experts Pick Conn Over Louis," New York Post, January 16, 1941.

1672. Feder, Sid, "Louis Batters Nova Helpless, Referee Stops Fight in 6th," Louisville Courier-Journal, September 30, 1941.

1673. "54,487 See Louis Conquer Conn After Weathering Heavy Blows," Detroit Free Press, June 19, 1941.

1674. Frank, Stanley, "Louis' Reign Shows How Times Change," New York Post, February 19, 1941.

1675. _____, "No Chance of Louis Losing Head in Ring," New York Post, June 12, 1941.

1676. "Joe Louis Named 'Fighter of the Year'," (Louisville) Courier-Journal, Decembe r 29, 1941.

1677. "Joe Not Sure About Retiring," Detroit Free Press, September 30, 1941.

1678. "Louis-B. Baer Bout Plans," New York Times, April 18, 1941, p. 28.

1679. "Louis-Baer: Letter," New York Times, May 10, 1941, p. 12.

1680. "Louis-Baer Bout: Louis Wins, Decision Contested," New York Times, May 24, 1941, p. 19.

1681. "Louis-B. Baer Bout Plans," New York Times, December 9, 1941, p. 50.

1682. "Louis-B. Baer" Contract Signed," New York Times, December 17, 1941, p. 41.

1683. "Louis-B. Baer Bout: Louis and Baer Train," New York Times, December 23, 1941, p. 31.

1684. "Joe Louis-C. Burman Bout: Men to Sign," New York Times, January 22, 1941, p. 25.

1685. "Louis-Burman Bout: Louis Retains Title," New York Times, February 1, 1941, p. 12.

1686. "Louis-Conn Bout Planned," New York Times, May 2, 1941, p. 31.

1687. "Louis-Conn Bout: Formal Article Signed," New York Times, June 4, 1941, p. 30.

1688. "Louis-Conn Bout: Louis Wins," New York Times, June 19, 1941, p. 1.

1689. "Louis-G. Dorazio Bout: Louis Signs," New York Times, February 4, 1941, p. 25.

1690. "Louis-Musto Bout: Training," New York Times, April 6, 1941, p. 2, sec. 5.

1691. "Louis-Musto Bout: Louis Wins," New York Times, April 9, 1941, p. 34.

1692. "Louis-Nova Bout: Detroit Makes Bid," New York Times, July 4, 1941, p. 10.

1693. "Louis-Nova Bout: Interviewed," New York Times, July 5, 1941, p. 19.

1694. "Louis-Nova Bout: Plans," New York Times, September 3, 1941, p. 29.

1695. "Louis-Nova Bout: Louis Wins, "New York Times, September 30, 1941, p. 1.

1696. "Louis-A. Simon Bout: Training," New York Times, March 16, 1941, p. 4, sec. 5.

1697. "Louis-Simon Bout Plans," New York Times, April 6, 1941, p. 2, sec. 5.

1698. "Louis Comments on Rivals," New York Times, November 20, 1941, p. 41.

1699. "Louis Objects to Plan to Keep Conn Out of Ring Till Last Minute," New York Times, June 6, 1941, p. 28.

1700. "Louis Kayoes Burman in Fifth Round," New York Daily News, February 1, 1941, pp. 1, 24.

1701. "Louis May Defend His Crown in Detroit Again in September: Hettcha Talk with Jacobs," Detroit Free Press, April 6, 1941.

1702. "Louis Reported Anxious to Meet Nova," New York Times, July 31, 1941, p. 21.

1703. "Louis 1942 Plans," New York Times, December 7, 1941, p. 1, sec. 5.

1704. "Louis 6-1 Over Buddy Bear Tonight in D.C.," Daily Worker, May 23, 1941.

1705. "Louis Sluggish in Musto Kayo: Punches Lack Old Power," New York Journal American, April 9, 1941.

1706. "Louis to Defend Title Gratis: Meets Buddy Baer Jan. 9 for Navy Relief Fund," New York Post, November 13, 1941.

1707. "Louis to Rest Till September," New York Times, June 20, 1941, p. 25.

1708. "Louis Wins in Seventh Round When Buddy Baer Is Disqualified by Referee: 35,000 See Bomber Triumph on a Foul," New York Times, May 24, 1941, p. 19.

1709. McCann, Dick, "Joe KO's Conn in 13th to Save Title He
       Was Losing on Points," New York Daily News, June 19,
       1941.

1710. Mahon, Jack, "Louis by TKO in 13th; (Abe) Simon Down
       5 Times," New York Daily News, March 22, 1941.

1711. Meany, Tom, "Baer-Louis Fight Pictures Get Six-Minute
       Trimming," PM, May 26, 1941.

1712. Nicholes, Joseph C., "Louis Wins in Seventh Round
       When Buddy Baer Is Disqualified by Referee: Louis
       Down for 4 in 1st; Louis Sent Through Ropes, He Comes
       Back to Punish Buddy, Who Is on Canvas 3 Times,"
       New York Times, May 24, 1941, p. 19.

1713. Nunn, William G., "Louis Turned Defeat into Victory
       with One Explosive Punch," Pittsburgh Courier, June 28,
       1941, p. 16.

1714. Own, Russell, "The Man Who Will Beat Joe Louis: The
       Champion Says It Will Be 'Somebody Who Can Hit Me
       Hard Enough to Hurt Me and Keep on Doing It,'" New York
       Times Magazine, September 28, 1941, pp. 1-3.

1715. Parker, Dan, "Title, Fortune in Conn's Grip at Kayo
       in 13th (By Joe Louis before 54,487)," New York Mirror,
       June 19, 1941, pp. 1, 32.

1716. Peterman, Cy, "All Signs Points Conn As Next Heavy
       Champ: Million-Dollar Return, Fading Louis Cast
       September's Shadows," Philadelphia Inquirer, June 20,
       1941.

1717. Rouzeau, Edgar, "Joe's 'Most Logical' Opponent Named
       for September Battle," Pittsburgh Courier, June 28,
       1941, p. 16.

1718. Sabo, John N., "Joe Fared to Hang on in Twelfth:
       Billy Conn Makes Mistake of Trying to Outslug Champ;
       54,487 Fans Cheer Loser," Detroit Free Press, June 19,
       1941.

1719. "Saying a Final Good-by to Max Baer," Kansas City Star,
       April 6, 1941.

1720. Seder, Sid, "Louis Knocks Out Nova in Sixth Round,"
       Detroit Free Press, September 30, 1941.

1721. "Should Joe Retire?" Pittsburgh Courier, July 19,
       1941, p. 1.

1722. "Should Joe Louis Retire? . . . . 'No!' Says Joe Louis
       . . . and That's That!" Pittsburgh Courier, August 9,
       1941, p. 17.

118   Joe Louis

1723. Smith, Jack, "'Had to KO Him So I Did'--Louis,"
       New York Daily News, June 19, 1941.

1724. Smith, Wendell, "Smitty's Sport Purts: Louis-Conn
       Broadcast," Pittsburgh Courier, June 28, 1941, p. 16.

1725. "Tsk, Tsk--Joe's Slipping Again!: $18,000 for Joe;
       $5,000 for Gus Dorazio," Daily Worker, February 19,
       1941.

1726. "Wilson Cops Open; 8,000 Turn Out to See Joe Louis
       Play," Pittsburgh Courier, July 12, 1941, p. 16.

1727. Wood, Wilbur, "Don't Have to Dive for Louis: Stock
       Market Guffaws at Pennsylvania State Senator's Charge
       Dorazio Went in Tank," New York Sun, February 19, 1941.

                    B. FAMILY

1728. "Gave Marva (Louis) $125,000, Champ Says," Pittsburgh
       Courier, July 19, 1941, p. 1.

1729. "Joe Louis and Wife Make Up, Divorce Off," New York
       Post, August 19, 1941.

1730. "Joe Louis and Wife on 2d Honeymoon," New York Post,
       August 20, 1941.

1731. "Joe Louis Answers Wife: He Denies Cruelty, Says
       Statement on Income Is Untrue," New York Times,
       July 10, 1941, p. 21.

1732. "Joe Louis Carries His Wife From Court As They Make
       Up," New York World-Telegram, August 19, 1941.

1733. "Joe Louis Ordered to Pay $200 a Week Temporary
       Alimony," Pittsburgh Courier, August 9, 1941, p. 1.

1734. "Joe Louis Unable to Pay Marva $200 Weekly Alimony,
       Claim," Pittsburgh Courier, August 23, 1941, p. 5.

1735. "Joe, Marva (Louis) May 'Make Up': Meet This Week
       to Talk about Reconciliation," Pittsburgh Courier,
       July 12, 1941, p. 1.

1736. "Louis and Wife Fail to Agree in Conference,"
       New York World-Telegram, July 22, 1941.

1737. "Louis Denies Striking Wife," New York World-Telegram,
       July 9, 1941.

1738. "Louis' Wife Gets $200 Alimony," New York World-
       Telegram, August 1, 1941.

1739. "Marva Unkind, Says Louis: Champ Files Answer in
       Divorce Suit," New York Post, July 19, 1941.

1740.   "'Not Making What Marva Claims'--Joe," <u>Pittsburgh Courier</u>, August 23, 1941, p. 1.

1741.   Prattis, P. L., "Marva and Joe Are Not to Blame for Domestic Rift," <u>Pittsburgh Courier</u>, July 12, 1941, p. 13.

1742.   Roger, J. A., "Adverse Publicity in Louis' Divorce Case May Hurt Champ," <u>Pittsburgh Courier</u>, July 26, 1941, p. 24.

1743.   "Spent $15,000 a Year As Champion's Wife: Mrs. Joe Louis Says She Had to Maintain Position," <u>New York Times</u>, August 19, 1941, p. 23.

1744.   "The Bill of a Champ's Wife: Mrs. Joe Louis Wore $50 Pajamas," <u>New York Post</u>, August 19, 1941.

1745.   "Wife Sues Joe Louis, Says He Socked Her," <u>New York Daily News</u>, July 3, 1941.

C.   FOLK HERO

1746.   "Four Thousand Hail Joe Louis in Front of Theresa Hotel in New York," <u>Pittsburgh Courier</u>, June 28, 1941, p. 20.

1747.   Johnson, Hugh S., "Joe Louis' Last Fight Not in Prize Ring But for His People Champ Deserves Aid, a Credit to Sport," <u>Philadelphia Inquirer</u>, October 4, 1941.

D.   GOLFER

1748.   "Joe Louis Trails in Golf Tourney (in Detroit)," <u>PM</u>, August 13, 1941.

E.   JOE LOUIS IN THE ARMY

1749.   Bromberg, Lester, "Louis-Buddy to Give Navy $50,000 Gift," <u>New York World-Telegram</u>, November 13, 1941.

1750.   Buck, Al, "Louis Anxious to Go into Army as Champ; Won't Give up Crown," <u>New York Post</u>, September 13, 1941.

1751.   _____, "Louis Gets Draft Questionaire: 'They Got Me,' Champion Says," <u>New York Post</u>, January 31, 1941.

1752.   "Drafting of Louis Costly to (New York) State," <u>New York Journal American</u>, October 10, 1941, p. 45.

1753.   Frank, Stanley, "Louis' Navy Benefit Bout Grand Gesture," <u>New York Post</u>, November 14, 1941.

1754. Graham, Frank, "Joe Louis and the Army," New York Sun,
       October 15, 1941.

1755. "Joe Louis Passes His Test for Army: Brown Bomber Now
       Subject to Immediate Call--Carriers on Exhibition Tour,"
       New York Times, October 15, 1941, p. 28.

1756. "Private Joe Louis Now in Uniform," New York Sun,
       January 16, 1941, p. 1.

1757. Rouzeac, Edgar T., "Army May Grab Joe After Nova Go,"
       Pittsburgh Courier, August 16, 1941, p. 17.

                    F. PERSONAL

1758. Buck, Al, "Louis Voted Writers' Trophy 'For Doing
       Most for Boxing,'" New York Post, December 10, 1941.

1759. "Clyde Martin Wins Joe Louis Open Golf Tournament,"
       Detroit News, August 15, 1941.

1760. "Hunter (College's Elementary School) Pupils Rate
       Joe Louis Above Hitler," New York World-Telegram,
       March 24, 1941.

1761. "Joe Louis Aids (Federal Council of the Church of
       Christ in America) Church: Establishes Fund for
       Race Relations Department of Council," New York Sun,
       October 1, 1941.

1762. "Joe Louis Rates Denby, Martin and Robinson Favorites
       in Golf Tourney," Pittsburgh Courier, August 9, 1941,
       p. 16.

1763. "Joe Louis Says 'No Pay': Not Responsible for Debts
       of Others, He Advertises," New York Times, July 17,
       1941, p. 27.

1764. "Program to Feature Joe This Sunday at 12:30 Over NBC,"
       Philadelphia Tribune, November 22, 1941.

1765. Igoe, Hype, "Louis to Sue for Million: Slurs on
       Health by Air Announcer Bring Court Action," New York
       Journal-American, September 5, 1941.

                    8. 1942

                    A. BOXER

1766. Bromberg, Lester, "Champ (Louis) Disposes of Baer in
       2:56 in Return Match," New York World-Telegram,
       January 10, 1942.

1767. Frank, Stanley, "No Fighter Ever Greater Than Louis,"
       New York Post, January 10, 1942.

1768. "J. Louis-B. Baer," New York Times, January 1, 1942, p.40.

1769. "J. Louis Benefit Exhibition Bout Planned for Polo
       Grounds All-Sports Carnival," New York Times, May 26,
       1942, p. 28.

1770. "Joe Louis Denies Report of Quitting Ring; Tells M.
       Jacobs Statement Misunderstood; Associate Press
       Quotes Louis on Original Report," New York Times,
       October 13, 1942, p. 27.

1771. "Joe Louis Plans to Retire From Ring Comment, Career,"
       New York Times, October 12, 1942, p. 1.

1772. "Louis Plans Another Title Bout," New York Times,
       January 7, 1942, p. 27.

1773. "Louis Wins; Comments," New York Times, January 10,
       1942, p. 19.

1774. Nicholas, Joseph C., "Louis Stops Simon in Sixth Round
       for 21st Successful Defense of Ring Title (Before
       18,220)," New York Times, March 28, 1942, p. 12.

1775. "(Gene) Tunney Hails Louis as Greatest Figher of All
       Time," New York Post, January 22, 1942.

                    B.   JOE LOUIS IN THE ARMY

1776. "Army Bars Joe Louis Fight This Summer: Can Only
       Appear in Exhibitions, (Sec.) Stimson Declares,"
       Daily Worker, June 19, 1942.

1777. "A New War Song Inspired by Corporal Joe Louis," New
       York Sunday Mirror, July 5, 1942, p. 2, 15.

1778. Buck, Al, "Louis Helps Boost Morale of Soldiers,"
       New York Post, March 17, 1942, p. 9.

1779. Burley, Dan, "Joe Joins Army After Slaughter of Baer
       Before 20,000 at Navy Show at Garden," New York
       Amsterdam Star-News, January 17, 1942.

1780. Editorial. "Joe Louis Typifies Negro Patriotism,"
       (Louisville) Courier-Journal, January 20, 1942.

1781. "Exhibition Tour of Camps and Forts in 2nd Corps
       Area Planned," New York Times, May 16, 1942, p. 19.

1782. "F.D.R., Mrs. Roosevelt Greet Pvt. Joe Louis,"
       New York Worker, May 24, 1942.

1783. "Furlough Sought for Joe Louis to Permit Him to
       Defend Title," New York Times, February 5, 1942, p. 28.

1784. "J. Louis Arrives, Los Angeles for Furlough: Comments,"
       New York Times, October 14, 1942, p. 30.

1785. "J. Louis: Camp Upton," New York Times, June 20, 1942, p. 18.

1786. "Joe Louis: Example of How to Beat Hitler," Daily Worker, April 1, 1942.

1787. "J. Louis Exhibition Bouts Fort Hamilton Arena Brooklyn," New York Times, June 16, 1942, p. 19.

1788. "Joe Louis in the Army," The Ring, Vol. 21, No. 4, May, 1942, p. 4.

1789. "J. Louis to Start Training," New York Times, May 23, 1942, p. 18.

1790. Levette, Harry, "Hollywood Puts Out Mat of Welcome for Joe Louis, Journal and Guide, October 31, 1942, p. 17.

1791. "Louis-A. Simon Bout: Joe Louis to Train at Fort Dix," New York Times, March 3, 1942, p. 19.

1792. "Louis Knocks Out Simon for Second Time and Keeps His Heavyweight Championship: Negro Donates Entire Purse (ca $45,000) to Army Emergency Relief," New York Herald-Tribune, March 28, 1942.

1793. "Louis Off to Don (U.S.) Army Uniform," New York Journal-American, January 14, 1942.

1794. "Louis Signs with Simon to Aid Army Relief Fund," Daily Worker, February 26, 1942.

1795. McCann, Dick, "Louis-Baer Gate to Hit $200,000 (for Navy Relief Fund)," New York Daily News, January 9, 1942.

1796. "N.Y. Boxing Ass'n to Honor Joe Louis with Scrolls at Polo Grounds All Sports Carnival for Contributions at Army and Navy Relief Funds," New York Times, June 9, 1942, p. 32.

1797. "Pair of Louis' Gloves Given at Negro 'Salute'," Daily Worker, March 24, 1942.

1798. Parker, Dan, "Louis Stops Baer in First, Bomber Floors Foe 3 Times Before 20,000; Navy Gets $100,000," New York Daily Mirror, January 10, 1942.

1799. "Sergt. Joe Louis Captivates Film Capital During Recent Leave (from Army)," Pittsburgh Courier, October 31, 1942.

C.   PERSONAL

1800.   Bostic, Joe, "Louis Boxes: Receives Scroll 12,648
        Cheer Champ, Stars," People's Voice, June 20, 1942,
        p. 34.

1801.   "Boston (Chronicle) Weekly Asks Award (NAACP Spingar
        Award) for Joe Louis," Daily Worker, January 26, 1942.

1802.   "Honored at Testimonial Dinner N.Y.C.," New York Times,
        May 22, 1942, p. 31.

1803.   "Joe Louis' Famous Words Now Used as Song Lyrics,"
        Journal and Guide, October 31, 1942, p. 17.

1804.   "Joe Louis Gets E. J. Neil Memorial Plaque," New York
        Times, January 22, 1942, p. 21.

1805.   "Joe Louis Has Drawn Over $1,000,000 in 8 Madison
        Square Garden Shows," Philadelphia Tribune, January 3,
        1942.

1806.   Suskind, Peter, "Virtue Will Triumph, Joe (Louis)!"
        Journal and Guide, October 21, 1942.

9.   1943

A.   FAMILY

1807.   "Marva Louis Confirms Split with Sergeant Joe,"
        People's Voice, October 2, 1943, p. 4.

B.   JOE LOUIS IN THE ARMY

1808.   "Dempsey Says Louis-Conn Fight Should Top Series of
        Big Fights in New War Loan Drive," Pittsburgh Courier,
        October 9, 1943.

1809.   "Joe Louis and His 'Buddies' Stop at Camp Carson,
        Colo.," Pittsburgh Courier, October 30, 1943, p. 16.

1810.   Jones, Lucius, "Joe Louis' Tour of Army Camps of Nation
        Rekindles Interest Among Soldiers in His Illustrious
        Career," Pittsburgh Courier, October 30, 1943, p. 17.

1811.   "Louis Boxing Troupe Has Performed Before 150,000,"
        Pittsburgh Courier, October 9, 1943, p. 17.

1812.   "Louis Pulls $40,000 at Loew's State Theatre in
        New York City," Pittsburgh Courier, November 13, 1943,
        p. 19.

1813.   Low, Nat, "The War Dep't Is Sending Joe Louis on an
        Exhibition Tour of the World," People's Voice, July 14,
        1943.

1814.   _____, "Will Joe Louis Be Too Old to Fight
         After the (World) War (Two)? We Doubt It?" Daily
         Worker, July 8, 1943.

1815.   Mercer, Sid, "Baseball Enthuses GI's, Louis Finds,"
         New York Journal-American, December 17, 1943.

1816.   "Sgt. (Joe) Louis' Army Tour Helps Negro-White
         Goodwill--Life," Daily Worker, Sport, September 11,
         1943, p. 6.

1817.   "Sgt. Joe Louis Boxes at Camp Lee on Tour," Chicago
         Defender, September 18, 1943, p. 17.

1818.   Smith, Wendell, "The King of Sock, Sgt. Joe Louis,
         Is Still the 'Big Guy'," Pittsburgh Courier, July 17,
         1943.

1819.   _____, "Why Should Louis Be Expected to Fight
         Billy Conn Another Title Fight Without Being Paid?"
         Pittsburgh Courier, October 9, 1943, p. 16.

1820.   "10,000 Soldiers Turn Out, Hail Sergt. Joe Louis, Ray
         Robinson," New York Amsterdam News, September 25, 1943.

1821.   "The Champ Visits Amarillo (Texas)," Pittsburgh Courier,
         December 11, 1943, p. 14.

10.   1944

A.   FOLK HERO

1822.   "Robeson Expects Majors to Drop Racial Ban Soon,"
         Pittsburgh Courier, January 8, 1944, p. 1. States
         that the example of Joe Louis is an inspiration to all
         Americans.

B.   JOE LOUIS IN THE ARMY

1823.   Effrat, Louis, "Joe Louis Returns After Long Tour:
         Champion, in 14-Month Trip of 30,000 Miles, Entertain-
         ed 2,000,000 Service Men," New York Times, October 11,
         1944, p. 25.

1824.   Harrington, Ollie, "Air Heroes Thrilled by Joe's
         Visit (in Italy)," Pittsburgh Courier, September 2,
         1944, p. 12.

1825.   _____, "Louis and Boxing Troupe Now Perform-
         ing in Italy," Pittsburgh Courier, August 26, 1944, p.
         12.

1826.   "Joe Louis at Garden Nov. 16," The Guardian, November
         11, 1944.

1827. "Joe Louis Back in U.S., Will Visit District," Evening Star, October 10, 1944.

1828. "Joe Louis Gloves Aid in $45,900 Bond Sale," Evening Star, July 9, 1944.

1829. "Joe Louis Visits Fliers in Italy," Norfolk Journal and Guide, September 2, 1944.

1830. Mardo, Bill, "Sgt. Joe Louis World Citizen, Is Home Again," Daily Worker, October 12, 1944.

1831. "Staff Sergeant Joe Louis Morale Builder for Our Soldiers at Front," Los Angeles Weekly, June 24, 1944.

11.   1945

A.   BOXER

1832. "Brazil Millionaire Wants Joe Louis and Billy Conn to 'Swing It Out in Rio (De Janeiro)," Pittsburgh Courier, December 15, 1945.

1833. Editorial, "So Joe Is Going to Quit the Ring!" New York Amsterdam News, January 27, 1945.

1834. Fentress, J. Cullen, "Want Louis-Conn Title Bout in L.A. Coliseum," Pittsburgh Courier, December 8, 1945.

1835. "(Jack) Dempsey Says Joe Will be Dethroned," Pittsburgh Courier, July 7, 1945.

1836. "Mike Jacobs Manages Louis," Pittsburgh Courier, November 3, 1945, pp. 1, 4.

1837. "Mike (Jacobs) Won't Boss Joe: Louis' Right Hand Man Says Champ Is in Safe Hands and That Jacobs Is Promoter and Nothing Else," Pittsburgh Courier, December 8, 1945, p. 16.

1838. "'No Rift' (Between Joe Louis and Me) Says Julian Black, Louis' Manager," Pittsburgh Courier, November 19, 1945, p. 10.

1839. Smith, Wendell, "Louis a Champion without a Manager," Pittsburgh Courier, October 27, 1945, p. 12.

1840. "Sports Editorial:--Who Is Doing Business for the Champion? (Joe Louis)," Pittsburgh Courier, October 27, 1945, p. 12.

1841. "Louis, Dempsey's Managerial Problems May Be Identical," Pittsburgh Courier, November 10, 1945, p. 10.

B. GOLFER

1842. "Louis, Vines in Golf Tourney," Pittsburgh Courier,
November 3, 1945, p. 12.

C. JOE LOUIS IN THE ARMY

1843. Adams, Julius J., "Medals for Louis, Gibson Revive
Talk of No 'Medal of Honor' for Negro GI," New York
Amsterdam News, October 6, 1945.

1844. Buck, Al, "Joe Louis' Decision to Quit Ring After Conn
Bout Meets Approval," New York Post, January 19, 1945.

1845. Carroll, Ted, "Huge Bankroll Is Joe's Ace: Louis
Has Right Kind of Financial Backing (as a Promoter),"
New York Age, March 12, 1945, pp. 16, 17.

1846. "Congressman Powell Ask FDR to Commission Sgt. Joe
Louis," Chicago Defender, March 17, 1945, p. 18.

1847. "Joe Louis, Boxer, Honored by Army: Legion of Merit
Presented for His Exhibition in Camps Here and Over-
Seas," New York Times, September 24, 1945.

1848. "Joe Louis Spars in Coast (Los Angeles and San
Francisco) Drills," Pittsburgh Courier, November 24,
1945, p. 12.

1849. "Joe Louis, Truman Gibson Army Merit Awards for
Outstanding Service," Pittsburgh Courier, September
29, 1945, pp, 1, 4.

1850. "Louis Lands GI Boxer in Alaska," Pittsburgh Courier,
September 8, 1945, p. 12.

1851. "No Commission for Joe Louis," Chicago Defender,
March 31, 1945.

1852. Sennate, A.C., "As Comic or Boxer, Joe's Still Their
Favorite Guy: Alaskan GI's Thrilled at Anything
Bomber Did on His Recent Jaunt," Afro-American,
September 1, 1945.

1853. Young, Fay, "Sgt. Joe Louis' Contribution Stands Out
as Greatest Single Effort in Second World War,"
Chicago Defender, May 12, 1945.

D. JOE LOUIS AS BUSINESSMAN

1854. "Joe Louis Buys Interest in Chicago's Rhumboogie Cafe:
Charlie Glenn Swings $25,000 Deal for Club," Pittsburgh
Courier, January 5, 1946, p. 16.

E.   PERSONAL

1855.   "Champ (Joe Louis) Stars in Movie 'Joe Palooka,'"
Pittsburgh Courier, December 15, 1945, p. 17.

1856.   "Heavyweight Champion Louis to Tour With (Luis)
Russell's Orchestra," Pittsburgh Courier, October 27,
1945, p. 5.

1857.   Hill, Herman, "Joe Louis, Lionel Hampton Take Honores
in Big Radio (Jubilee) Show," Pittsburgh Courier,
December 1, 1945.

1858.   "Joe Louis and Eddie 'Rochester' Anderson Turn
'Angel': Financial Backers of Variety Show, 'Jump,
Jive and Jam,'" Pittsburgh Courier, November 24,
1945, p. 16.

1859.   "Joe Louis Awarded Legion of Merit," Norfolk Journal
and Guide, September 29, 1945, p. 1.

1860.   "Joe Louis Faces Movie Cameras (in 'Joe Palooka'),"
Pittsburgh Courier, December 22, 1945, p. 18.

1861.   "Joe Louis' Story in 'Headlines' Mag," Chicago Defender,
November 3, 1945.

1862.   "Joe Louis to Be Guest on Jack Benny Show Soon,"
Norfolk Journal and Guide, November 3, 1945.

12.   1946

A.   BOXER

1863.   "Braddock Picks Conn (Over Joe Louis)," Pittsburgh
Courier, February 16, 1946, p. 13.

1864.   Breit, Harvey, "Louis Versus Conn--And 'Old Age,'"
New York Times Magazine, June 16, 1946, p. 16.

1865.   Davis, Charlie, "Louis Confident That He'll Defeat
Conn," Pittsburgh Courier, February 9, 1946, p. 16.

1866.   _____, "Seamon Is Directing Louis Drills,"
Pittsburgh Courier, March 30, 1946, p. 16.

1867.   Dawson, James P., "Louis Knocks Out Mauriello in First,
for 23d Successful Defense of Title (Before 39,000),"
New York Times, September 19, 1946.

1868.   "Joe Louis-B. Conn Bout," New York Times, June 3, 1946,
p. 31.

1869.   "J. Louis-Billy Conn Bout: Louis Training Plans,"
New York Times, January 1, 1946, p. 30.

1870. "Joe Louis-B. Conn Bout: Louis Wins by Knockout in
       8th Round," New York Times, June 20, 1946, pp. 1,27,29.

1871. "Joe Louis-T. Maunello Bout: Training Plans,"
       New York Times, August 7, 1946, p. 24.

1872. "Joe Louis-C. Sheppard Bout Proposed for Baltimore
       Next Spring," New York Times, November 16, 1946, p. 12.

1873. "J. Louis Plans Central and South American Exhibition
       Tour," New York Times, December 23, 1946, p. 26.

1874. "'Louis' Age No Problem,' Says Dempsey," Pittsburgh
       Courier, February 2, 1946, p. 12.

1875. "Louis Arriges in Indiana Camp: Champ Set for Drills,"
       Pittsburgh Courier, March 9, 1946, p. 16.

1876. "Louis-Conn Bout: Louis to Open Pompton Lakes, N.J.
       Training Site," New York Times, May 1, 1946, p. 34.

1877. "Louis-Conn Promoter Jacobs Drops Plans for $100 Ring
       Side Seats Applicants from 40 States and 3 Foreign
       Countries Seek Tickets," New York Times, February 1,
       1946, p. 26.

1878. "Louis Denies Reports He Will Retire After Conn Bout,"
       New York Times, April 13, 1946, p. 21.

1879. "Louis Interview by Moscow Pravda Reporter," New York
       Times, June 16, 1946, p. 5, sec. 3.

1880. "Louis Opens French Lick Spring Camp on March 1,"
       Pittsburgh Courier, January 19, 1946, p. 16.

1881. "Louis Says He Must Knock Out Conn to Win," New York
       Times, January 12, 1946, p. 19.

1882. "Louis Training Plans," New York Times, January 1,
       1946, p. 30.

1883. "Louis Undergoes Physical Exam," New York Times,
       September 11, 1946, p. 10.

1884. Mardo, Bill, "Joe to KO Slugger Tami (Mauriello) in
       3 or Less," Daily Worker, September 18, 1946, p. 7.

1885. "Miles Isn't Manager: 'Roxborough Is Still My Pilot'--
       Louis," Pittsburgh Courier, February 9, 1946, p. 1.

1886. Povich, Shirley, "45,266 See Short Rights, Left Hook
       End Fight," Washington Post, June 19, 1946, p. 1, 19.

1887. Smith, Wendell, "Challenger (Billy Conn) Says Joe Was
       Lucky," Pittsburgh Courier, January 5, 1946, p. 12.

1888. Washington, Chester, "Jolting Joe's Famous Fights: Louis Tackles the Towering Primo Carnera in His Toughest Test," Pittsburgh Courier, March 2, 1946, p. 13.

B. FOLK HERO

1889. "Harlem in Frenzy of Joy at Knockout (of Louis Over Conn)," New York Times, June 2, 1946, p. 28.

C. GOLFER

1890. Cannon, Jimmy, "Louis Worried--About Golf," New York Post, December 11, 1946.

1891. "Joe Louis a Good Golfer," People's Voice, June 15, 1946, p. 20.

D. PERSONAL

1892. Cannon, Jimmy, "Meet Joe Louis, the Host," New York Post, September 5, 1946.

1893. "Joe Louis Named Head of Interracial Vets' Committee," Chicago Defender, April 16, 1946.

1894. "Joe Louis Turns Divot Digger in Los Angeles," Pittsburgh Courier, February 23, 1945, p. 12.

1895. "J. Louis to Box Exhibition Bout Honululu," New York Times, October 24, 1946, p. 38.

1896. Smith, Wendell, "Joe Louis to Sue Ebony Magazine: Denies 'Spendthrift Charges,'" Pittsburgh Courier, May 25, 1946.

1897. Stephens, Louise, "Refuse Joe Louis as Candidate for Who's Who," Chicago Defender, September 21, 1946, p. 1.

1898. "When Joe Louis Was in England . . .," Daily Worker, April, 1946.

13. 1947

A. BOXER

1899. Cannon, Jimmy, "Joe Louis a True Champ In and Out of Ring," New York Home News, June 22, 1947.

1900. Cole, Haskell, "Louis Sharp in Camp Drills: Champion Preps for Walcott," Pittsburgh Courier, November 15, 1947, p. 18.

1901. Hurt, Rick, "Sports Train: Did Joe Louis Wait too Long to Retire?" People's Voice, December 13, 1947, p. 36.

1902.   "Joe Louis Honored As One of Ten Young Men of Past
Year," Pittsburgh Courier, January 25, 1947, p. 17.

1903.   "Joe Louis May Fight Bruce Woodcock in June: Bout Seen
If Bruce Can Beat Joe Baksi," Pittsburgh Courier,
February 22, 1947, Section Two, p. 17.

1904.   "Joe Louis to Retire After June Fight," People's
Voice, December 20, 1947, p. 36.

1905.   "Louis Arrives in Mexico City for Exhibition Tour,"
Pittsburgh Courier, February 8, 1947, Section Two,
p. 5.

1906.   "Louis' June Bout Off, Champ Lacks Real Foe," People's
Voice, May 3, 1947, p. 29.

1907.   "Louis Meets Mexican President; Godoy Bout Tame,"
Pittsburgh Courier, February 15, 1947, Section Two,
p. 16.

1908.   "Louis Meets San Salvador President," Pittsburgh
Courier, February 15, 1947, Section Two, p. 16.

1909.   "Louis Signs for London Exhibition," Daily Worker,
December 3, 1947.

1910.   "Record Crowd Watches Louis Batter Godoy in Chile,"
Pittsburgh Courier, March 1, 1947, Section Two, p. 16.

1911.   "The Champ's Punch . . . South of the Border (Mexico),"
Pittsburgh Courier, February 15, 1947, p. 5.

1912.   "Time Marches On . . . So Does Louis as Heavyweight
King," Pittsburgh Courier, February 15, 1947, Section
Tow, p. 17.

B. BUSINESSMAN

1913.   "Champ Turns Producer (of a Broadway Play) with
Canada Lee," Pittsburgh Courier, February 15, 1947,
p. 14.

C. FAMILY

1914.   "Joe Louis' Marriage Headed for Rocks," People's Voice,
December 20, 1947, p. 3.

1915.   "Marva, Joe Have Son; Remarriage Is Reported," People's
Voice, June 14, 1947, p. 3.

D.   FOLK HERO

1916.   Robeson, Paul, "Louis Is Still Our Champion," People's Voice, December 20, 1947, p. 14.

E.   GOLFER

1917.   "Joe Louis Knocked Out of Negro National Golf," New York Herald Tribune, August 29, 1947.

F.   PERSONAL

1918.   "Joe Louis Narrowly Escapes Death in Airplane Crash (in Ecaudor)," Pittsburgh Courier, February 22, 1947, p. 1.

1919.   "Joe Louis Tops List of Ideal Americans at N.Y. Youth Clubs," Afro-American, January 25, 1947, p. 5.

1920.   "Joe Louis Writes His Autobiography," Louisiana Weekly, April 8, 1947.

1921.   "The Joe Louis Super Market Will Open in Harlem, N.Y.," People's Voice, December 13, 1947, p. 35.

14.   1948

A.   BOXER

1922.   "Big Crowd Greets Louis on His Arrival in London," Evening Star, February 25, 1948.

1923.   "A. Daley on Louis Career," New York Times, June 20, 1948, p. 16.

1924.   Dawson, James P., "Louis Rallies to Stop Walcott in 11th and Retain Title as 42,667 Look On," New York Times, June 26, 1948, pp. 1, 11.

1925.   "Has Louis Changed His Mind on Quitting After June Go?" People's Voice, January 31, 1948.

1926.   Heinz, W. C., "Louis Talks About Walcott," New York Sun, May 21, 1948.

1927.   "Joe Louis Cancels Plans to Retire, to Defend Title, June '49," New York Times, October 20, 1948, p. 41.

1928.   "Joe Louis Denies Plan to Box Lesnevich; Insists His Retirement Is Definite," New York Times, July 21, 1948, p. 32.

1929.   "Louis Earns $80,000 in London," People's Voice, April 17, 1948, p. 24.

1930. "Joe Louis Postpones Retirement," New York Times, September 18, 1948, p. 13.

1931. "Joe Louis to Announce Official Retirement Soon," New York Times, August 21, 1948, p. 13.

1932. "Joe Louis to Box Godoy: Six-Round Exhibition Set for Philadelphia on Dec. 14," New York Times, November 24, 1948.

1933. "Joe Louis Uncertain about Retirement," New York Times, September 15, 1948, p. 44.

1934. "L. Firps Seeks a Cestac-Joe Louis Bout," New York Times, January 3, 1948, p. 19.

1935. "Lesnevich's Bout with Walcott Is Canceled," Washington Post, September 18, 1948.

1936. "Louis Again Says He Will Retire," New York Times, June 29, 1948, p. 28.

1937. "Louis a Grand Guy, Says Walcott, 'But' . . . I Aim to Win," Daily Worker, June 13, 1948, p. 16.

1938. "Louis Chooses Six He Thinks Should Tangle for Title Shot," Evening Star, December 5, 1948.

1939. "Louis 5-13 Favorite," New York Times, June 23, 1948, p. 35.

1940. "Louis Found Fit; Comments," New York Times, June 16, 1948, p. 39.

1941. "Louis Gets Enthusiastic Reception on Arrival for London Exhibitions: Champion to Make Three Appearances Daily for a Month," New York Times, February 25, 1948.

1942. "Louis Picks French Lick Training Site," New York Times, January 30, 1946, p. 21.

1943. "Louis Kayoes 'One More Fight' Talk," Daily Worker, July 22, 1948, p. 15.

1944. "Louis Knocks Out Walcott in 11th," New York Star, June 26, 1948, p. 6.

1945. "Louis Praised-Editorial," New York Times, June 27, 1948, p. 8, Sec. 4.

1946. "Louis Proves to Self and Fans He Really Could Fight Again," Evening Star, September 21, 1948.

1947. "Louis Reiterates Intention to Retire," New York Times, June 26, 1948, p. 11.

1948.   "Louis Reiterates Plans to Retire After Bout," New York
        Times, February 25, 1948, p. 30; February 26, 1948, p.
        29.

1949.   "Louis Reported in Good Condition," New York Times,
        June 2, 1948, p. 41.

1950.   "Louis Says England Tour Will Be Training Ground,"
        Daily Worker, February 18, 1948, p. 26.

1951.   "Louis Signs to Defend in N.Y.; Walcott Holding Out for
        30%," People's Voice, January 17, 1948, p. 29.

1952.   "Louis-Walcott Bout--Agreement Reported Near," New
        York Times, January 29, 1948, p. 29.

1953.   "Louis-Walcott Bout Promoters Fail to Agree on Purse
        Divison," New York Times, January 27, 1948, p. 34.

1954.   "Louis-Walcott Bout Radio and Telecast Plans," New
        York Times, March 11, 1948, p. 54.

1955.   "Louis-Walcott Bout--Louis Wins by Knockout in 11th
        Round," New York Times, June 25, 1948, p. 1.

1956.   "Louis and Walcott Sign for June 23 Bout," New York
        Times, April 15, 1948, p. 32.

1957.   "Louis-Walcott Ticket Prices Set," New York Times,
        March 23, 1948, p. 33.

1958.   "Louis Warns Walcott to Accept Terms or Lose Bout,"
        New York Times, February 20, 1948, p. 22.

1959.   Matthews, Leslie, "Ezzard Charles Not Ready for Joe
        Louis," New York Age, December 18, 1948, p. 16.

1960.   Miller, Buster, "Joe Louis to Defend His Title Next
        June," New York Age, October 23, 1948, p. 1.

1961.   "Walcott Failure to Sign Draws Louis Attack," Evening
        Star, February 19, 1948.

1962.   Walsh, Jack, "Joe Louis' Decision to Fight Again Makes
        Ahearn Happy," Washington Post, September 18, 1948.

1963.   Young, A. S. (Doc), "(Jimmy) Bivins Tough Foe Says
        Louis," New York Age, November 27, 1948, p. 17.

B.   FAMILY

1964.   O'Neill, Edward and James Desmond, "Joe Louis Love
        Thief, Model's Hubby (Rev. Matthew C. Faulkner)
        Says," New York Daily News, April 2, 1948.

C. PERSONAL

1965. "Joe Louis and Noble Sissle in Cancer Drive," People's
       Voice, January 17, 1948, p. 27.

1966. "Joe Louis and Paul Robeson Judge Beauty Match,"
       New York Age, September 24, 1948, p. 8.

1967. "Joe Louis Blamed in Traffic Snarl," Washington Post,
       July 26, 1948.

1968. "Joe Louis Gives $5,000 to Sydenham Hospital,"
       People's Voice, March 20, 1948, p. 5.

1969. "Joe Louis Honored: Special Deputy Sheriff of Wayne
       County, Michigan," New York Age, July 24, 1948, p. 1.

1970. "Louis to Open Trade School in Chicago: Founder and
       President of Insitituion of This $100,000 New Building,"
       New York Age, October 30, 1948, p. 2.

1971. "Love-Thief Case Point Won by Joe," Afro-American,
       May 7, 1948.

1972. Nunn, Bill, "An Open Letter to Joe Louis," Pittsburgh
       Courier, July 3, 1948.

1973. Rodney, Lester, "After Louis--Who?: Look at Long Range
       Field Brings One Voice for Cincy's Ezzard Charles,"
       Daily Worker, June 6, 1948, p. 11.

D. POLITICS

1974. "Joe Louis 'Admires' Henry Wallace," People's Voice,
       February 21, 1948, p. 4.

1975. "Joe Louis Backs Sherman for Harlem Mayor," People's
       Voice, February 14, 1948.

1976. "Joe Louis Enlists Mayor O'Dwyer in Sydenham Appeal,"
       People's Voice, February 14, 1948, p. 31.

1977. "Louis Reported Considering Political Career," New
       York Times, June 27, 1948, p. 1, Sec. 5.

15. 1949

A. BOXER

1978. Bourne-Vanneck, V. P., "Why Was Joe Louis Snubbed?"
       (By the New York State Athletic Commission),"
       New York Age, March 19, 1949, p. 1.

1979. Bromberg, Lester, "How Long Joe Louis Will Last,"
       National Police Gazette, Vol. 154, No. 3, March,
       1949, pp. 16-17.

1980. _____ , "Just How Good Is Ezzard Charles?: New Champ Has Tough Road Ahead, Following in Footsteps of Joe Louis . . . ," National Police Gazette, Vol. 154, No. 11, November, 1949, p. 19.

1981. _____ , "Who Can Fill Joe Louis' Gloves?" National Police Gazette, Vol. 154, No. 6, June, 1949, pp. 16-17.

1982. Burley, Dan, "Louis Beat 'Em All to the Punch," New York Age, March 12, 1949, p. 16.

1983. Carroll, Ted, "(Jack) Johnson or (Joe) Louis? Nat (Fleisher) Rates Them 1-2," New York Age, February 19, 1949, p. 12.

1984. Cohen, Sam, "Title Comeback Bout to Climax Louis Tour," Boston Daily Record, November 2, 1949.

1985. Daniel, Daniel M., "Louis-Dempsey 'Fight' Becomes Vibrant Again," The Ring, Vol. 28, No. 3, April, 1949, pp. 16-18, 36.

1986. Devine, Tommy, "Ezzard Charles? He's 'Palooka' to Joe Louis," Detroit Free Press, December 16, 1949, p. 26.

1987. "'I Mean to Win,' Says Joe Louis of Fighting for Staff Elevators," New York Age, April 16, 1949, p. 15.

1988. "Jersey Journal Says it 'Owns' a Bit of Joe Louis, Too," New York Age, March 12, 1949, p. 11.

1989. "Joe Louis Exhibition Tour, Boston," New York Times, November 15, 1949, p. 34.

1990. "Joe Louis Exhibition, Manila," New York Times, May 6, 1949, p. 35.

1991. "Joe Louis Exhibitions; Michigan State Comm. Scores Detroit Show," New York Times, December 16, 1949, p. 39.

1992. "Joe Louis Exhibition, Newark," New York Times, November 23, 1949, p. 22.

1993. "Joe Louis Exhibition Tour, Dallas," New York Times, March 20, 1949, p. 2, sec. 5.

1994. "Joe Louis Gets B'rith Shalom Award," New York Times, October 6, 1949, p. 45.

1995. "Joe Louis Officially Retires," New York Times, March 2, 1949, p. 1.

1996. "Joe Louis Ring Record," New York Times, March 2, 1949, p. 35.

1997.   "Joe Louis Squelches 'Comeback' Rumors: Says He Will
        Never Fight for Title Again!" Pittsburgh Courier,
        October 22, 1949, p. 1.

1998.   "Joe Louis Tour, Nassau," New York Times, March 2,
        1949, p. 35.

1999.   "Law May Ban Louis in Hub: Retired Champion Too
        Old (at 35) to Box Here (Boston)," Boston Post,
        October 12, 1949.

2000.   "Left Eye Bothering Joe Louis: Injured Optic
        Bothers Louis," New York Age, February 5, 1949, p. 12.

2001.   "Louis-Musto Bout: Banned, Cleveland," New York Times,
        March 11, 1949, p. 12.

2002.   "Louis Officially Retires: to Promote Charles-Walcott
        Bout," Daily Worker, March 2, 1949.

2003.   "Louis Retirement Sets Off Struggle for Control of
        Title," Washington Post, March 2, 1949, p. 19.

2004.   "Near Certainty: Joe Louis Will Vs. Ezzard Charles,"
        New York Age, December 31, 1949.

2005.   "20th Century Sporting Club to Relinquish Rights to
        Madison Square Garden: New Corporation to Be
        Associated with International Boxing Club Headed by
        Joe Louis," New York Times, May 6, 1949, p. 33.

2006.   "Vancouver Bans Joe Louis Exhibitions," New York Times,
        December 20, 1949, p. 40.

2007.   Walker, Mickey, "Could Louis Have Beaten Jack Johnson,"
        National Police Gazette, Vol. 154, No. 8, August, 1949,
        p. 20.

2008.   _____, "Why Tunney Could Have Licked Louis,"
        National Police Gazette, Vol. 154, No. 4, April, 1949,
        p. 19.

2009.   Webber, Harry B., "Say Jersey 'Owns' a Bit of Louis,
        Too," New York Age, March 12, 1949, p. 11.

B.   FAMILY

2010.   Burley, Dan, "Joe Louis Nixes Marriage Rumors: Denies
        Giving Her (Rudy Dallas) $40,000 Home: She Confirms
        All His Statements," New York Age, February 12, 1949,
        pp. 1, 2.

C.   GOLFER

2011.   "Joe Louis Wins Cleveland (Golf) Play," New York Age,
        July 23, 1949, p. 23.

D. JOE LOUIS AS BOXING PROMOTER

2012.   Burnett, Bill, "Dempsey Here, See Louis a Flop as
        Fighter Promoter," Washington Post, March 27, 1949.

2013.   Carroll, Ted, "Huge Bankroll Is Joe's Ace: Louis Has
        Right Kind of Financial Backing," New York Age,
        March 12, 1949, pp. 16, 17.

2014.   _____, "Joe Louis and Markson Top Team: Ted
        Carroll Praises New Fight Promotion Lineup As Bomber
        Proves Mettle," New York Age, August 6, 1949, p. 25.

2015.   _____, "Joe Louis Boss (as a promoter) at
        Madison Square Garden," New York Age, May 14, 1949,
        pp. 1, 9.

2016.   _____, "Joe Louis Future Brighter (as a boxing
        promoter)," New York Age, May 21, 1949, p. 24.

2017.   Edinboro, Ollie, "N.Y. Nixes Out Louis Title Go:
        Promoter Joe Draws Frown of Col. Eagan," New York Age,
        March 12, 1949, pp. 1, 9.

2018.   Editorial, "Good Luck, Joe (as a promoter)," New York
        Age, March 19, 1949, p. 12.

2019.   Effrat, Louis, "Louis Officially Resigns World Title;
        Will Become Boxing Promoter," New York Times, March 2,
        1949, p. 1.

2020.   "Louis Quits Ring, Joins Chicagoans As Promoter,"
        Washington Post, March 2, 1949, pp. 17, 19.

2021.   "N.Y. Nixes Out Louis Title Go: Promoter Joe Draws
        Frowns of Col. Eagan," New York Age, March 12, 1949,
        p. 1.

2022.   "Promoter Joe Eyes Saddler and Pep Bout," New York
        Age, March 19, 1949, p. 17.

2023.   Burley, Dan, "Louis Moves in on Madison Square Garden,"
        New York Age, May 14, 1949, p. 16.

2024.   "Champ (Louis) Aids Fighters: Gives $100 to the
        National Committee for Labor Israel," New York Age,
        February 5, 1949, p. 12.

2025.   "Joe Louis Asks New Your State Athletic Commission
        Championship Recognition," New York Times, July 29,
        1949, p. 16.

2026.   "Joe Louis' $500,000 Suit Against Look," Atlanta
        Daily World, January 6, 1949, p. 1.

138   Joe Louis

2027.   "Louis Calls Off Look (Magazine) Libel Suit," New York
        Age, April 16, 1949, p. 2.

2028.   "Louis Comments," New York Times, May 11, 1949, p. 42.

2029.   "Louis' Earnings Top All at $3,887,323," Washington
        Post, March 2, 1949.

2030.   "Louis Opens War Against Self-Service Elevator Apts,"
        New York Age, March 19, 1949, pp. 1-9.

2031.   "Louis Sues Look for $500,000 Libel," Chicago Daily
        Worker, January 5, 1949.

2032.   "Louis Sues Look Magazine for $500,000 Libel (Over
        False, Untrue and Exceedingly Harmful Statements About
        the Champion's Financial Condition)," Daily Worker,
        January 5, 1949.

2033.   "Robeson Statements are Repudiated on Telecast,"
        New York Age, May 14, 1949, p. 2.

2034.   Robinson, Will, "Ted Rhodes' Monopoly on Joe Louis
        (Golf) Open Continues," Pittsburgh Courier, September
        10, 1949, p. 18.

2035.   Roswell, H. H., "Joe Louis Is No Miser," National
        Police Gazette, Vol., 154, No. 2, February, 1949,
        p. 19.

2036.   "Tenants Join Louis Elevator Campaign," New York Age,
        April 2, 1949, p. 11.

2037.   "Wishes for a Joyous Season From Joe Louis," New York
        Age, December 24, 1949, p. 18.

2038.   "Cleric (Rev. Matthew C. Faulkner) Names Louis in
        Divorce Suit," New York Sun, June 7, 1949.

                        16.   1950

                        A.   BOXER

2039.   Bromberg, Lester, "Ezzard Charles Says--'I Can Beat
        Joe Louis!'" National Police Gazette, Vol. 155, No. 5.,
        May, 1950, pp. 20-21.

2040.   _____, "Joe Louis--Myth or Marvel?" National
        Police Gazette, Vol. 155, No. 8, August, 1950, pp.
        20-21, 28.

2041.   _____, "Joe Louis' Punch--How It Feels!" National
        Police Gazette, Vol. 155, No. 1, January 1950, pp.
        16-17.

2042.   _____ , "Warning to Joe Louis--Stay Retired!"
National Police Gazette, Vol. 155, No. 3, March,
1950, pp. 20-21.

2043.   _____ , "What Will Joe Louis Do Now?" National
Police Gazette, Vol. 155, No. 12, December, 1950,
pp. 20-21.

2044.   Carroll, Ted, "Louis' Spectacular Success on His Rich
Exhibition Trail," The Ring, Vol. 29, No. 9, October,
1950, pp. 18-19.

2045.   "Comment on Louis-Charles Bout," New York Times,
October 1, 1950, p. 2, Sec. 4.

2046.   "Decides to Return to Ring," New York Times, October
15, 1950, p. 4, Sec. 5.

2047.   "J. Da Grosa Plans to Bar Louis Bouts," New York
Times, December 11, 1950, p. 33.

2048.   "Joe Louis-Charles Bout Set; Louis to Get 35% of Net,"
New York Times, August 18, 1940, p. 25.

2049.   "Joe Louis Exhibition Salt Lake City," New York Times,
January 26, 1950, p. 32.

2050.   "Joe Louis Exhibition St. Petersburgh, Florida," New
York Times, February 9, 1950, p. 37.

2051.   "Joe Louis Decides on Comeback," New York Times,
July 25, 1950, p. 34.

2052.   "Joe Louis Defeats Caesar Brion in Chicago, But Makes
Poor Showing," Chicago Defender, December 9, 1950, pp.
16, 17.

2053.   "Joe Louis Hangs 'Em Up for Good," New York Age, April
8, 1950, p. 8.

2054.   "Joe Louis Rejects Ezzard Charles Challenge," New York
Times, January 22, 1950, p. 2, sec. 5.

2055.   "Joe Louis to Continue Comeback," New York Times,
December 1, 1950, p. 35.

2056.   "Joe Louis Undecided on Retirement," New York Times,
October 3, 1950, p. 38.

2057.   Povich, Shirley, "(Ezzard) Charles Wins Unanimous
Decision Over Louis: Tired, Aged Joe No Match for
Ez, Who Almost KO's Him in 14th," Washington Post,
September 28, 1950, pp. 1, 12.

B.   INCOME PROBLEMS

2058.   "Louis Gets $100,458, (Ezzard) Charles $57,405,"
Washington Post, September 28, 1950, p. 12.

2059.   "Hurry! See Joe Louis Box All Sports Carnival Sunday,"
People's Voice, June 13, 1950, p. 33.

2060.   "(Louis) Explains His Relation with Cleric's Wife:
Says He Mixed with Her (Mrs. Carrole Drake Faulkner)
to Help Build-Up Popularity of Model," New York
Amsterdam News, January 3, 1948.

2061.   "Federal Government Files $58,938 Income Tax Lien for
Unpaid '47 Tax, Chicago," New York Times, May 20, 1950,
p. 72.

2062.   "Seeks Bout to Pay Tax Arrears," New York Times,
July 25, 1950, p. 34; July 29, 1950, p. 8.

2063.   "Seeks Compromise on Income Tax Arrears," New York
Times, October 3, 1950, p. 38.

C.   PERSONAL

2064.   "It Happened in (Griffin), Ga.: Joe Louis Boxes White
Cop in Exhibition," Afro-American, March 18, 1950.

2065.   "Joe Louis Walks Out on Exhibition Fight in Augusta,
Ga. Because Negroes Not Allowed to Sit at Ringside,"
New York Amsterdam News, March 11, 1950, p. 1.

2066.   "Rev. M.C. Faulkner Drops Alienating of Affection
Suit After Settlement," New York Times, June 28,
1950, p. 15.

17.   1951

A.   BOXER

2067.   Cannon, Jimmy, "Joe Louis Through, a Tired Old Man,"
New York Post, October 28, 1951.

2068.   "(Ezzard) Charles Doesn't Think Louis Can Really Come
Back," Daily Worker, January 5, 1951.

2069.   Dawson, James P., "Louis Knocks Out Savold in Sixth and
Gains Chance for Another Title: 18,179 See Ring Battle,"
New York Times, June 16, 1951, p. 10.

2070.   Egan, Dave, "Men Who Know See End for Louis," Boston
Daily Record, October 25, 1951, p. 46.

2071.   Hern, Gerry, "Louis Gave His All to the End,"
Boston Post, October 30, 1951.

2072. Jennings, Jim, "Walcott Will Beat the Louis Jinx!"
       National Police Observer, Vol. 156, No. 11, November
       1951, pp. 16-17.

2073. "Joe Louis Defeated by (Rocky) Marciano," New York
       Amsterdam News, November 3, 1951, p. 30.

2074. "Louis, Happy Over Latest Win, Faces One More
       Stepping Stone," Washington (D.C.) Evening Star,
       February 8, 1951, pp. C-1, C-2.

2075. Nichols, Joseph C., "Marciano Knocks Out (Joe)
       Louis in Eighth Round of Heavyweight Fight," New York
       Times, October 27, 1951, p. 12.

2076. Nichols, Joseph C., "(Rocky) Marciano Knocks Out Louis
       in Eighth Round of Heavyweight Fight in Garden; 17,241
       See Fight," New York Times, October 27, 1951, p. 12.

2077. "Pleased Louis Now Sees Return with Ezzard Charles,"
       Daily Worker, January 5, 1951.

2078. Rice, Grantland, "Big Question: How Long Can Louis
       Last?" Boston Globe, October 26, 1951.

                     B. PERSONAL

2079. "For Champion Visits Baby Home in Japan," New York
       Times, December 17, 1951.

2080. Hirshberg, Al, "'You Placed a Red Rose on Abe Lincoln's
       Grave,' Tribute to Joe Louis," Boston Post, January
       26, 1951.

2081. "Louis in $$ Daze," New York Post, October 29,1951.

                     18. 1952

                     A. PERSONAL

2082. Berg, Louis, "The Champ (Joe Louis) and His Double
       (Actor Coley Wallace)(in 'The Joe Louis Story'),
       New York Herald Tribune, March 29, 1952, p. 13.

2083. "IBC Holding Position at $15,000 for Him (Louis)
       When Retirement Is Final," Chicago Defender, January
       12, 1952, p. 16.

2084. "'Joe Louis Story' to Be Filmed in 1953," Daily Worker,
       August 6, 1952.

B.   JOE LOUIS AND POLITICS

2085.   "Joe Louis Favors (Harold E.) Stassen, Backs Civil Rights Stand," Washington (D.C.) Evening Star, April 7, 1952, p. A-5.

2086.   "Joe Louis Quits G.O.P. Ranks, Says He'll Vote for Stevenson," Washington (D.C.) Evening Star, October 16, 1952.

19.   1953

A.   BOXER

2087.   "Name Louis Best (Boxer) in Half-Century," Pittsburgh Courier, October 17, 1953.

20.   1954

A.   BUSINESSMAN

2088.   "Joe Louis Selling Milk," Chicago Defender, October 16, 1954, p. 3.

2089.   "Champ Was Paid Cash ($150,000) to Resign Says Justice Dept.," Afro-American, July 17, 1954, p. 1.

B.   PERSONAL

2090.   Rodney, Lester, "(Joe Louis) a Fine 'Rookie' Referee," Daily Worker, November 3, 1954.

2091.   "Louis Returns to Ring . . . to Teach (Paul Andrews) Protege," New York Post, February 2, 1954, p. 76.

21.   1955

A.   BUSINESSMAN

2092.   "Joe Louis Involved in Interracial Hotel in Las Vegas, Nev., The Moulin Rouge," Afro-American, May 21, 1955, p. 7.

B.   FAMILY

2093.   Sullivan, Ed and Robert McCarthy, "Joe Louis Takes Rich Bride (Rose Morgan); She's 'Helen Rubinstein of Harlem'," New York Daily News, December 4, 1955, p. 3.

22.   1956

A.   FAMILY

2094.   "'Joe's the Boss,' New Mrs. Admits (Formerly Rose Morgan)," Pittsburgh Courier, July 7, 1956, p. 2.

B. INCOME TAX PROBLEM

2095.   "How Joe Louis' Kids Lost $64,000 to U.S. (U.S. Internal Revenue)," Afro-American, December 29, 1956, p. 15.

2096.   "Joe Louis Taxes Due U.S. Gov't Amount of $1,210,789," Chicago Defender, February 11, 1956, p. 1.

2097.   "Amsterdam News Fights to Have His (Joe Louis) Tax Debts Forgiven by the U.S. Government," New York Amsterdam News, January 21, 1956, p. 1.

2098.   "Rep. Alfred E. Siemanski (Dem, N.J.) Has Introduced a Bill in House of Rep. for Tax Relief of Joe Louis," Afro-American, June 9, 1956, p. 1.

2099.   "U.S. Acts to Seize $66,000 Trust of Joe Louis' Kids," New York Post, December 17, 1956.

2100.   "U.S. Government Claims All of His (Joe Louis) Income," Chicago Defender, December 15, 1956, p. 1.

2101.   "Will U.S. Seize Fund of Joe Louis' Kids?" New York Post, December 16, 1956.

2102.   "Joe Sidelined by Heart Condition," Daily Worker, July 25, 1956, p. 1.

2103.   Kilgallen, James L., "Champ's 4-1/2 Million Just Slipped Away," New York Journal American, April 10, 1956.

2104.   Poston, Ted, "His (Joe Louis) Heart's in the Right Place," New York Post, July 29, 1956.

C. PROFESSIONAL WRESTLER

2105.   Gross, Milton, "Why Louis Wrestled 'For Whites Only' (in St. Petersburgh, Florida)," New York Post, April 5, 1956, pp. 32-33.

2106.   _____, "Joe Louis and the South," New York Post, April 9, 1956, pp. 33, 54.

2107.   _____, "Joe Louis and the South," New York Post, April 10, 1956, pp. 63-64.

2108.   _____, "Joe Louis and the South," New York Post, April 11, 1956, pp. 63-64.

2109.   "Small Crowd (4,410) Sees Louis Wrestle (in Detroit, Michigan)," New York Post, May 25, 1956.

2110.   Walsh, Jack, "Louis Down to Wrestling Weight--240 (Lbs.)," Washington Post, March 15, 1956.

23. 1957

A. BOXER

2111. "NBA Rates Louis 'Tentative 4th'; Expects He'll Retire," Daily Compass, December 27, 1957.

B. INCOME TAX PROBLEM

2112. "Labor Unions (AFL-CIO) Back Joe Louis in Taxes," Daily Worker, February 3, 1957.

2113. Rodney, Lester, "Short Memories (United States Government) in Washington," The Worker, January 6, 1957.

2114. "The Short Memories in Washington," Daily Worker, February 17, 1957.

2115. "Work Pushed on Income Tax Settlement for Louis," New York Post, January 24, 1957.

C. PERSONAL

2116. Cannon, Jimmie, "Joe, Nice Guy," New York Post, December 26, 1957.

2117. _____, "Couple of Quick Ones," New York Post, December 26, 1957.

2118. "Hoffa May Hire Joe Louis," Pittsburgh Courier, October 19, 1957, p. 3.

2119. "Joe Louis' Hotel Bill From Union Funds," New York Age, August 21, 1957, p. 7.

2120. "Joe Louis Sues Tom Galento for TV Libel for $250,000," New York Amsterdam News, March 30, 1957, p. 3.

24. 1958

A. FAMILY

2121. Albelli, Alfred, "Wife (Rose Morgan) Claims Joe Louis KOs Family Hopes, Sues," New York News, October 24, 1958.

2122. "Mrs. Joe Louis (Rose Morgan) Sues, Says He Bars the Stork," New York Post, October 23, 1958.

2123. "Wife (Rose Morgan) Is Suing Joe Louis for Annulment," New York Post, August 27, 1958.

B.   INCOME TAX PROBLEM

2124.   "Joe Louis Children Lose $100,000 Trust Fund for Back Taxes," Afro-American, April 3, 1958, p. 1.

2125.   "Joe Louis Gets Tax Break; Pays $20,000 a Year," Pittsburgh Courier, January 18, 1958, p. 2.

2126.   "Tax Pact Hits Joe Louis for $20,000 a Year," New York Journal American, January 10, 1958.

2127.   "Tax Plan Set for Joe Louis," New York Post, January 10, 1958.

C.   PERSONAL

2128.   "Joe Louis to Film His Life Story for TV," Chicago Defender, December 2, 1958, p. 19.

25.   1960

A.   AWARD

2129.   "Joe Louis to Get Top (100% Wrong) Award," California Eagle, February 25, 1960.

B.   BUSINESSMAN

2130.   "Joe Louis Agency Gives up Cuban Account," Afro-American, July 16, 1960, p. 1.

2131.   "Joe Louis Denies Tie with Castro," New York Times, June 2, 1960, p. 14.

2132.   "Joe Louis Named Union Organizer," New York Post, January 10, 1960.

2133.   "Louis Set to Toss the Towel in Cuba," New York Daily News, June 2, 1960.

2134.   Poston, Ted, "Joe Louis Giving Up Cuban Promoter Job," New York Post, June 1, 1960.

2135.   Robinson, Jackie, "Joe Louis and Cuba," New York Post, June 6, 1960.

C.   PERSONAL

2136.   "Louis Kayoed Walcott; Made Vow to Mother!" Pittsburgh Courier, November 12, 1960, Magazine Section, p. 3.

2137.   "Louis Sets Off Clash in Kenya," Chicago Defender, November 12, 1960, p. 1.

2138.   Smith, Gene, "The Joe Louis Story," <u>New York Post</u>,
         June 27, 1960, p. 28, Part I.

2139.   _____, "The Joe Louis Story," <u>New York Post</u>,
         June 28, 1960, p. 56, Part II.

2140.   _____, "The Joe Louis Story," <u>New York Post</u>,
         June 29, 1960, p. 60, Part III.

2141.   _____, "The Joe Louis Story," <u>New York Post</u>,
         June 30, 1960, p. 46, Part IV.

2142.   _____, "The Joe Louis Story," <u>New York Post</u>,
         July 1, 1960, p. 32, Part V.

26. 1961

A. BOXING CRITIC

2143.   "Joe Louis Calls Boxing 'A Disgrace'," <u>Chicago Defender</u>,
         June 9, 1961, p. 1.

2144.   "Joe Louis Raps N.Y. Commission in Testimony at Boxing
         Inquiry," <u>Afro-American</u>, June 10, 1961, p. 13.

2145.   "Louis Calling New York Lax, Supports Bill on Boxing
         'Czar'," <u>New York Times</u>, June 2, 1961, p. 26.

B. BUSINESSMAN

2146.   "Joe Louis Describes Detail Deal with Castro,"
         <u>Afro-American</u>, June 17, 1961, p. 13.

2147.   "Joe Louis Says PR Firm Lost Money on Cuba," <u>Afro-American</u>, September 2, 1961, p. 17.

2148.   "Louis Considers New Promotions," <u>New York Post</u>,
         December 22, 1961.

2149.   "Joe Louis Makes Debut as Nite Club Comedian,"
         <u>Journal and Guide</u>, August 19, 1961, p. 45.

27. 1962

A. PERSONAL

2150.   "Joe Louis Is Interested in Golf, TV and Business,"
         <u>New York Amsterdam News</u>, May 26, 1962, p. 33.

28. 1963

A. PERSONAL

2151.   "Top American Leaders Join Big 'Salute to Joe Louis,'"
         <u>New York Courier</u>, July 6, 1963.

29.   1964

A.   INCOME TAX PROBLEM

2152.   Wallace, William N., "Joe Louis' Main Bout at 50: Par and Taxes," New York Times, May 14, 1964, p. 45.

2153.   "Joe Louis at 50 Reminisces on Past," Afro-American, May 23, 1964, p. 9.

30.   1966

A.   BOXER

2154.   "The Night the Bomber Whipped 'Der Schlager,'" New York Amsterdam News, April 23, 1966, Section G, p. 8.

B.   BUSINESSMAN

2155.   Blair, W. Granger, "Louis Leads with His Right: Ex-Champion Greets Patrons at Gaming Club (Piccadilly) in London," New York Times, September 17, 1966, p. 56.

31.   1968

A.   HEALTH CONDITION

2156.   Bromberg, Lester, "Brown Bomber Set for a Surgical Bout," New York Post, March 27, 1968.

32.   1969

A.   FAMILY

2157.   "Joe Louis, Wife to Divorce," New York Amsterdam News, January 11, 1969, p. 1.

B.   PERSONAL

2158.   Bromberg, Lester, "Louis' Memory of (Abe) Simon Has Tough but Nice Ring," New York Post, October 28, 1969.

2159.   "Joe Louis Collapses on Street," Washington Evening Star, June 26, 1969.

2160.   "Louis Counters the Low Blow--with a Laugh," New York Post, September 27, 1969.

33.   1970

A.   FOLK HERO

2161.   "From One Champ to Another," Winston-Salem Journal and Sentinel, February 1, 1970.

2162. "Joe Louis Unchallenged Champion of the People," Michigan Chronicle, August 22, 1970.

2163. Murray, Jim, "The One and Only Joe Louis," Michigan Chronicle, August 15, 1970.

2164. "Russ Cowans Talks About Joe Louis," Michigan Chronicle, August 22, 1970.

2165. Santos, Frank, "Brown Bomber Was Indeed the Greatest," Pittsburgh Courier, August 15, 1970.

2166. "We Let Joe Know We Still Love Him," Michigan Chronicle, August 22, 1970.

B.   HEALTH CONDITION

2167. "Admitted to Denver Psychiatric Hospital on Court Order; No Reason for Action Given," New York Times, May 2, 1970, p. 20.

2168. "Are Head Punches Taking Toll Now on Joe Louis?" New York Amsterdam News, May 9, 1970, pp. 1, 43.

2169. Bromberg, Lester, "Joe Louis' New Fight (Hospitalized in a Psychiatric Asylum)," New York Post, May 4, 1970.

34.   1971

A.   HONORS

2170. "Celebrities Honor Joe Louis in Las Vegas," Pittsburgh Courier, May 29, 1971.

2171. "Joe Louis Honored as 'The Man of the Century' by the Rinkeydinks," New York Amsterdam News, December 4, 19-71, pp. A1, A5.

2172. Slack, Sara, "Joe Louis 'Man of the Century,'" New York Amsterdam News, December 4, 1971, pp. 1, 5.

B.   PERSONAL

2173. "D. Anderson Comments on B. Nagler's Book on Former World Heavyweight Boxing Champ Joe Louis, His Boxing Career and His Alleged Use of Drugs," New York Times, June 3, 1972, p. 23.

35.   1973

A.   HONORS

2174. "Bethune-Cookman College on May 22 Cites Boxer Joe Louis for His Efforts to Help Blacks Achieve Equality in World of Sports," New York Times, May 23, 1973, p. 55.

B.   PERSONAL

2175.   Eskenazi, Gerald, "An Epilogue: Joe Louis and Max
        Schmeling Meet Again," New York Times, August 9, 1973.

36.   1975

A.   FOLK HERO

2176.   Green, Bob, "Yesterday's Hero," New York Post,
        December 24, 1975.

37.   1976

A.   HONORS

2177.   "Benefit Show Salute to the Champ, Joe Louis Set,"
        New York Times, August 2, 1976, p. 2.

2178.   "Bomber's Salute Here Wednesday," Michigan Chronicle,
        August 15, 1976.

2179.   "City Pays Tribute to Champ of Champs," Michigan
        Chronicle, August 22, 1976.

2180.   "Detroit Council Joins Joe Louis Salute, Renames Wash-
        ington Blvd. in His Honor," Pittsburgh Courier, August
        15, 1976.

2181.   "Former Champion Joe Louis to Be Honored," The Carolina
        Times, August 15, 1976.

2182.   "It Was a Salute to Joe Louis," New York Amsterdam News,
        August 15, 1976, p. 2.

2183.   "Salute to Champ a Success," Pittsburgh Courier, August
        15, 1976.

B.   PERSONAL

2184.   Anderson, Dave, "Joe Louis Would Kill Clay?" New York
        Times, November 10, 1976.

2185.   Edwards, Dick, "Joe Louis Ripped Off Again?" News World,
        November 10, 1976.

2186.   "Court Medical Exam for Louis Canceled by Agreement of
        Attorneys; He Will Be Transferred to VA Hospital," New
        York Times, May 13, 1976, p. 7.

2187.   "Joe Louis Put in an Asylum," New York Post, May 2,
        1976.

2188.   Lewin, Leonard, "Louis Hears Familiar Ring," New York
        Post, September 21, 1976.

2189.   "Louis Earned Over $4 Million in Ring," _Michigan Chronicle_, May 16, 1976.

2190.   "Psychiatrists Treat Joe Louis," _Afro-American_, May 9, 1976.

2191.   "Released from Hospital; Was There Since May Because of Emotional Disorder," _New York Times_, October 16, 1976, p. 32.

2192.   "The 'Establishment' Let Joe Louis Down," _The Michigan Chronicle_, August 29, 1976.

2193.   "What Joe Louis Did for Jimmy Hoffa," _New York Amsterdam News_, August 18, 1976, p. A-5.

2194.   Ziegel, Vic, "The Violinist," _New York Post_, November 30, 1976.

38.   1977

A.   HEALTH CONDITION

2195.   "George J. Friedman Letter Held Roger Wilkins Misquoted Joe Louis on His Famous Statement About Winning WWII in His November 13th Article on Reggie Jackson," _New York Times_, November 27, 1977, p. 2, sec. 5.

2196.   Trescott, Jacqueline, "Joe Louis' Birthday Party: A Winning Night," _Washington Post_, May 16, 1977, pp. B1, B6.

2197.   "Condition Noted," _New York Times_, November 10, 1977, p. 10, sec. 4.

2198.   "In Stable Condition After Being Operated on by Heart Specialist, Dr. Michael E. DeBakey," _New York Times_, November 4, 1977, p. 26.

2199.   "Joe Louis Hospitalized After Heart Attack," _News World_, October 24, 1977.

2200.   "Joe Louis in Critical Condition," _New York Amsterdam News_," October 29, 1977, p. A-1.

2201.   "Joe Louis Under Care of DeBakey in Houston," _Staten Island Advance_, October 30, 1977.

2202.   Rubin, Jeff, "Docs Call Louis' Condition Guarded," _New York Post_, October 24, 1977.

39.   1978

A.   FOLK HERO

2203.   Hart, Jeffrey, "Joe Louis: Tower of Class," _New York Press_, September 12, 1978.

2204. Izenberg, Jerry, "Tribute to Louis Can't Begin to Pay the Debt," New York Advance, November 5, 1978.

2205. "Joe Louis Honored at Caesar's Palace," Washington Post, November, 1978, p. 1, sec. 5.

2206. "Joe Louis Seeks Better Film Fee," New York Post, March 30, 1978.

2207. Murray, Jim, "Brown Bomber Finally Finds a Foe He Can't Handle: Time," New York Advance, March 29, 1978.

2208. Pye, Brad, Jr., "'The Brown Bomber' in Las Vegas," Los Angeles (Calif.) Sentinel, November 16, 1978, p. 1B.

2209. Smith, Red, "Happy Birthday, Joe," New York Times, May 14, 1978.

2210. "Still Punching," News World, January 17, 1978.

2211. Will, George F., "Joe Louis Story Recalls Heyday of Racism," New York News World, August 19, 1978.

2212. _____, "The World That Made the Brown Bomber," Newsday, August 7, 1978.

2213. Williams, Bob, "Louis Gets Tiny Slice From Show," New York Post, January 30, 1978.

B. HONORS

2214. "Detroit Votes to Name New Stadium after Louis," New York Times, June 23, 1978.

2215. Izenberg, Jerry, "It's Time to Heal Joe Louis' Scar," New York Post, November 7, 1978.

2216. Katz, Michael, "Stars Came Out to Honor Louis, But Some of Them Didn't Shine," New York Times, November 11, 1978.

2217. Jackson, Jesse, "'Brown Bomber' Still the Champ," News World, February 28, 1978.

2218. "Joe Louis--A Champion Inside and Outside Ring," New York Daily News, November 11, 1978.

2219. Rosenthal, Harold, "End of a Hero," News World, July 15, 1978.

2220. Trescott, Jacqueline, "Joe Louis a Winner by Unanimous Decision: For an Assemblage of Heavyweights, He's Still Undisputed Champ," Washington Post, November 11, 1978, pp. F1, F4.

40. 1979

A. PERSONAL

2221. "Brown Bomber's 65th Birthday," New York Amsterdam News,
May 19, 1979, pp. 66, 72.

2222. "E.D.G.E.S. Organization in Joe Louis Corner," New
York Amsterdam News, July 21, 1979, p. 61.

2223. Gallo, Bill, "Punchlines: Joe Louis is 65 Today," New
York Daily News, May 13, 1979.

2224. "Joe Louis is 65 Today and Not a Forgotten Hero,"
New York Times, May 13, 1979.

2225. Waters, Bob, "The Simple Dignity of Joe Louis, Champion,"
Newsday, May 13, 1979.

41. 1980

A. BOXER

2226. Editorial, "Black Pioneers in Sports," Sporting News,
April 19, 1980, p. 14.

B. HEALTH PROBLEMS

2227. "Brown Bomber Enters Hospital," News World, October
8, 1980.

2228. "Joe Louis Gets a Pacemaker," News World, December 25,
1980.

2229. "Illustration with Wife Leaving Hospital," New York
Times, October 17, 1980, p. 36.

2230. Pepe, Phil, "Joe Louis' Final--and Toughest--Battle,"
New York Daily News, February 4, 1980, p. 50.

C. HONORS

2231. "Cong. Louis Stokes of Cleveland, Ohio, Is Launching
a Drive to Get the Presidential Medal of Freedom, the
Nation's Highest Civilian Honor, for Joe Louis," Jet,
February 14, 1980, p. 6.

2232. "Detroit to Honor Louis at New Arena," Jet, February
28, 1980, p. 50.

2233. "'Joe Louis Arena'--New 18,000-Seat Arena in Detroit,
Mich. Will be Dedicated Officially on March 2, 1980,"
Jet, February 28, 1980, p. 50.

2234. "Joe Louis Has 'Welcome Back Home' Party in Detroit,
Mich. to Christen Arena Named for Him," Jet, March 27,
1980, pp. 31, 52-53.

2235.   "Joe Louis Plans to Visit Hall Named in His Honor,"
         Winston-Salem Journal, July 15, 1980.

2236.   Katz, Michael, "Louis Homecoming Stirs Old Memories,"
         New York Times, February 29, 1980, p. 22.

2237.   "Navy Honors Joe Louis for Gift During WWII," Jet,
         March 13, 1980, p. 56.

2238.   "Rep. Stokes Seeks Freedom Medal for Champ Joe Louis,"
         Jet, February 14, 1980, p. 6.

2239.   "U.S. Navy Honors Joe Louis for $47,000 Gift to Navy
         Relief Fund 30 Years Ago During World War II," Jet,
         March 13, 1980, p. 56.

D.   PERSONAL

2240.   "Joe Louis' Good Works Often Went Unheralded," New
         York News, December 28, 1980.

V
Periodicals about Joe Louis

''Tell Adolf [Hitler] that if he wants to send any more henchmen
to England a la Hess, please let it be Max Schmeling.''

Joe Louis

A SELECTED LIST

1. 1935

A. BOXER

2241. "Boxing: Writers Grant Louis the Title Braddock
       Still Holds," Newsweek, Vol. 6, No. 14, October 15,
       1935, p. 25.

2242. "'Brown Bomber' From Detroit," Literary Digest, Vol.
       119, No. 2351, May 4, 1935, p. 35.

2243. "'Brown Bomber,' Gets the Notices: Lives up to Advance
       Raves by Toppling Primo Carnera in the Sixth,"
       Literary Digest, Vol. 120, No. 1, July 6, 1935, pp.
       32-33.

2244. Editorial, "Joseph Louis Barrows," Opportunity, Vol.
       13, No. 10, October, 1935, p. 295.

2245. "Fighting Morale of Joe Louis," Newsweek, Vol. 6, No.
       14, October 5, 1935, p. 24.

2246. "Joe Louis and Jesse Owens," Crisis, Vol. 42, No.
       8, August, 1935, p. 241.

2247. "Joe Louis Beats Levinsky," Literary Digest, Vol. 120,
       No. 7, August 17, 1935, p. 33.

2248. "Louis Wins Again (Over Paulino Uzcudun)," Literary
       Digest, Vol. 120, No. 25, December 21, 1935, p. 41.

2249. "Joe Louis Wins Over Max Baer," Literary Digest, Vol.
       120, No. 14, October, 1935, p. 32.

2250. "Louis Wins $47,000 and Puts His Camp on the Wagon,"
       Newsweek, Vol. 6, No. 7, August 17, 1935, p. 24.

2251.   Reynolds, Quentin, "Dark Dynamite," Collier's, Vol. 95, June 22, 1935, p. 16.

2252.   Schmeling, Max as Told to Paul Gallico,'This Way I Beat Joe Louis,'" Saturday Evening Post, Vol. 209, No. 9, August 29, 1936, pp. 5, 7, 40; Vol. 209, No. 10, September 5, 1935, pp. 10-11, 32-34.

2253.   Scully, Frank, "Young Black Joe," Esquire, Vol. 4, No. 4, October, 1935, p. 36.

B.   PERSONAL

2254.   "Bible-Reading Louis Takes Leaf From Book of David," Newsweek, Vol. 6, No. 1, July 6, 1935, pp. 22-23.

2255.   "Brown Bomber's Birthday Celebrated in Detroit," Literary Digest, Vol. 110, No. 21, May 25, 1935, p. 25.

2256.   "Joe Louis Engaged (to Marva Trotter)," Literary Digest, Vol. 120, No. 11, September 14, 1935, p. 37.

2257.   "Joe Louis Made First Bank Deposit--$75--August, 1934," Literary Digest, Vol. 120, No. 24, December 14, 1935, p. 41.

2258.   "Louis Gives $100 to Church; East Side Wants Him to Run For Senator," Newsweek, Vol. 6, No. 15, October 12, 1935, p. 25.

2259.   Mitchell, Jonathan, "Joe Louis Never Smiles," New Republic, Vol. 84, No. 1088, October 9, 1935, pp. 239-240.

2.   1936

A.   BOXER

2260.   Braddock, James J., "Louis'Bubble Has Burst," The Ring, Vol. 14, No. 8, September, 1936.

2261.   Daniel, Daniel M., "Slugging Louis Eager for Vacation Days," The Ring, Vol. 15, No. 3, April, 1936, p. 2.

2262.   "Dusky Meteor: Joe Louis of the Dead Pan, Marvel of the Prize-Ring," Literary Digest, Vol. 121, No. 24, June 13, 1936, p. 36.

2263.   Farrell, James T., "The Fall of Joe Louis," Nation, Vol. 142, No. 3704, June 27, 1936, pp. 834-836.

2264.   Fleischer, Nat, "Louis Starts Anew," The Ring, Vol. 14, No. 9, October, 1936.

2265.   Garvey, Marcus, "Schmeling and Joe Louis," The Black Man, July-August, 1936, Vol. II, No. II, pp. 19-20.

2266.   Hannagan, Steve, "Black Gold," Saturday Evening Post,
         Vol. 208, No. 2, June 20, 1936, p. 14.

2267.   "Joe Louis," Brown American, Vol. 1, June 1936, p. 21.

2268.   "Joe Louis and the Negro Press," Crisis, Vol. 43,
         No. 8, August, 1936, p. 241.

2269.   "Joe Louis Denies Being Doped for the Max Schmeling's
         Fight," Literary Digest," Vol. 122, No. 4, July 25, 1936,
         p. 35.

2270.   "Joe Louis-Isadore Gastanaga Fight Off," Literary
         Digest, Vol. 121, No. 1, January 4, 1936, p. 34.

2271.   "Joe Louis' Next Two Fights Between Max Schmeling
         and James J. Braddock," Literary Digest, Vol. 121,
         No. 6, February 8, 1936, p. 38.

2272.   "Joe Louis Wins Over (Al) Ettore," Literary Digest,
         Vol. 122, No. 14, October 3, 1936, p. 39.

2273.   "Paradoxical Louis: The Brown Bomber Has Prize-Ring
         Scribes All Upset Again," Literary Digest, Vol. 122,
         August 29, 1936, p. 34.

2274.   Roche, Billy, "Let's Not Go Haywire on This Lad Louis,"
         The Ring, Vol. 14, No. 1, January, 1936, pp. 6-7.

2275.   Schmeling, Max, "How I Shall Beat Joe Louis Where All
         Others Failed," Liberty, June 13, 1936.

2276.   "Schmeling v. Louis," Time, Vol. 27, No. 26, June 29,
         1936, pp. 35-36.

2277.   "Shadows Behind Joe Louis," Brown American, Vol. 1,
         November, 1936, pp. 18, 26.

2278.   Tillery, Floyd, "Untold Chapters in the Life of Joe
         Louis," The Ring, Vol. 15, No. 4, May, 1936.

3.   1937

A.   BOXER

2279.   "Black Fists: Bomber Louis in Good Negro Company as
         Boxing Champion," Literary Digest, Vol. 123, No. 1,
         July 3, 1937, pp. 34-35.

2280.   "Boxing: Braddock Skips Schmeling for Louis--and a
         Bigger Gate," Literary Digest, Vol. 123, No. 7,
         February 13, 1937, pp. 38-39.

2281.   "Braddock to Fight Louis in Chicago on June 22, 1937,"
         Literary Digest, Vol. 123, No. 15, April 10, 1937,
         p. 40.

2282.   Broun, Heywood, "Joe Louis and John Lewis," Nation, Vol. 144, No. 6, February 6, 1937, p. 156.

2283.   Carroll, Ted, "Joe Louis Compared to Titans of the Past," The Ring, Vol. 17, No. 9, October, 1938, pp. 8-10.

2284.   _____, "Schmeling vs. Louis, Right vs. Left," The Ring, Vol. 17, No. 6, July, 1938, pp. 16, 44.

2285.   "Hardest Punch Joe Ever Threw . . ." Look, December 20, 1938, pp. 33-34.

2286.   "Joe Louis," Sport, Vol. 4, No. 3, March, 1938, p. 77.

2287.   "Joe Louis, Brown Bomber," Brown American, Vol. 2, May, 1938, p. 16.

2288.   "Joe Louis Defeats Natie Brown," Literay Digest, Vol. 123, No. 9, February 27, 1938, p. 34.

2289.   "Joe Louis, 1935's No. 1 Athlete," Literary Digest, Vol. 123, No. 1, January 2, 1938, p. 32.

2290.   "Louis Whips Braddock; Scorned by (Jack) Johnson and Europe," Newsweek, Vol. 10, No. 1, July 3, 1938, pp. 22-23.

2291.   McLemore, Henry, "Joe Louis," Look, December 20, 1938, p. 30.

2292.   "Sports: Joe Louis," Brown American, Vol. 2, No. 4, July, 1938, p. 6.

2293.   "The Championship, It Is a Joke: So Grumbles Schmeling As Braddock and Joe Louis Square Off," Literary Digest, June 19, 1937, pp. 33-34.

2294.   "With the Exception of Joe Louis, Colored Fighters are Notorious for Elaborate Superstitions," Literary Digest, Vol. 123, No. 2, July 10, 1938, p. 32.

4.   1938

A.   ACTOR

2295.   Miller, Loren, "Hollywood's New Negro Films," Crisis, Vol. 45, No. 1, January, 1938, pp. 8-9. Discusses Joe Louis starring in the movie, "Spirit of Youth."

2296.   "Joe Louis Wins Ribbons in America's First All-Negro Horse Show at Detroit," Life, Vol. 5, No. 2, July 11, 1938, pp. 44-45.

B.   BOXER

2297.   Daniel, Daniel M., "Joe Favorite Over German Challenger (Max Schmeling)," The Ring, Vol. 17, No. 6, July,
1938, pp. 13, 16.

2298.   _____, "Joe Louis Fistic Puzzle--Now Marvel,
Now Mediocre," The Ring, Vol. 17, No. 5, June, 1938,
pp. 10-11.

2299.   _____, "Studies in Black (Louis) and White
(Schmeling)," The Ring, Vol. 17, No. 7, August,
1938, pp. 6, 28.

2300.   Fleischer, Nat, "Fleischer Picks Louis to Stop
Schmeling," The Ring, Vol. 17, No. 6, July, 1938,
pp. 2, 16.

2301.   Louis, Joe, "It's Revenge I'm After: My Way to Beat
Schmeling," Liberty, June 25, 1938, p. 8.

2302.   McNeil, T. W., "Gun Shyness (of Joe Louis)," The Ring,
Vol. 17, No. 5, June, 1938, p. 18.

2303.   Schmeling, Max, "I'll Do It Again: How I Will Knock
Out Louis," Liberty, June 25, 1938.

2304.   Tickell, George, "Big Break for Barlund in Louis Challenge Lineup," The Ring, Vol. 17, No. 10, November 10,
1938, pp. 8-9, 33.

C.   EDUCATION

2305.   Bromberg, Lester, "Joe Louis Deplores Lack of Schooling," The Ring, Vol. 17, No. 7, August, 1938, pp. 12-
13.

5.   1939

A.   BOXER

2306.   "A Real Champion: Joe Louis," Opportunity, Vol. 17,
No. 11, October, 1939, pp. 290-291.

2307.   Bliven, Bryce, Jr., "Humpty Dumpty Had a Great Fall,"
New Republic, Vol. 99, No. 1284, July 12, 1939, p.
277.

2308.   Garvey, Marcus, "Joe Louis and the Germans," The Black
Man, February, 1939, Vol. IV, No. 1, pp. 19-20.

2309.   Kessler, Gene, "Joe Louis' Ghost Talks," Esquire, Vol.
12, No. 4, October, 1939, pp. 59, 104.

B.   PERSONAL

2310. "Joe Louis Earned $1,551,322," Brown American, Vol. 3,
       No. 4, October, 1939, p. 16.

6.   1940

A.   BOXER

2311. Brown, Earl, "Joe Louis the Champion, Idol of His Race,
       Sets a Good Example of Conduct," Life, Vol. 8, No. 25,
       June 17, 1940, pp. 48, 56.

2312. Brumby, Bob, "Conn Sees Louis Triumph, Gets Title Shot
       in June," PM, December 17, 1940.

2313. _____, "Here's How . . . And Why . . . Joe Louis,
       Who Can't Find an Opponent Takes Up Golf with a Bang,"
       PM, September 9, 1940.

2314. _____, "Joe Louis Says Billy Conn Is Too Small
       to Fight Him," PM, August 4, 1940.

2315. _____, "Louis Marches on Stillman's: On Lookers
       See Only Champ, Pass up Hollow Shells of Oldtime
       Fighters," PM, August 2, 1940.

2316. _____, "Mike Jacobs' Headache Project: A Fight
       a Month for Joe Louis," PM, December 2, 1940.

2317. Carroll, Ted, "Louis Proves Greatness," The Ring,
       Vol. 19, No. 8, September, 1940, pp. 14-15, 48.

2318. Dempsey, Jack, "Warning to Joe Louis!--Beware Godoy's
       South American Punch . . .," Liberty, Vol. 17, No. 5.,
       February 5, 1940, p. 4.

2319. Fleischer, Nat, "Godoy Brings Out Joe Louis' Faults,"
       The Ring, Vol. 19, No. 3, April, 1940, p. 3.

2320. _____, "Louis Slipping? Asks Godoy; Champ
       Surly and Vengeful," The Ring, Vol. 19, No. 8,
       September, 1940, p. 12.

2320a. "Godoy Asks Donovan Ban . . . Fears Official Favors
       Joe," PM, June 20, 1940.

2320b. "Sham Battle," Time, Vol. 36, No. 27, December 30,
       1940, p. 33.

2321. Vidner, R., "In This Corner: Facts About the
       Champion," Current History, Vol. 51, March, 1940, pp.
       49-50.

7.   1941

A.   ARMY

2322.   Brumby, Bob, "Louis, 1-A in Army Draft, Will Fight for Navy First," PM, November 13, 1941.

2323.   _____, ". . . Louis Is Ready for the Army: Champion, to Be Called Next Month, Will Go Through With Title Defense," PM, September 10, 1941, p. 37.

2324.   _____, "Louis Says Boxing Must Give All for Defense," PM, December 16, 1941.

2325.   Daniel, Daniel M., "Louis in Army? No He's in 3A," The Ring, Vol. 20, No. 8, September, 1941, pp. 3-4, 41.

2326.   "Louis Army Bound," PM, August 13, 1941.

B.   BOXER

2327.   "Abe Simon Gets the Louis Ax Tonight," PM, March 21, 1941.

2328.   Adams, Caswell, "Introducing the New Joe Louis," Saturday Evening Post, Vol. 213, No. 45, May 10, 1941, pp. 26, 27, 106.

2329.   "'Brown Bomber' -- The Story of Joe Louis," Brown American, Vol. 4, No. 21, March, 1941, p. 10.

2330.   Brumby, Bob, "A Sore Right Hand Kept Louis From Chilling Musto," PM, April 9, 1941.

2331.   _____, "Louis Can't Help But Make His Opponents Look Bad," PM, June 8, 1941.

2332.   _____, "Joe Louis Takes Time Out to Meet a Few Camp Callers: Louis Determined He'll Quit the Ring a Champ," PM, September 21, 1941, p. 29.

2333.   _____, "Louis Insists He's Worried About Conn," PM, January 23, 1941, p. 37.

2334.   _____, "Louis Only Real Champion," PM, November 3, 1941.

2335.   _____, "Louis Out to Polish Off Nova in a Hurry: Too Dangerous to Fool With, Joe Says," PM, September 24, 1941, p. 4.

2335a.   _____, "Louis Tires of Ring . . . May Not Go Through with Nova Fight; Seventh Defense of Title in Year May Strike Champion as One Too Many . . . He'd Win Though," PM, August 31, 1941.

2336.   Brumby, Bob, "Lush Era of Boxing Goes Out With Louis," PM, September 11, 1941.

2336a.   _____, "That Burman Was Game But Louis Is Still Louis," PM, February 2, 1941.

2337.   "Champion Joe Louis: Black Moses," Time, Vol. 38, No. 13, September 29, 1941, Cover of Magazine, pp, 60-61.

2338.   Daniel, Daniel M., "Joe Wearing Out," The Ring, Vol. 20, No. 5, June, 1941, pp. 12-13, 55.

2339.   Dawson, James P. and Daniel M. Daniel, "Louis-Conn Fight Gets Expert Preview," The Ring, Vol. 20, No. 6, July, 1941, pp. 3, 27.

2340.   Daniel, Daniel M. "Louis-Nova Battle Ends Outdoor Season," The Ring, Vol. 20, No. 9, October, 1941, pp. 3-4, 47.

2340a.   _____, "Louis in Army, Will Aid Morale," The Ring, Vol. 20, No. 10, November, 1941, pp. 3-5, 41.

2340b.   _____, "Louis Rests Until Second Conn Fight," The Ring, Vol. 20, No. 11, December, 1941, pp. 10-11.

2341.   _____, "Six Fights for Louis Feature 1941 Plans of Mike Jacobs," The Ring, Vol. 20, No. 2, March, 1941, pp. 3-4, 43.

2342.   Fleischer, Nat, "All (Challengers) Look Alike to Joe," The Ring, Vol. 20, No. 4, May, 1941, pp. 12, 44.

2342a.   "Louis Toll Rises," The Ring, Vol. 20, No. 5, June, 1941, p. 11.

2343.   "Is Louis Slipping," The Ring, Vol. 20, No. 3, April, 1941, pp. 10, 11.

2344.   Meany, Tom, "Louis Had to Put Away Nova When He Did . . . or Die Laughing," PM, September 30, 1941.

2345.   "Not So Simple Simon," Time, Vol. 37, No. 13, March 31, 1941, pp. 38-39.

2346.   Pardy, George, "(Joe Louis) A Busy Champion," The Ring, Vol. 20, No. 9, October, 1941, pp. 10-11, 46.

2347.   _____, "When Champ (Joe Louis) Is Champ," The Ring, Vol. 19, No. 4, May, 1940, pp. 10, 41.

2348.   "Sport: Baby Baer," Time, Vol. 37, No. 22, June 2, 1941, p. 55.

2349.   "Sport: Heartbreaker," Time, Vol. 37, No. 26, June 30, 1941, pp. 56-57.

2350.   "The Champ and the Church," <u>Brown American</u>, September-
        October, 1941, p. 15.

2351.   "The Philadelphia Story: Louis Executes Gus Dorazio,"
        <u>PM</u>, February 18, 1941.

C. BUSINESSMAN

2352.   Igoe, Hype, "Louis' Dude Ranch Shows Joe at His Best,"
        <u>The Ring</u>, Vol. 20, No. 7, August, 1941, pp. 19-21.

D. GOLFER

2353.   "Joe's Open (Louis is Bobby Jones, Golfer, of His
        Race)," <u>Time</u>, Vol. 38, No. 8, August 25, 1941, p. 41.

E. PERSONAL

2354.   "Mrs. Joe (Louis) Sues for Divorce," <u>PM</u>, July 31,
        1941.

8.   1942

A.   ARMY

2355.   "Fighter Joe Louis Signs Up to Fight for the U.S.,"
        <u>Life</u>, Vol. 12, No. 4, January 26, 1942, p. 24.

2356.   Gallico, Paul, "The Private Life of Private Joe Louis,"
        <u>Liberty</u>, May 23, 1942, pp. 39-41, 52-54.

2357.   Albertanti, Francis, "Louis-Conn Fight Holds Attention,"
        <u>The Ring</u>, Vol. 21, No. 10, November, 1942, pp. 5-7.

2358.   _____, "Ring, Neil Awards: Memorable for Joe,"
        <u>The Ring</u>, Vol. 21, No. 3, April, 1942, pp. 8-9.

2359.   Carroll, Ted, "On World Boxing Tour (With Joe Louis),"
        <u>The Ring</u>, Vol. 21, No. 10, November, 1942, pp. 6-7, 42.

2360.   Daniel, Daniel M., "Knockout of Schmeling Louis'
        Masterpiece," <u>The Ring</u>, Vol. 20, No. 12, January
        1942, pp. 3-4, 42.

2361.   _____, "Louis Confronts Title, 'Freezing,'"
        <u>The Ring</u>, Vol. 21, No. 7, August, 1942, pp. 8-9,
        47.

2362.   _____, "Louis-Conn Bout, Boxing's Triumph
        for All-Time," <u>The Ring</u>, Vol. 21, No. 10, November,
        1942, pp. 3-4.

2363.   Dempsey, Jack as told to Med Brown, "Is Joe Louis'
        Crown in Danger at Last?" <u>Liberty</u>, October 17, 1942,
        pp. 43-45.

2364. Fleischer, Nat, "Man of the House: Joe Louis," <u>The Ring</u>, Vol. 21, No. 5, June, 1942, pp. 3-7.

2365. Gallico, Paul, "Citizen Barrow," <u>Liberty</u>, May 23, 1942.

2366. _____, "Citizen Barrow," <u>Readers Digest</u>, Vol. 40, No. 242, June, 1942, pp. 21-25.

2367. Graffis, Herb, "The Sporting Scene (Development of the Louis Heir Is Complicated)," <u>Esquire</u>, Vol. 17, No. 1, January, 1942, p. 93.

2368. "The Sportsman, Louis Revives Old Question of Years: When Is a Fighter Too Old to Fight?" <u>The Ring</u>, Vol. 22, No. 10, November, 1942, pp. 3-4, 36.

2369. "The Champ in Camp: A Day with Joe Louis at Fort Riley," <u>The Ring</u>, Vol. 21, No. 9, October, 1942, p. 5, 7.

B. BOXER

2370. Ackerman, Meyer, "Joe Louis Fighter of the Month," <u>The Ring</u>, Vol. 21, No. 5, June, 1942, pp. 32-33.

2371. "Joe Louis Is Out to Make Good (as a soldier)," <u>PM</u>, July 18, 1942, p. 9.

2372. "Joe Louis--The Nonpareil," <u>Service</u>, Vol. 6, March, 1942, p. 7.

2373. "Private Joe Louis Goes to Work (For the Army)," <u>The Ring</u>, Vol. 21, No. 3, April, 1942, pp. 2, 4, 7.

9. 1943

A. ARMY

2374. "Louis on Tour: Sergeant Joe Starts 100-Day Boxing Swing Around Nation's Army Posts," <u>Life</u>, Vol. 15, No. 11, September 13, 1943, pp. 34-35.

B. BOXER

2375. Graham, Frank, "Louis Will Fight Again," <u>Look</u>, November 30, 1943.

2376. "Joe Louis: Man of the Month," <u>Negro Digest</u>, Vol. 2, No. 3, May, 1943, p. 44.

10. 1944

A. ARMY

2377.   Dwyer, Harry, "Brown Bomber Makes Happy Landing
        (in London)," The Ring, Vol. 23, No. 6, July, 1944,
        pp. 10-11.

2378.   "Joe Louis Back Home at Fort Riley," The Ring, Vol. 22,
        No. 12, January, 1944, p. 8.

2379.   "Joe Louis Right: 'We're on God's Side,'" Brown
        American, Winter-Spring, 1944, p. 6.

2380.   "Joe Louis Visits Army Hospital in England," Pulse,
        Vol. 2, August, 1944, p. 31.

2381.   "Morale Builders (Joe Louis and Others) in Armed
        Forces," The Ring, Vol. 23, No. 11, December, 1944,
        p. 5.

B. BOXER

2382.   Fannon, Mark, "Louis, Conn, Mills," The Ring, Vol. 23,
        No. 9, October, 1944, p. 3.

2383.   Green, Abe, Jr.,"Let Louis Fight Conn," Negro Digest,
        Vol. 3, No. 2, April, 1944, pp. 85-86.

2384.   Tickell, George T., "Toughest (Max Baer) Foe of Joe
        Louis," The Ring, Vol. 23, No. 8, September, 1944,
        pp. 3-6.

11. 1945

A. ARMY

2385.   "How Sgt. Joe Louis Sees the War," PM, April 8, 1945.

2386.   Peebles, Dick, "Joe's Post-War Plans," Yank, August
        3, 1945.

2387.   "Sgt. Joe Louis Wins Promotion," PM, April 10, 1945.

B. BOXER

2388.   Cummiskey, Joe, "Conn Signs for Fight with Louis
        Next June," PM, October 19, 1945.

2389.   Fleischer, Nat, "How Joe Shapes Up," The Ring, Vol.
        23, No. 12, January, 1945, pp. 3, 35.

2390.   "Louis Calls His Shot: He'll Chill Conn Again," PM,
        October 24, 1945.

2391. O'Reilly, Tom, "Louis Didn't Play Possum," <u>PM</u>,
       April 2, 1945.

2392. Tickell, George, "Louis Takes No Chances (Quickly
       Knocks Out Opponents)," <u>The Ring</u>, Vol. 24, No. 23,
       March, 1945, pp. 5-7, 43.

                    C. PERSONAL

2393. "Marva and Joe Louis: Story of a Marriage," <u>Headlines
       and Pictures</u>, May, 1945, pp. 8-9.

2394. "How Joe Louis Lost 2 Million," <u>Ebony</u>, May, 1946, pp.
       10-14.

                    12. 1946

                    A. ARMY

2395. Cannon, Jimmy, "What the Army Has Done to Louis and
       Conn," <u>Salute</u>, April, 1946.

2396. Seeley, Evelyn, "Joe Louis on Racial Democracy: 'It's
       Got to Be . . . Negro, Whites Alongside One Another,'"
       <u>PM</u>, August 16, 1946, p. 14.

                    B. BOXER

2397. "Boxing: Bombed Out" (Fight Between Joe Louis and
       Billy Conn), <u>Newsweek</u>, Vol. 28, No. 1, July 1, 1946,
       pp. 73-74.

2398. "Conn-Louis Gate to Fall Far Under 3 Million," <u>PM</u>,
       June 19, 1946.

2399. Crossett, Jim, "The <u>Esquire</u> Poll on Sports Personalities:
       12.6% Favorites Joe Louis," <u>Esquire</u>, Vol. 26, No. 3,
       September, 1946, p. 108.

2400. Cumminskey, Joe, "Conn & Louis Can Still React,"
       <u>PM</u>, May 5, 1946.

2401. _____, "Mike Jacobs Sets $100 Top," <u>PM</u>, April
       2, 1946.

2402. Daniel, Daniel M., "Nine Warn Against Second Louis
       Fights," <u>The Ring</u>, Vol. 25, No. 8, September, 1946,
       pp. 3-4, 19.

2403. _____, "How Louis Wrested Title from Braddock,"
       <u>The Ring</u>, Vol. 25, No. 3, April, 1946, pp. 14-16,
       32.

2404. _____, "Louis and Conn in N.Y.," <u>The Ring</u>, Vol.
       23, No. 11, January, 1946, pp. 3, 27.

2405.   _____, "Louis Recreated Tex's Golden Era,"
        The Ring, Vol. 25, No. 6, July, 1946, pp.6-8.

2405a. _____, "Louis Kept Belting Those Baer Boys,"
        The Ring, Vol. 25, No. 7, August, 1946, pp. 14-16.

2406.   _____, "The First Louis-Conn Fight Reconstructed,"
        The Ring, Vo. 25, No. 5, June, 1946, pp. 12-14, 27.

2407.   _____, "Louis-Schmeling Bouts Studies in
        Contrasts," The Ring, Vol. 25, No. 4, May, 1946, pp.
        19-26.

2408.   Dawson, James P., "Sizing up Joe's Conqueror," The
        Ring, Vol. 25, No. 9, October, 1946, pp. 12-13.

2409.   Feder, Sid, "Why Now for Joe Louis?" The Ring, Vol. 25,
        No. 11, December, 1946, pp. 12, 43.

2410.   Fleischer, Nat, "Age No Criterion in Louis-Conn Battle,"
        The Ring, Vol. 25, No. 4, May, 1946, pp. 14-17.

2411.   _____, "Billy Conn Blows Chance; Overcome by
        Fear (against Joe Louis)," The Ring, Vol. 25, No. 8,
        September, 1946, pp. 5-9.

2412.   _____, "How Much Has Long Layoff Hurt Joe Louis?"
        The Ring, Vol. 25, No. 3, April, 1946, pp. 3-6, 35.

2413.   _____, "Louis Again Kayoes Conn," The Ring,
        Vol. 25, No. 7, August, 1946, p. 3.

2414.   _____, "Louis Again Victor by Kayoe (over Tami
        Mauriello)," The Ring, Vol. 25, No. 10, November, 1946,
        pp. 4-5.

2415.   _____, "Louis Versus Conn," The Ring, Vol. 25,
        No. 6, July, 1946, pp. 3-4, 22.

2416.   _____, "The Fighting Fury Repeats (Between
        Louis and Mauriello)," The Ring, Vol. 25, No. 11,
        December, 1946, pp. 3-8.

2417.   Gibbs, Wolcott, "A Reporter at Large (Louis vs.
        Conn)," New Yorker, Vol. 22, No. 20, June 29, 1946,
        pp. 40-46.

2418.   Lardner, John, "There Seems to Have Been a Fight (Be-
        tween Louis and Conn)," Newsweek, Vol. 28, No. 1, July
        1, 1946, p. 72.

2419.   "Louis, Conn End Training," PM, June 18, 1946.

2420.   "Louis Wins by KO in 1st," PM, September 19, 1946, p.
        24.

2421. Peck, Seymour, "An Easy Win for Joe Louis," PM, May 9, 1946.

2422. Rudd, Irving, "Louis in 3 Rounds," The Ring, Vol. 25, No. 4, May, 1946, pp. 10, 35.

C. FOLK HERO

2423. "Harlem Hails Its No. 1, Hero (Joe Louis) with Mammoth Parade," PM, June 20, 1946.

D. PERSONAL

2424. Feder, Sid, "Little Things Build Joe Louis Legend," The Ring, Vol. 25, No. 7, August, 1946, pp. 4-5, 39.

2425. Hohenberg, John, "Now He (Joe Louis) Slays 'Em--with Wisecracks," Liberty, January 12, 1946, pp. 18, 74-75.

13. 1947

A. BOXER

2426. "Adamant Champ," Newsweek, Vol. 29, No. 18, May 5, 1947, p. 83.

2427. "Big Joe vs. Jersey Joe," Newsweek, Vol. 30, No. 6, August 11, 1947, p. 81.

2428. Broun, Heywood Hale, "About That Figure Again," PM, December 12, 1947.

2429. Carroll, Ted, "Joe a Real Champ, Has Met 'Em All," The Ring, Vol. 26, No. 11, December, 1947, pp. 6-7, 43.

2430. "Champion's Crown Totters: Louis and Walcott," Life, Vol. 23, No. 24, December 15, 1947, pp. 36-37.

2431. "Joe vs. Joe, Who Won?" Newsweek, Vol. 30, No. 24, December 15, 1947, p. 77.

2432. Jones, Jersey, "(Joe Louis) Ten Years a Champ," The Ring, Vol. 26, No. 8, September, 1947, pp. 3, 35.

2433. "Louis Is 10-1 Favorite: 18,000 Expected for Garden Bout Tonight," PM, December 5, 1947.

2434. "Louis Will Retire After Walcott Bout, 'Win, Lose, or Draw,'" PM, December 12, 1947.

2435. Medford, Jack, "Joe Louis," Sportfolio, Vol. 2, No. 1, July, 1947, pp. 60-72.

2436. "Money Ain't Everything," Time, Vol. 49, No. 9, March 3, 1947, p. 52.

2437. The Observer, "The Scramble Is on (To Find Boxer to
       Fight Louis)," The Ring, Vol. 26, No. 5, June, 1947,
       pp. 3, 34.

2438. The "Sportsman,""Joe Louis Goes Aloft on Lucrative
       Tour," The Ring, Vol. 26, No. 3, April, 1947, pp. 8, 14.

2439. "$30 Top Announced for Louis-Walcott Bout," PM,
       October 28, 1947.

B.   PERSONAL

2440. Daniel, Daniel M., "Louis Talks Retirement," The Ring,
       Vol. 26, No. 6, June, 1947, pp. 3, 35.

2441. Fleischer, Nat, "Louis' Tour a Financial Success for
       Joe Not Promoters," The Ring, Vol. 26, No. 4, May,
       1947, pp. 3, 32.

2442. "Louises Agree on Trust Fund," PM, October 23, 1947.

14.   1948

A.   BOXER

2443. Buck, Al, "Louis and (Gene) Tunney Are Ring Counter-
       parts," The Ring, Vol. 27, No. 8, September,1948,
       pp. 17, 34.

2444. Daniel, Daniel M., "Heavyweight Division Faces Incred-
       ible Low: Joe Louis Fading, Walcott No Terror . . .,"
       The Ring, Vol. 27, No. 4, May, 1948, pp. 3, 4, 36.

2445. _____, "Joe Louis Retires; Glitter Era Ends,"
       The Ring, Vol. 27, No. 9, October, 1948, pp. 3-4,
       34.

2446. _____, "Louis and Walcott Fight for New York,"
       The Ring, Vol. 27, No. 2, March, 1948, pp. 3-4, 33.

2447. _____, "Louis' 2nd Time 'Hex' Threatens
       Walcott," The Ring, Vol. 27, No. 6, July, 1948, pp.
       3-5.

2447a. Feder, Sid, "Pride and Gold Delay Bomber's Retire-
       ment," The Ring, Vol. 27, No. 1, February, 1948,
       pp. 18, 48.

2448. Fleischer, Nat, "Handwriting on the Wall for Champion
       Joe Louis," The Ring, Vol. 27, No. 1, February, 1948,
       pp. 15-17, 47-48.

2449. _____, "Louis' K.O. Punch Saved a Bad Fight,"
       The Ring, Vol. 27, No. 8, September, 1948, pp. 12-15.

2450. _____, "'Louis vs. Gus,' Says The Ring," The Ring, Vol. 27, No. 8, September, 1948, pp. 3-5.

2451. "Joe's Last Fight (Louis vs. Walcott)," Time, Vol. 52, No. 1, July 5, 1948, p. 40.

2452. Jones, Jersey, "Louis' Retirement Leaves a Sad Mess," The Ring, Vol. 27, No. 8, September, 1948, pp. 6-9.

2453. Lardner, John, "Final (It Better Be) Curtain," Newsweek, Vol. 32, No. 1, July 5, 1948, p. 65.

2454. _____, "Great Louis Mystery," Newsweek, Vol. 31, No. 25, June 21, 1948, p. 84.

2455. "Louis Sings for 2nd Bout with Walcott," PM, April 15, 1948.

2456. "Louis Wins, Retires," Life, Vol. 25, No. 1, July 5, 1948, pp. 57-58.

2457. Martin, Whitney, "Louis Camp a Sleepy Hollow," PM, June 4, 1948.

2458. Martin, Whitney, "Louis Talk Against Walcott Ill Advised," PM, May 25, 1948.

2459. "On the Ropes," Time, Vol. 52, No. 18, November 1, 1948, p. 44.

2460. The Observer, "Who's Next? (If Joe Louis Defeats Walcott)," The Ring, Vol. 26, No. 12, January, 1948, pp. 19-22.

B.   PERSONAL

2461. Fay, B., "Why Did Joe Louis Change His Mind About Retiring?" Collier's, Vol. 122, No. 21, November 20, 1948, p. 74.

2462. "Louis Takes Fight Films Seriously," PM, June 7, 1948.

2463. "The Louis Legend," Negro Digest, Vol. 7, No. 3, July, 1948, p. 16.

2464. "The New Joe Louis," Life, Vol. 24, No. 25, June 21, 1948, pp. 61-62.

15.   1949

A.   BOXER

2465. Cohane, Tim, "Joe Louis Is Going to Lose His Title," Look, Vol. 13, No. 1, January 4, 1949, pp. 29-30.

2466.   Feder, Sid, "Joe Louis Remembers 'Forgotten Man' Walcott," The Ring, Vol. 28, No. 4, May, 1949, pp. 8-9.

2467.   Fleischer, Nat, "Louis Retirement Meets with Approval," The Ring, Vol. 28, No. 4, May, 1949, p. 12.

2468.   _____, "Savold vs. Louis in June," The Ring, Vol. 28, No. 2, March, 1949, pp. 3, 34.

2469.   "Gentlemen's Agreement," Time, Vol. 53, No. 11, March 14, 1949, p. 82.

2470.   Jones, Jersey, "Good Luck, Joe!: Retiring From Ring, Louis Follows Promotional Trail Blazed by Another Great Heavyweight Champion, Jack Dempsey," The Ring, Vol. 28, No. 4, May, 1949, pp. 10-11, 43.

2471.   _____, "Help Wanted - Male: Louis Retirement, Like (Jim) Jeffries' 45 Years Ago, Leaves Heavyweight Ranks Sadly in Need of Good Fighters," The Ring, Vo. 28, No. 5, June, 1949, pp. 6-8, 37.

2472.   Salak, Johnny, "Kayo Averages List Joe Louis Tops (Among Heavyweights)," The Ring, Vol. 28, No. 5, June, 1949, pp. 16-17.

2473.   Sher, Jack, "Brown Bomber," Sport, Vol. 1, No. 1, 1949, p. 60.

B.   BOXING PROMOTER

2474.   "Boxing: Promoter (Joe Louis)," Newsweek, Vol. 33, No. 11, March 14, 1949, pp. 75-76.

2475.   Bromberg, Lester, "Can Joe Louis Last as a Boxing Promoter?" Negro Digest, Vol. 8, No. , November, 1949, pp. 47-49.

2476.   "Can Joe Louis Make Good in Business," Ebony, June, 1949, pp. 20-29.

2477.   Editorial, "Joe Louis, Promoter: He Will Need 24-Hour Vigilance in His New Enterprise," Life, Vol. 26, No. 11, March 14, 1949, p. 32.

16.   1950

A.   BOXER

2478.   Bright, Harvey, "Study in Contrasts (Joe Louis and Jack Dempsey)," The Ring, Vol. 29, No. 10, November, 1950, pp. 10, 34.

2479.   Bromberg, Lester, "How Joe Louis' Punch Feels," Negro Digest, Vol. 8, No. 2, April, 1950, pp. 11, 14.

2480.   Daniel, Daniel M., "Joe in Big Climax," The Ring,
        Vol. 24, No. 9, October, 1950, pp. 4-5.

2480a. _____, "Joe Louis and Ezz Charles Stir Boxing,"
        The Ring, Vol. 24, No. 10, November, 1950, pp. 6-7.

2481.   Every, Ed Van. "Veteran Sees Ezzard Win (Over Louis),"
        The Ring, Vol. 24, No. 3, April, 1950, pp. 6, 39.

2482.   Fleischer, Nat, "Hail King Charles (Ezzard Gains
        World Title Like a Real Champion and Joe Louis Makes
        His Exit in Same Manner," The Ring, Vol. 24, No. 11,
        December, 1950, pp. 6-7, 35.

2483.   _____, "Louis Will Fight Charles," The Ring,
        Vol. 24, No. 3, April, 1950, p. 6.

2484.   Heintz, W. C., "I Remember Joe," The Ring, Vol. 24,
        No. 11, December, 1950, pp. 24, 43.

2485.   "Joe Will Fight Ezzard Charles," The Ring, Vol. 29,
        No. 8, September, 1950, pp. 3-4, 36.

2486.   "Louis to Fight Again?" The Ring, Vol. 28, No. 12,
        January, 1950, pp. 3, 44.

2487.   "Pictures That Tell Story of Louis' Defeat," The Ring,
        Vol. 24, No. 11, December, 1950, pp. 8-9.

2488.   Tunney, Gene, "Was Joe Louis the Greatest?" Collier's,
        Vol. 125, No. 2, January 14, 1950, pp. 17, 53, 54.

2489.   Schulberg, Budd, "Uncle Mike and the Big Strike--Joe
        Louis," Collier's, Vol. 125, No. 18, May 6, 1950,
        pp. 30-31, 67-69.

2490.   "They (Ex-Heavyweight Champs) Never Come Back," Time,
        Vol. 56, No. 15, October 9, 1950, p. 55.

2491.   "Why I'm (Joe Louis) Fighting Again," Ebony, October,
        1950, pp. 15-18.

B.   FAMILY

2492.   Nagler, Barney, "Charles' and Louis' Moms Suffered,"
        The Ring, Vol. 24, No. 11, December, 1950, pp.16, 39.

C.   PERSONAL

2493.   Heinz, W. C., "What Happened to Joe Louis' $4,000,000!"
        Cosmopolitan, December, 1950, pp. 70-73, 176.

17.   1951

A.   BOXER

2494.   Buck, Al, "The Louis Fadeout: A Major Event in Fistic Affairs of 1950," The Ring, Vol. 30, No. 1, February, 1951, pp. 28, 45.

2495.   Daniel, Daniel M., "Joe and Lee (Savold) in Another Big Interlude," The Ring, Vol. 30, No. 6, July, 1951, pp. 3, 31.

2496.   _____, "Joe Louis Sidetracked," The Ring, Vol. 30, No. 9, October, 1951, pp. 10-11.

2497.   _____, "Louis Still Shades Ezz From Sun," The Ring, Vol. 30, No. 4, May, 1951, pp. 6, 48.

2498.   Edwards, L. M., Reply, Vol. 152, April 17, 1965, p. 44.

2499.   Every, Ed Van, "(Gene) Tunney Decries Joe Louis Comeback," The Ring, Vol. 24, No. 12, January, 1951, pp. 9, 48.

2500.   Fleischer, Nat, "(British Board of Boxing Control) B.B.B.C.--'Louis Is Champ,'" The Ring, Vol. 30, No. 9, October, 1951, p. 5.

2501.   _____, and Stanley Weston, "Joe Louis Fighter of the Month," The Ring, Vol. 30, No. 7, August, 1951, p. 34.

2502.   _____, "Joe's Poundage (210 Pounds) Amazes Boxing Critics," The Ring, Vol. 30, No. 7, March, 1951, p. 14.

2503.   _____, "Walcott Upsets Joe Louis' Plans (To Fight Ezzard Charles)," The Ring, Vol. 30, No. 4, May, 1951, pp. 3-5, 53.

2504.   Parker, Dan, "Champ Who Was Born Too Late," Negro Digest, Vol. 9, June, 1951, pp. 64, 66.

2505.   Salak, Johnny, "Louis, Pep, Robinson, Standout of the Decade," The Ring, Vol. 30, No. 3, April, 1951, pp. 12-13.

2506.   "Why Louis Will Whip Charles," Color, July, 1951, p. 53.

B.   BUSINESSMAN

2507.   "Didn't Beat Drums for Fidel's Cuba--Joe Louis," Jet, June 22, 1951, p. 56.

C.   FAMILY

2508. "I Didn't Raise My Boy to Be a Fighter," Negro
Digest, Vol. 9, February, 1951, pp. 3, 6.

D.   PERSONAL

2509. Burley, Dan, "Love Life of Joe Louis: Romances of
Most Eligible Negro Bachelor Have Involved Beautiful
Women Around the Nation," Ebony, Vol. 6, July, 1951,
pp. 22-26.

2510. Cohane, Tim, "The Sad Story of Joe Louis," Look
Vol. 15, No. 2, February 27, 1951, pp.

2511. Fleischer, Nat, "Louis Vanished Fortune Explained,"
The Ring, Vol. 30, No. 6, July, 1951, pp. 18-19, 41.

2512. Heinz, W. C., "What Happened to Joe Louis' $4,000,000,"
Negro Digest, Vol. 9, March, 1951, pp. 87, 94.

2513. Moley, Raymond, "Joe Louis' Greatest Fight (The In-
ternal Revenue Office)," Newsweek, Vol. 38,No. 20,
November 12, 1951, p. 116.

18.   1952

A.   BOXER

2514. Fleischer, Nat, "Louis K.O. Starts New Era: Marciano's
Eight Round Knockout of Joe Closes One of Ring's
Most Lustrous Careers," The Ring, Vol. 30, No. 12,
January, 1952, pp. 3-6.

B.   BUSINESSMAN

2515. "Joe Louis in Distillery Business," Color, December,
1952, pp. 24-25.

2516. "Joe Louis Launces Whiskey Business," Jet, June 19,
1952, p. 44.

C.   ENTERTAINER

2517. "Joe Louis Stages a Comeback as a Dancer and
Showman," Sepia Record, September, 1952, pp. 8-10.

D.   GOLFER

2518. "Joe's Fight (First Black Ever to Play in a P.G.A.
Co-Sponsored Tournament, San Diego Open)," Time,
Vol. 59, No. 4, January 28, 1952, p. 65.

E. PERSONAL

2519. Cohen, Philip, "Joe Louis Picks a Fight," Labor, January 21, 1952.

2520. "Who Will Joe Louis Marry?" Tan, September, 1952, pp. 31-34.

2521. "Pageant Salutes Joe Louis--A great Guy, An Epic Fighter, an American Legend," Negro History Bulletin, Vol. 16, June, 1953, p. 201.

19. 1953

A. PERSONAL

2522. "Ten Biggest Lies About Joe Louis," Ebony, Vol. 8, August, 1953, pp. 52-58.

20. 1954

A. BOXER

2523. Roxborough, J. W., "How I Discovered Joe Louis," Ebony, Vol. 9, October, 1954, pp. 64-70.

B. PERSONAL

2524. "Why Joe Won't Become a Boxing Bum," Jet, February, 1954, pp. 56-58.

2525. "Why He (Louis) Won't Marry," Hue, December, 1954, pp. 4-8.

21. 1955

A. PERSONAL

2526. "I'd Do It All Over Again Says Joe Louis," Ebony, Vol. 11, November, 1955, pp. 65, 70.

2527. "Will Taxes Put Joe Louis in Jail?" Jet, July 14, 1955, pp. 52-54.

22. 1956

A. HEALTH CONDITIONS

2528. "Will a Bad Heart End His (Louis) Career?" Jet, August 9, 1956, pp. 52-55.

B. INCOME TAX PROBLEMS

2529. "Boxer Tax Troubles," U.S. News and World Report, Vol. 41, No. 26, December 28, 1956, p. 8.

2530. Lardner, John, "Pathos of Taxes," Newsweek, Vol. 47, No. 3, January 16, 1956, p. 73.

C. JOE LOUIS AS WRESTLER

2531. "Can Louis Make It As a Wrestler?" Jet, April 5, 1956, pp. 52-55.

D. PERSONAL

2532. "Can Joe's New Marriage (to Rose Morgan) Last?" Tan, April, 1956, pp. 38-40.

2533. "Gov't (Federal) Charges Louis 'Sold Out' Heavyweight Title," Jet, May 10, 1956, pp. 54-55, 57.

2534. "Joe Louis Philosophy: Ex-Champ's Most Notable Quotations Are as Treasured as His Phenomenal Boxing Record," Ebony, Vol. 11, September, 1956, pp. 52, 54.

2535. "Joe Louis 1 of 2 Negro Faces in Wax at Waxwork Museum in London (Haile Selassie is the other)," Hue, October, 1956, pp. 54-56.

2536. "Joe Louis Says 'Go Slow' in Dixie (South) Desegregation Fight," Jet, April 26, 1956, pp. 6-7.

2537. "Joe Takes a Wife," Ebony, Vol. 11, March, 1956, pp. 45-46.

2538. Linn, Edward, "Joe Louis: Oh, Where Did My Money Go?" Saturday Evening Post, Vol. 228, No. 28, January 7, 1956, pp. 22, 23.

2539. "Why Joe Decided to Marry," Jet, January 5,1956, pp. 14-17.

23. 1957

A. BUSINESSMAN

2540. "Joe Louis Loses $10,000 Yearly in Break Up of International Boxing Club of N.Y. and Ill.," Jet, July 11, 1957, pp. 52-53.

B. PERSONAL

2541. "Blow That K.O.'D Joe Louis," U.S. News and World Report, Vol. 42, No. 4, January 25, 1957, pp. 63-64.

2542. "Joe Louis' Marriage to Rose Morgan on the Ropes," Jet, January 17, 1957, p. 20.

2543. "Joe Wins One for Uncle Sam," Ebony, Vol. 12, January, 1957, pp. 42-43.

2544. "New Fund Started to Pay Off Louis' Income Tax Debt," Jet, January 31, 1957, pp. 50-51.

2545. "What Happened to Joe Louis Tax Fund?" Jet, April 18, 1957, pp. 8-11.

2546. "What Happened to Joe Louis' Marriage?" Jet, June 27, 1957, pp. 18-21.

24. 1958

A. PERSONAL

2547. "How Joe Louis Lost 43 Pounds: Low Calorie Protein Diet Changes Bulging 263 Pound Ex-Champ into Stream-lined 220," Ebony, Vol. 13, May, 1958, pp. 55-57.

2548. "Little Joe Louis, Joe Brown," Ebony, Vol. 13, July, 1958, pp. 88-91.

25. 1959

A. MARRIAGE

2549. "Joe Louis Marries 3rd Time--Martha Malone Jefferson of Los Angeles, Calif.," Jet, April 2, 1959, pp. 48-53.

26. 1962

A. PERSONAL

2550. Pye, B., "Joe Louis and Wife Score K.O. as Promoters," Sepia, Vol. 11, July, 1962, pp. 39, 41.

2551. Talese, Gay, "Joe Louis: The King as a Middle-Aged Man," Esquire, Vol. 57, No. 6, June, 1962, pp. 92-98.

27. 1970

A. HEALTH CONDITION

2552. Cassidy, Joseph, "Story Behind the K.O. of a Champion: Why They Put Joe Louis into a Mental Hospital," Inquirer, June 14, 1970, p. 1.

B. PERSONAL

2553. Editorial, "Of Boxers and Boxing: Then Came Joe Louis," Ebony, October, 1970, Vol. 25, No. 12, p. 164.

2554. Higgins, Chester, "A Salute to the Champion," Ebony, Vol. 25, No. 12, October, 1970, pp. 158-163.

2555. _____, "The Joe Louis Story Nobody Talks About," Jet, May 28, 1970, pp. 46-57.

28.   1971

A.   HEALTH CONDITION

2556.   Nagler, B., "How Joe Louis Got 'Hooked' on Cocaine,"
Sepia, Vol. 21, September, 1972, pp. 22-24.

B.   HONORS

2557.   "Celebrity-Studded Crowd Honors Joe Louis in Vegas on
His 57th Birthday," Jet, June 30, 1971, pp. 50-51.

C.   PERSONAL

2558.   Lucas, Bob, "The Truth About Joe Louis," Sepia,
Vol. 22, December, 1971, pp. 14.

29.   1973

A.   PERSONAL

2559.   Robinson, Louie, "Joe Louis at Sixty," Ebony, Vol. 28,
No. 12, October, 1973, pp. 64-72.

30.   1977

A.   FRIENDSHIP

2560.   "Frank Sinatra Proves a Real 'Friend' Pays Louis'
Hospital and Doctor's Bill," Jet, December 1, 1977,
p. 11.

31.   1978

A.   AUTOBIOGRAPHY

2561.   "Startling and Frank, Louis Tells All in New Intimate
Book," (Joe Louis: My Story), Jet, Vol. 54, July 13,
1978, pp. 52-57.

B.   BOXER

2562.   Coburn, Mark D., "America's Great Black Hope (Joe
Louis-Max Schmeling Fight)," American Heritage,
Vol. 29, No. 6, October-November, 1978, pp. 82-91.

2563.   Smith, Red, "It Was More Than Just Louis vs. Schmeling
(Had International Impact)," TV Guide, January 28,
1978, p. 28.

C.   HEALTH CONDITION

2564.   Lucas, Bob and Isaac Sutton, "Joe Louis Fights to
Walk Again," Jet, Vol. 54, June 22, 1978, pp. 44-50.

D.   HONORS

2565.   "Sinatra's Fete for Joe Louis Raises Over 1/2 Million,"
        Jet, Vol. 55, November 30, 1978, pp. 8-9.

2566.   "Sinatra to Host Las Vegas Fund-Raiser for Joe Louis,"
        Jet, September 28, 1978, p. 59.

2567.   "The Bomber Cast in Stone," News World, November 14,
        1978.

E.   PERSONAL

2568.   "Loves of Joe Louis," Ebony, Vol. 34, No. 1, November,
        1978, pp. 43-46.

32.   1979

A.   TRIBUTES

2569.   "A Tribute to Joe Louis," Sports, Vol. 68, May,1979,
        pp. 90-97.

2570.   "Heavyweights Come to Joe Louis on His 65th Birthday,"
        Jet, Vol. 56, June 7, 1979, pp. 30-31.

2571.   Tyler, Tim, "A Tribute to Joe Louis," Sports, Vol. 68,
        No. 5, May, 1979, pp. 90-93.

33.   1980

A.   GOODWILL AMBASSADOR

2572.   "Where Were They Then? Ebony Takes a Look at What 11
        Prominent Blacks Were Doing in 1945:   Joe Louis,"
        Ebony, Vol. 36, November, 1980, p. 54.   Was
        Heavyweight Champion of the World in 1945.   In 1980
        Louis worked as "Goodwill Ambassador" at Caesars
        Palace in Las Vegas.

34.   1981

A.   HONORS

2573.   "Former Boxer Ken Norton Stars in "Joe Louis Story","
        Jet, Vol. 61, October 1, 1981, p. 56.

2574.   "Joe Louis, RIP," National Review, May 1, 1981, p. 472.

2575.   "Joe Louis Statue Fund in Detroit Gets $50,000," Jet,
        Vol. 60, June 25, 1981, p. 50.

35.   1982

A.   BOXER

2576.   Cohane, Tim, "I Was There: Joe Louis' Greatest
Fight," <u>Modern Maturity</u>, June/July, 1982, pp. 72-74.
Author discusses fight between Joe Louis and Billy
Conn.

VI
Obituaries

"All that I am as a fighter, a champion, I owe to Jack Blackburn. He was teacher, father, brother, nurse, best pal to me and I'll never get over his going away [his death] from here."

Joe Louis

A. STATES

A SELECTED LIST

1. CALIFORNIA

2577. Brown, Jessie Mae, "Joe Louis: Man of Very Few Words,"
       Los Angeles (Calif.) Sentinel, April 16, 1981, p. 18.

2578. Buchwald, Art, "When Joe Louis Blitzed the Nazis,"
       Los Angeles Sunday Times, April 19, 1981, Part 6, p.
       3.

2579. Editorial, "A Giant (Joe Louis) Has Fallen," Los
       Angeles (Calif.) Sentinel, April 16, 1981, p. 6.

2580. Hill, Herman, "Joe Louis Was a True Friend," Los
       Angeles (Calif.) Sentinel, April 16, 1981, p. 1B.

2581. "Louis Answered 'A Higher Calling'," Los Angeles
       (Calif.) Sentinel, April 16, 1981, p. 3.

2582. Norwood, Chico C., "The (Los Angeles) Community
       Remembers Joe (Louis)," Los Angeles (Calif.) Sentinel,
       April 16, 1981, p. 3B.

2583. _____, "We're Gonna Miss (Joe Louis) You,"
       Los Angeles (Calif.) Sentinel, April 16, 1981, pp. 1B,
       4B.

2584. "Pictorial Salute to Joe Louis Barrow: The 'Brown
       Bomber,'" Los Angeles (Calif.) Sentinel, April 16,
       1981, p. 5.

2585. Pye, Brad, Jr., "World Bids Joe Louis Goodbye," Los
       Angeles (Calif.) Sentinel, April 16, 1981, pp. 1, 13.

2586. Taylor, Sharon, "Death (of Joe Louis) Shocks Mother,"
       Los Angeles (Calif.) Sentinel, April 16, 1981, p. 1B.

2587. Young, A. S. "Doc", "Louis Was One of Three (Jesse
       Owens, Jackie Robinson) Supermen," Los Angeles (Calif.)
       Sentinel, April 16, 1981, pp. 1B, 4B.

2. DELAWARE

2588. "Louis Was Ring Genius: Schmeling," Wilmington (Del.)
       Evening Journal, April 13, 1981, p. 4.

3. GEORGIA

2589. Editorial, "The Greatest (Joe Louis)," Atlanta (Ga.)
       Constitution, April 14, 1981, p. 4.

2590. "Reagan Statement Praises (Joe) Louis," Atlanta
       Constitution, April 14, 1981, p. 4D.

4. ILLINOIS

2591. "A Salute to the Champ Joe Louis (May 13, 1914-
       April 12, 1981)," Ebony, June, 1981, pp. 132-138.

2592. Benson, Chris, "Joe Louis Laid to Rest with Heroes
       in Arlington," Jet, May 7, 1981, pp. 54-59.

2593. "Boxing Community Mourns the Loss of One of Its
       Greatest Heroes," Chicago Tribune, April 13, 1981,
       Section 4, p. 4.

2594. "Champ (Joe Louis) Used His Influence to Destroy 'Jim
       Crow'," Jet, April 30, 1981, p. 56.

2595. Condon, David, "A Fitting Requiem for the Heavyweight--
       Joe Louis," Chicago Tribune, April 13, 1981, Section 4,
       pp. 1, 7.

2596. "Commentary on Joe Louis," Chicago Defender, April 13,
       1981, p. 10.

2597. Editorial, "Requiem for a Heavyweight--Joe Louis,"
       Chicago Tribune, April 15, 1981, p. 17.

2598. Greene, Bob, "Standing Room Only for a Forgotten
       Hero (Joe Louis)," Chicago Tribune, April 15, 1981,
       p. 19.

2599. Higgins, Chester, "A Salute to the Champ: Joe Louis,
       May 13, 1914-April 12, 1981," Ebony, June, 1981, pp.
       132-136, 138. Reprint of same article that
       appeared in Ebony, October, 1970, pp. 158-163.

2600. Jarrett, Vernon, "What Joe Louis Gave to Us,"
       Chicago Tribune, April 15, 1981, p. 16.

2601. "Joe Louis Is Dead," Chicago Tribune, April 13, 1981,
       pp. 1, 21.

2602. "Joe Louis' Heart Gives, Ex-Champion Dies at 66,"
       Chicago Defender, April 13, 1981, p. 28.

2603. "Joe Louis' Most Famous Adversaries (Max Schmeling,
       Billy Conn and Jersey Joe Walcott)," Chicago Tribune,
       April 13, 1981, Section 4, p. 4.

2604. "Joe Louis Jr. Grieves Because He Could Not Help His
       Famous Father," Jet, May 7, 1981, pp. 16-18, 52-53.

2605. "Joe Louis Recuperating from Heart Surgery," Jet,
       January 22, 1981, p. 49.

2606. Johnson, Robert E., "Joe Louis 'A Credit to His Race--
       Human Race,' Is Dead at Age 66," Jet, April 30, 1981,
       pp. 16, 58, 59.

2607. "Louis-Schmeling Bout Will Never Die," Chicago Defender,
       April 13, 1981, p. 26.

2608. "Nation Mourns 'Brown Bomber,'" Chicago Defender,
       April 13, 1981, pp. 1, 2.

2609. "(President) Reagan Lauds Joe Louis," Jet, April 30,
       1981, p. 59.

2610. Sanders, Charles L., "The Job that Joe Louis Was Not
       Proud of," Jet, April 30, 1981, pp. 60-61.

2611. Terry, Don, "Sadness, Joy Greet Boxer's (Joe Louis)
       Death," Chicago Defender, April 13, 1981, p. 2.

2612. "The 'Brown Bomber,'" Chicago Defender, April 13,1981,
       p. 24.

2613. "The 'Final Bell' for Joe Louis," Chicago Defender,
       April 18, 1981, p. 64.

2614. Unger, Norman O., "'Brown Bomber' Dies Day After
       Viewing Heavyweight Fight," Jet, April 30, 1981, pp.
       12-15.

2615. "The Saying--Gems of Wisdom of Joe Louis--A Credit
       to His Race--The Human Race--Dead at Age 66," Jet,
       April 30, 1981, pp. 11-17, 52-61.

2616. "Wit and Humor: Joe Louis Dropped Gems of Wisdom,
       Too," Jet, April 30, 1981, pp. 52-54.

2617. "Joe Louis Lived Up to What Stars (Taurus, April 21-
       May 21) Foretold," Jet, April 30, 1981, p. 5-7.

5. MARYLAND

2618. Borders, Myran, "Nation Says 'Farewell' Joe Louis:
       Boxing Great Will Rest in Arlington Cemetery,"
       Baltimore Afro-American, April 21, 1981, p. 1, 23.

2619. "'Brown Bomber' Inspired Those in and out of Boxing,"
       Baltimore Sun, April 13, 1981, pp. 1C, 6C.

2620. Editorial, "Always a Champion: Joe Louis,"
       Baltimore Afro-American, April 21, 1981, p. 4.

2621. Editorial, "(Joe Louis) a Credit to His Race,'"
       Baltimore Sun, April 14, 1981, p. 18A.

2622. "Ex-Champion Joe Louis Dies of Heart Failure at 66,"
       Baltimore Sun, April 13, 1981, pp. 1, 12.

2623. Hatter, Lou, "(Red) Burman Remembers Louis as 'Nice
       Man', Despite Being the Victims of Kayo Punch,"
       Baltimore Sun, April 14, 1981, pp. 7C, 9C.

2624. Lacy, Sam, "It was THE Champion Who Died Sunday in
       Las Vegas," Baltimore Afro-American, April 18, 1981, p.
       20.

2625. Tosches, Rich, "Boxing Great Joe Louis Dead at 66,"
       Baltimore Afro-American, April 14, 1981, p.

6. MASSACHUSETTS

2626. Angelou, Maya, "A Day to Remember . . . (Joe Louis),"
       Boston Globe, April 14, 1981, p. 15.

2627. "Change of Pace-Boxer Joe Louis Recalled," Christian
       Science Monitor, April 23, 1981, p. 16.

2628. Editorial, "Joe Louis, 1914-1981," Boston Globe,
       April 14, 1981, p. 14.

2629. Elderldn, Phi, "Champion Joe Louis Wore Greatness
       Wtihout Frills," Christian Science Monitor, April 23,
       1981.

2630. Fitzgerald, Ray, "To a Kid in the 30's, He (Joe
       Louis) Was the Best," Boston Globe, April 13, 1981,
       pp. 1, 28.

2631. "Joe Louis Is Dead at 66," Boston Globe, April 13,
       1981, pp. 1, 20.

2632. Scripps, Cindy, "'Brown Bomber' Is Dead," Boston Globe,
       April 13, 1981, p. 20.

7. MICHIGAN

2633. "'A Great Soldier': Friends Praise Louis for Inspiring a Generation," Detroit Free Press, April 13, 1981, pp. 1F, 6F.

2634. "Another Side of the Bomber (Joe Louis)," Detroit Free Press, April 13, 1981, p. 12A.

2635. "Blow by Blow, He Rebuilt Boxing," Detroit Free Press, April 13, 1981, p. 13A.

2636. Bowles, Billy and Remer Tyson, "Joe Louis: How He Touched a Generation," Detroit Free Press, April 13, 1981, p. 3E.

2637. "'Brown Bomber' Joe Louis Dead at 66," Detroit Free Press, April 13, 1981, pp. 1A, 5A.

2638. "Dave Clark: 'The First Schmeling Fight: A Sad Night . . . It Was Like a Funeral,'" Detroit Free Press, April 13, 1981, p. 6E.

2639. "Ex-Athletes, Others Recall Boxing Great," Detroit Free Press, April 13, 1981, p. 15A.

2640. "Joe Louis 1914-1981: And Still Heavyweight Champion of the World," Detroit Free Press, April 13, 1981, p. 1E.

2641. "(Joe Louis) 54 Fights, 50 Victories, 43 KO's," Detroit Free Press, April 13, 1981, p. 2E.

2642. "June 22, 1938: World Is Shaken in Two Minutes and Four Seconds," Detroit Free Press, April 13, 1981, p. 5E.

2643. Puscas, George, "Joe Louis: He Was More Than a Champion," Detroit Free Press, April 13, 1981, p. 6E.

2644. "Stanley Evans: 'I Knew If He Hit You, You Were Down . . . I Had to Outsmart Him,'" Detroit Free Press, April 13, 1981, p. 6E.

2645. Sylvester, Curt, "They Remember a Young Fighter," Detroit Free Press, April 13, 1981, p. 6E.

2646. "The Champion of Champions: Joe Louis," Michigan Chronicle, April 18, 1981, Section D, p. 8.

2647. "The Schmeling Fights: June 19, 1936: It's Over in the 12th; Joe Hides His Face as He Leaves Stadium," Detroit Free Press, April 13, 1981, p. 5E.

2648. Vincent, Charlie, "Billy Conn: 'People Don't Realize How Great He Was,'" Detroit Free Press, April 13, 1981, p. 5E.

2649. Vincent, Charlie, "Louis Had Sad Final Days: Pain Ends for an 'Institution,'" Detroit Free Press, April 13, 1981, p. 5E.

2650. "Walter Smith: "Joe's Face Was All Skinned Up . . . He Took a Bad Whipping,'" Detroit Free Press, April 13, 1981, p. 6E.

2651. "We'll Just Call You Joe Louis," Detroit Free Press, April 13, 1981, p. 12A.

2652. White, Jonathan and Frank Saunders, "Bittersweet Week for City's Blacks: NAACP Dinner Triumph, Louis' Death," Michigan Chronicle, April 18, 1981, pp. 1, 4.

2653. Wright, Richard, "Black Pride Popped Loose on the Day (May 24, 1935) Joe Louis Won," Detroit Free Press, April 13, 1981, pp. 1B, 3B.

8. MISSOURI

2654. "'Boxing Genius' Led Black Athlete's Rise," St. Louis (Missouri) Post-Dispatch, April 13, 1981, p. 2D.

2655. Broeg, Bob, "Louis Leaves Legacy of Warmth and Deep Appreciation," St. Louis (Missouri) Post-Dispatch, April 13, 1981, p. 2D.

2656. Fall, Joe, "To Boy in '30, Brown Bomber Was an Idol," Sporting News, Vol. 191, May 2, 1981, p. 472.

2657. "Joe Louis, His Legend Lives On," Sporting News, Vol. 191, April 25, 1981, p. 54.

2658. "Louis' Death Recalls the Way We Were," Sporting News, Vol. 191, May 2, 1981, p. 16.

9. NEVADA

2659. Arnold, Patrick, "Crowds Always Lauded the Arrival of Louis," Valley Times (North Las Vegas, Nevada), April 14, 1981, pp. 23-24.

2660. "Joe Louis' Ring Record," Valley Times (North Las Vegas, Nevada), April 13, 1981, p. 24.

2661. "Joe Louis: Is Mourned," Las Vegas, April 13, 1981, p. 22.

2662. Feour, Royce and A. D. Hopkins, "Joe Mourned by World," Las Vegas Review-Journal, April 13, 1981, pp. 1A, 2A.

2663. Guthrie, Bill, "Joe Louis Dies at 66: Champ Was Las Vegas Resident," Las Vegas Sun, April 13, 1981, pp. 1, 19.

2664.   Koch, Ed, "Final Bell Rings for Joe Louis: Boxing
        Great Dies in Vegas," Valley Times (North Las Vegas,
        Nevada), April 13, 1981, pp. 1, 2.

2665.   _____, "Joe's Last Words," Valley Times (North
        Las Vegas, Nevada), April 13, 1981, p. 26. Joe
        reportedly told his wife Martha, on Sunday, June 12th,
        "I want to see the Diana Ross show tomorrow."

2666.   _____, "Joe's Last Words: The Legend Dies
        Hard," Valley Times (North Las Vegas, Nevada),
        April 13, 1981, pp. 1, 26.

2667.   _____, "Joe Louis Deserves Dignity & Respect,"
        Valley Times (North Las Vegas, Nevada), April 13,
        1981, p. 26. This is a reprint of an article that
        appeared in the May 20, 1980 issue of the same
        newspaper.

2668.   _____, "'Louis Was Finest Human that Lived':
        Close Friend Ash Resnick Remembers the Brown Bomber,"
        Valley Times (North Las Vegas, Nevada), April 13,
        1981, p. 28.

2669.   _____, "Rev. (Jesse) Jackson to Eulogize Louis
        Friday at Caesars," Valley Times (North Las Vegas,
        Nevada), April 14, 1981, pp. 23-24.

2670.   _____, "Wrestling Injury Linked to Louis' Heart
        Problems: Brown Bomber Recalled Fight with 360-Pound
        Matman," Valley Times (North Las Vegas, Nevada),
        April 14, 1981, p. 24.

2671.   "Highlights of Brown Bomber's Career," Valley Times
        (North Las Vegas, Nevada), April 13, 1981, p. 25.

2672.   "Louis Drew Great Respect from His Foes: Max
        Schmeling and Buddy Baer and Billy Conn," Las
        Vegas Review-Journal, April 13, 1981, p. 1C.

2673.   "Louis 'Greatest Champion Who Ever Lived,'" Nevada
        State Journal, April 13, 1981, p. 25.

2674.   "Louis Inspired Black Athletes Everywhere," Valley
        Times (North Las Vegas, Nevada), April 13, 1981,
        pp. 27-28.

2675.   "Louis, Schmeling at War," Valley Times (North Las
        Vegas, Nevada), April 13, 1981, p. 24.

2676.   "Louis Services Set for Friday," Las Vegas Review-
        Journal, April 14, 1981, p. 2B.

2677.   "Louis Was an Inspiration to the Young," Las Vegas
        Review-Journal, April 14, 1981, p. 1C.

2678. "Louis Watches His Last Bout," Valley Times (North Las Vegas, Nevada), April 13, 1981, p. 27. This was the Larry Holmes-Trever Berbick Fight that was fought about 13 hours before Joe Louis died.

2679. "Quotes, Anecdotes About Joe Louis," Las Vegas Sun, April 13, 1981, p. 22.

2680. Rose, Murray, "Memories of Ring Legend Louis by Ex-Boxing Writer (Murray Rose)," Valley Times (North Las Vegas, Nevada)," April 14, 1981, p. 21.

2681. Scripps, Cindy, "Boxing Great Joe Louis Dies in Las Vegas at 66," Nevada State Journal, April 13, 1981, pp. 1, 7.

2682. Staresinic, George, "To Joe Louis: Friends Pay Last Respects," Las Vegas Sun, April 17, 1981, pp. 25, 27.

10. NEW YORK

2683. Anderson, Dave, "A Corporal (Joe Louis) for Arlington (National Cemetery)," New York Times, April 20, 1981.

2684. Berkow, Ira, "Louis Demonstrated His Style in and out of the Ring," New York Times, April 14, 1981, p. 24.

2685. Bonventre, Peter, "Joe Louis, 1914-1981," Newsweek, Vol. 97, April 27, 1981, pp. 101-102.

2686. "Boxer Joe Louis Dead at 66," Staten Island Advance, April 13, 1981, pp. A1, A2.

2687. "Brown Bomber Gets the Funeral of a Champion," New York Times, April 22, 1981, p. 1.

2688. Buchwald, Art, "Joe Louis Saved America's Honor," Long Island (N.Y.) Newsday, April 18, 1981.

2689. _____, "The Day Joe Louis Beat the Nazi Hope (Max Schmeling)," New York Post, April 18, 1981.

2690. Chadwick, Bruce, "Seek a Place (in New York City) to Name in Memory of Joe Louis," New York Daily News, April 29, 1982.

2691. Clines, Francis X., "Hundreds Present for Joe Louis Rites at Arlington," New York Times, April 22, 1981, pp. A1, B8.

2692. Coombs, Orde, "For Joe Louis, Black Glory But Not the White Gold," New York Daily News, April 17,1981.

2693. "Distorting Joe Louis' Importance," New York Amsterdam News, April 25, 1981, p. 17.

2694. Editorial, "A Modern Hero," New York Times, April 14, 1981, p. 26.

2695. Editorial, "Farewell to Joe Louis: A Great American," New York Amsterdam News, May 2, 1981, p. 61.

2696. Editorial, "Joe Louis," New York Amsterdam News, April 18, 1981, p. 18.

2697. Gardner, Marilyn and Hy Gardner, "Joe Louis' One-Liners as Sharp as His Jab," Staten Island (N.Y.) Advance, May 29, 1981.

2698. Greene, Bob, "Remembering Another Joe Louis," New York Daily News, April 20, 1981.

2699. Greer, Thom, "U.S. Loses Its Greatest Hero," New York News, April 13, 1981, p. 50.

2700. Fearon, Peter, "Louis Will Be Buried in Arlington," New York Post, April 16, 1981, p. 1.

2701. "Heavyweight Champion Joe Louis Dies at 66," New York World, April 13, 1981, p. 1.

2702. "I Remember Joe," New York Amsterdam News, April 18, 1981, p. 72.

2703. Gallo, Bill, "Louis-Ali? Joe Wins It," New York Daily News, April 19, 1981.

2704. "In Memory of Joe Louis," New York Post, April 18, 1981.

2705. Izenberg, Jerry, "Heart Attack Claims Life of Brown Bomber," New York Post, April 13, 1981, pp. 52-53.

2706. _____, "The Day Joe Louis Died," New York Post, April 13, 1981, pp. 1, 52.

2707. _____, "Tragedy KO's an Appointment with the Champ," Staten Island Advance, April 13, 1981.

2708. _____, "Too Few Americans Knew the Real Brown Bomber," New York Post, April 17, 1981.

2708a. _____, "Joe Louis: So Much that So Few Knew About Him," Staten Island (N.Y.) Advance, April 17, 1981.

2709. "Joe Louis: American Folk Hero," New York Amsterdam News, April 18, 1981, p. 72.

2710. "Joe Louis," Current Biography, Vol. 42, No. 6, June, 1981, p. 42.

2711. "Joe Louis," Current Biography, Vol. 42, June, 1981, p. 42.

2712. "Joe Louis," New Yorker, April 27, 1981, pp. 36-38.

2713. "Joe Louis, 1914-1981," Newsweek, Vol. 97, April 27, 1981, p. 101.

2714. "Joe Louis: A Hit in Harlem," New York Amsterdam News, April 18, 1981, p. 6.

2715. "Joe Louis: America's Boxing Legend: 'Brown Bomber' A Great Champ," New York World, April 13, 1981.

2716. "Joe Louis Buried as Hero in Arlington (National Cemetery)," The (New York) News World, April 22, 1981, p. 1.

2717. "Joe Louis Dead at 66," New York Daily News, April 13, 1981, pp. 23, 28.

2718. "Joe Louis: The Immortal Heavyweight," New York Amsterdam News, April 18, 1981, p. 7.

2719. "Joe Louis, Legend and Man," News World, April 15, 1981, p. 1.

2720. "Joe Was Their Man!" New York Amsterdam News, April 18, 1981, p. 72.

2721. Katz, Michael, "Walcott, Hearns Call (Joe) Louis Inspiration," New York Times, April 13, 1981, Sports, p. C12.

2722. "Last Bell Rung for Joe Louis," News World, April 18, 1981, p. 1.

2723. "Louis an 'Inspiration to Millions': Pres. Reagan," News World, April 14, 1981, p. 1.

2724. Markson, Harry, "Joe Louis: A Man of Innate Dignity, Integrity and Grace," New York Times, April 19, 1981.

2725. Marley, Mike, "Legend of the Boxing Hero was America's Symbol of Class and Dignity," New York Post, April 13, 1981.

2726. _____, "The Legend of the Brown Bomber," New York Post, April 13, 1981.

2727. McGowen, Deane, "Joe Louis 66, Heavyweight King Who Reigned 12 Years, Is Dead," New York Times, April 13, 1981, pp. 1, D11.

2728. "Memories of Joe," New York Amsterdam News, April 18, 1981, p. 5.

2729.   Moore, Mike, "Rose Morgan: Success in Grand Style," Essence, Vol. 12, No. 2, June 1981, pp. 34, 38, 40, 44. Rose Morgan discusses her marriage to Joe Louis. They were married from 1955 to 1957.

2730.   "Requiem for a Legendary Champion," New York Amsterdam News, April 18, 1981, p. 24.

2731.   Rosenbohn, Sam, "Joe Louis Loses Final Fight, Dies of Heart Attack," New York Post, April 13, 1981, p. 1.

2732.   "Scholarship Fund Set (at the Mini Institute of City College) to Honor Joe Louis," The (New York) News World, May 8, 1981.

2733.   Smith, Red, "Joe Louis Through the Years," New York Times, April 13, 1981, Sports, pp. C1, C12.

2734.   Sobran, Joseph, "Joe Louis--Portrait of a Tax Martyr," New York Post, April 23, 1981.

2735.   Sowell, Thomas, "A Real Champion--He Was a Credit to the Human Race," Long Island (N.Y.) Newsday, April 15, 1981.

2736.   "The Brown Bomber (Joe Louis)," Sports Illustrated, Vol. 54, No. 17, April 20, 1981, p. 29.

2737.   "The New York Post Remembers Joe Louis," New York Post, April 18, 1981, p. 8.

2738.   "Thousands Mourn the Passing of a Champ," New York Post, April 21, 1981, p. 1.

2739.   "True Story of Joe Louis' Last 'Fight,'" The (New York) News World, May 6, 1981.

2740.   Verigan, Bill, "Joe Louis: 1914-1981," New York Daily News, April 13, 1981, pp. 1, 64.

2741.   _____, "Joe Louis: 1914-1981," New York Daily News, April 14, 1981, pp. 24, 28.

2742.   Waldman, Myron S., "A Hero's Farewell for Joe Louis," Long Island (N.Y.) Newsday, April 22, 1981, pp. 1, 29.

2743.   Waters, Bob, "Close to a King," Long Island (N.Y.) News Day, April 13, 1981, p. 1.

2744.   _____, "A Reminiscence of Joe Louis," Long Island Newsday, April 13, 1981.

2744a.   "Joe Louis 12-Year Champ Dies," Long Island Newsday, April 13, 1981, p. 1.

2745. Young, Dick, "Joe Louis' Deeds Live on," New York Daily News, April 13, 1981, pp. 50-51.

2746. _____, "The Great Joe Louis Has Passed on, But He Will Live in Minds of Fight Fans," New York Daily News, April 13, 1981, pp. 22, 23.

11.   NORTH CAROLINA

2747. "Boxers Pay Tribute to Joe Louis," Lexington (N.C.) Dispatch, April 13, 1981, p. 12.

2748. "Boxing Great Louis Dies at 66," Winston-Salem (N.C.) Journal, April 13, 1981, pp. 1, 2.

2749. "Boxing's Joe Louis Dies of Heart Attack," Raleigh (N.C.) News and Observer, April 13, 1981, p. 1, 6.

2750. "'Brown Bomber' Called Greatest," Durham (N.C.) Morning Herald, April 13, 1981, p. 2A.

2751. Claiborne, Jack, "(Joe) Louis Helped Us Conquer Hate," Charlotte (N.C.) Observer, April 14, 1981, p. 16.

2752. "Death Claims Boxing Great Joe Louis, 66," Asheville (N.C.) Citizen, April 13, 1981, pp. 11, 13.

2753. Editorial, "America Loses a Great Man: Joe Louis-- Dignity and Candor," Charlotte (N.C.) Post, April 16, 1981, p. 2.

2754. Editorial, "The First Black Superstar (Joe Louis)," The (Raleigh) Carolinian, April 16, 1981, pp. 4, 8.

2755. "Ex-Boxing Champion Joe Louis Dies at 66," Charlotte (N.C.) Observer, April 13, 1981, pp. 1, 7A.

2756. "Final Rites Set Friday for Joe Louis," The (Raleigh) Carolinian, April 16, 1981, pp. 1, 2.

2757. "Fight World Mourns Louis," Fayetteville (N.C.) Observer, April 13, 1981, p. 2B.

2758. "Followers Mourn 'Mr.' Boxing," Winston-Salem (N.C.) Journal, April 13, 1981, p. 33.

2759. "Friends, Foes Remember Louis as Inspiration," High Point (N.C.) Enterprise, April 13, 1981, p. 3B.

2760. "Joe Louis, Champion, Dies at 66," Fayetteville (N.C.) Observer, April 13, 1981, pp. 1, 2.

2761. "Joe Louis Knocked Out Hitler's Super-Race Theory: Was Hero to All Americans," Wilmington (N.C.) Journal, April 16, 1981, pp. 1, 2.

2762. "Last Rites Held for Joe Louis," The (Durham) Carolina Times, April 18, 1981, pp. 1, 3.

2763. "Louis Fought to Keep Dignity in Fight Game," Charlotte (N.C.) Observer, April 13, 1981, pp. 5B, 10B.

2764. "Louis Leaves Fan Legacy of Warmth," Charlotte (N.C.) Observer, April 14, 1981, pp. 11, 13.

2765. "Pictorial Highlights in Life of Joe Louis," The (Raleigh) Carolinian, April 16, 1981, p. 13.

2766. Smith, Red, "Louis Was Not a Complainer; Just a Champ," Winston-Salem (N.C.) Journal, April 13, 1981, Sports, pp. 1, 33.

2767. "The Brown Bomber Hears His Last Bell," Durham (N.C.) Morning Herald, April 13, 1981, pp. 1, 2.

12.   PENNSYLVANIA

2768. Harrison, Claude, "Louis Reigned Record 12 Years as Heavyweight King," Philadelphia Tribune, April 14, 1981, p. 11.

2769. Jefferies, Eddie, "Brown Bomber Fell at 66," Pittsburgh Courier, April 25, 1981, pp. 1, 9.

2770. "Joe Gramby Calls Louis 'Greatest Champion' Ever," Philadelphia Tribune, April 14, 1981, p. 11.

2771. "Joe Louis Married 4 Times," Philadelphia Tribune, April 14, 1981, p. 11.

2772. "Joe Louis Rites Set," Philadelphia Tribune, April 14, 1981, pp. 1, 20.

2773. "NAACP Mourns Louis," Pittsburgh Courier, April 25, 1981, p. 9.

13.   SOUTH CAROLINA

2774. "American Hero Joe Louis Dies," Columbia (S.C.) Record, April 13, 1981, pp. 1D, 9D.

14.   VIRGINIA

2775. "Boxing Lost a 'Friend'," Roanoke (Va.) Times & World-News, (Sports), April 13, 1981, p. 1.

2776. Grimsley, Will, "To Those Who Recall the 40's, Louis Is Still 'The Champ'," Richmond (Va.) News Leader, April 14, 1981, p. 17.

2777. "Heart Attack Fells 'Brown Bomber', Joe Louis, 66," Roanoke (Va.) Times and World-News, April 13, 1981, pp. 1, 8.

2778. Wyche, Lindsay, "Last Bell Rings for Brown Bomber," Norfolk Journal and Guide, April 15, 1981, pp. 1, 3.

15. WASHINGTON, D.C.

2779. Addie, Bob, "Joe Louis, Boxing's 'Brown Bomber,' Dies at 66," Washington Post, April 13, 1981, p. B4.

2780. Alexander, Clifford L., "Fighters Together: Joe Louis," Washington Post, April 22, 1981.

2781. Ashe, Arthur, "The Passing of the Last Idol," Washington Post, April 14, 1981, pp. 1D, 3D.

2782. Berkow, Ira, "Louis Demonstrated His Style in and out of the Ring," Washington Post, April 14, 1821.

2783. Buchwald, Art, "Thanks, Joe, For Saving Our National Pride," Washington Post, April 19, 1981.

2784. Callahan, Tom, "They All Knew Joe Louis," Washington Star, April 13, 1981, p. B4.

2785. Cohen, Ricahrd, "When We Were Winners with the Brown Bomber," Washington Post, April 14, 1981, pp. C-1, C-3.

2786. Editorial, "Joe Louis," Washington Post, April 14, 1981, p. 20.

2787. Heller, Dick, "Joe Louis, Ex-Champ, Dies of Heart Attack," Washington Star, April 13, 1981, p. B-4.

2788. "Joe Louis Dead at 66 of Heart Attack," Washington Post, April 13, 1981, pp. A-1, A-18.

2789. "Joe Louis Dies in Las Vegas: Boxing's Greatest Legend," Washington Post, April 13, 1981, pp. 1, 18.

2790. Kindred, Dave, "A Loving Son Talks About His Father: Joe Louis Jr. Wishes He Could Have Helped Years Earlier," Washington Post, April 17, 1981, pp. E1, E5.

2791. _____, "A Sad Funeral for 'Poor Joe' Ends as Celebration of a Hero," Washington Post, April 18, 1981, pp. C1, C5.

2792. Kornheiser, Tony, "Bereft of Dollars, Dignity, He Was Still Joe Louis: Heavyweight Champion an Original Hero," Washington Post, April 13, 1981, pp. D-1, D-3.

2793. Povich, Shirley, "Louis: Always a Champion," Washington Post, April 14, 1981, pp. 1D, 3D.

2794. "President (Ronald Reagan) Pays Tribute to Louis,"
      Washington Post, April 14, 1981, p. D-4.

2795. Siegel, Morris, "Boxing's Best Went Out Way Ahead,"
      Washington Star, April 13, 1981, p. D-6.

B.   COUNTRIES

A SELECTED LIST

1.   CANADA

2796. Editorial, "Joe Louis," The Globe and Mail (Toronto,
      Canada), April 14, 1981, p. 6.

2797. "Deaths" Joe Louis," MacLean's, Vol. 94, No. 52,
      December 28, 1981, pp. 47-48.

2798. "Joe Louis: Heavyweight Champ Ring Legend," The Globe
      and Mail (Toronto, Canada), April 13, 1981, p. 15.

2.   ENGLAND

2799. Rodda, John, "Death of Joe Louis, the Greatest
      Heavyweight," The Manchester (England) Guardian,
      April 19, 1981, p. 7.

Appendices

A
Book Reviews

1.   1947

Bostwick, R. O. My Life Story, by Joe Louis, Library
    Journal, Vol. 72, March 1, 1947, p. 393.

Gobbins, Dennis. My Life Story by Joe Louis, June 3, 1947.

Lardner, John. My Life Story, by Joe Louis, New York Times,
    April 13, 1947, p. 33.

My Life Story, by Joe Louis, Kirkus, Vol. 15, January 15,
    1947, p. 56.

My Life Story, by Joe Louis, New Yorker, Vol. 23, April 26,
    1947, p. 99.

My Life Story, by Joe Louis, Booklist, Vol. 43, May 1, 1947,
    p. 1.

My Life Story, by Joe Louis, New York Herald Tribune Weekly
    Book Review, May 11, 1947, p. 36.

My Life Story, by Joe Louis, Wilson Library Bulletin, Vol. 43,
    May, 1947, p. 81.

2.   1978

Baker, J. N. Joe Louis: My Life, by Joe Louis, Newsweek,
    Vol. 92, July 17, 1978, p. 83.

Gluck, Herb. Book Review. Joe Louis: My Life, by Joe Louis,
    New York Times Book Reviews, Vol. 83, July 23, 1978, p. 13.

Joe Louis: My Life, by Joe Louis, Essence, Vol. 9, February,
    1979, p. 27.

Joe Louis: My Life, by Joe Louis, School Library Journal,
    Vol. 25, February, 1979, p. 68.

Joe Louis: My Story, by Joe Louis, Kirkus Reviews, Vol. 46,
    April 15, 1978, p. 477.

Joe Louis: My Story, by Joe Louis, Publishers Weekly, Vol.
    213, May 8, 1978, p. 66.

Joe Louis: My Story, by Joe Louis, Booklist, Vol. 74, June 1,
    1978, p. 1094.

Joe Louis: My Story, by Joe Louis, Library Journal, Vol. 103,
    June 1, 1978, p. 1190.

Joe Louis: My Story, by Joe Louis, Newsweek, Vol. 92, July 17,
    1978, p. 83.

Joe Louis: My Life, by Joe Louis, Sporting News, Vol. 186,
    August 12, 1978, p. 48.

Joe Louis, My Life, by Joe Louis, West Coast Review of Books,
    Vol. 4, September, 1978, p. 63.

Joe Louis: My Story, by Joe Louis, Best Sellers, Vol. 38,
    November 1978, p. 246.

Johnson, Glenderlyn. Joe Louis: My Life, by Joe Louis,
    Black American, September 26, 1979.

Lehmann-Haput, C. Joe Louis: My Story, by Joe Louis, New
    York Times, June 20, 1978, p. C7.

Nunn, M. E. Joe Louis: My Life, by Joe Louis, Library
    Journal, Vol. 103, June 1, 1978, p. 1190.

Pollack, Joe. Joe Louis: My Life, by Joe Louis, Sporting
    News, Vol. 186, No. 6, August 12, 1978, p. 48.

B. BOOKS BY OTHERS

A SELECTED LIST

Joe Louis, Man and Super Fighter, by Edward Van Every, Brown
    American, Vol. 1, June, 1936, p. 1.

2. 1945

Joe Louis: American, by Margery Miller, Saturday Review of
    Literature, Vol. 28, December 8, 1945, p. 28.

Joe Louis: American, by Margery Miller, Boston Chronicle,
    December 1, 1945.

3.   1980

Joe Louis: The Brown Bomber, by Bill Libby, Publishers
    Weekly, Vol. 218, No. 25, December 19, 1980, p. 51.

B
Nicknames, Foreign Boxing Exhibitions, and Winners of *Ring Magazine*'s Merit Award

A. NICKNAMES GIVEN TO JOE LOUIS
   BY THE PRESS AND OTHERS

"African Avenger"

"Bible Belter"

"Black Atlas"

"Black Bomber"

"Black Blaster"

"Black Boomber"

"Black Lightning"

"Black Master"

"Black Menace"

"Chocolate Soldier"

"Choochoo"

"Colored Galahad"

"Dark Angel"

"Dark Destroyer"

"David From Detroit"

"Detroit Battler"

"Detroit Bomber"

"Detroit Destroyer"

"Detroit Dynamiter"

"Dusky Puncher"

"Ethiopian Exploder"

"Great Detroiter"

"The Greatest"

"Jolting Joe Louis"

"King Joe"

"Kingfish"

"K.K.K." (Kruel Kolored Klouter)

"Lethal Lambaster"

"Master in Black"

"Midnight"

"Ring Robot"

"Royal Highness of Sock"

"Sepia Sphinx"

"Somnolent Senegambian"

"Surprised Sepian"

"Tan Bomber"

"Tan Thunderbolt"

"Tan Tornado"

B. BOXING EXHIBITIONS IN FOREIGN COUNTRIES

A SELECTED LIST

Bogata, Columbia

Brussels, Belgium

Havana, Cuba

Kingston, Jamaica

Lima, Peru

London, England

Manila, Phillipines

Medellin, Columbia

Mexicali, Mexico

Mexico City, Mexico

Nassau (Bahamas)

Oriente, Cuba

Panama City, Panama

Port-of-Spain, Trinidad

Quito, Ecuador

Rio de Janeiro, Brazil

San Salvador, (Bahama)

Santiago, Chile

Vancouver, British Columbia

Victoria, British Columbia

C. WINNER OF RING MAGAZINE'S MERIT AWARD

(1928-1951)

1928 - Gene Tunney

1929 - Tommy Longhran

1930 - Max Schmeling

1931 - Tommy Longhran

1932 - Jack Sharkey

1933 - No Award

1934 - Barney Ross and Tony Canzoneri

1935 - Barney Ross

1936 - JOE LOUIS

1937 - Henry Armstrong

1938 - JOE LOUIS

1939 - JOE LOUIS

1940 - Billy Conn

1941 - JOE LOUIS

1942 - Ray Robinson

1943 - Fred Apostoli

1944 - Beau Jack

1945 - Willie Pep

1946 - Tony Zale

1947 - Gus Lesnevich

1948 - Ike Williams

1949 - Ezzard Charles

1950 - Ezzard Charles

1951 - Ray Robinson

C
Joe Louis's Ring Record

A. MAJOR FIGHTS

YEAR BY YEAR

1934

July 4	Jack Kracken, Chicago	KO-1
July 11	Willie Davis, Chicago	KO-3
July 29	Larry Udell, Chicago	KO-2
Aug. 13	Jack Kranz, Chicago	W-8
Aug. 27	Buck Everett, Chicago	KO-2
Sept. 11	Alex Borchuk, Detroit	KO-4
Sept. 25	Adolph Walter, Chicago	W-10
Oct. 24	Art Sykes, Chicago	KO-8
Oct. 30	Jack O'Dowd, Detroit	KO-2
Nov. 14	Stanley Poreda, Chicago	KO-1
Nov. 30	Charley Massera, Chicago	KO-3
Dec. 14	Lee Ramage, Chicago	KO-8

1935

Jan. 4	Patsy Perroni, Detroit	W-10
Jan. 11	Hans Birkje, Pittsburgh	KO-10
Feb. 21	Lee Ramage, Los Angeles	KO-2
Mar. 8	Donald Barry, S. Francisco	KO-3
Mar. 28	Natie Brown, Detroit	W-10
Apr. 12	Roy Lazer, Chicago	KO-3
Apr. 22	Biff Benton, Dayton	KO-2
Apr. 27	Roscoe Toles, Flint, Mich.	KO-6
Mar. 3	Willie David, Peoria, Ill.	KO-2
May 7	Gene Stanton, Kalamazoo	KO-3
June 25	Primo Carnera, New York	KO-6
Aug. 7	King Levinsky, Chicago	KO-1
Sept. 24	Max Baer, New York	KO-4
Dec. 13	Paolino Uzcudn, New York	KO-4

1936

Jan. 17	Charley Retzlaff, Chicago	KO-1
June 19	Max Schmeling, N.Y.	L-KO-12
Aug. 18	Jack Sharkey, New York	KO-3
Sept. 22	Al Ettore, Philadelphia	KO-5
Oct. 9	Jorge Brescia, New York	KO-3
Dec. 14	Eddie Simms, Cleveland	KO-1

1937

Jan. 11	Steve Ketchel, Buffalo	KO-2
Jan. 29	Bob Pastor, New York	W-10
Feb. 17	Natie Brown, Kansas City	KO-4
June 22	James Braddock, Chicago	KO-8
	Won World Heavyweight Championship	
Aug. 30	Tommy Farr, New York	W-15

1938

Feb. 23	Nathan Mann, New York	KO-3
Apr. 1	Harry Thomas, Chicago	KO-5
June 22	Max Schmeling, New York	KO-1

1939

Jan. 25	John Henry Lews, N.Y.	KO-1
Apr. 17	Jack Roper, Los Angeles	KO-1
June 28	Tony Galento, New York	KO-4
Sept. 20	Bob Pastor, Detroit	KO-11

1940

Feb. 9	Arturo Godoy, New York	W-15
Mar. 29	Johnny Paycheck, New York	KO-2
June 20	Arturo Gody, New York	KO-8
Dec. 16	Al McCoy, Boston	KO-6

1941

Jan. 31	Red Burman, New York	KO-5
Feb. 17	Gus Dorazio, Philadelphia	KO-2
Mar. 21	Abe Simon, Detroit	KO-13
Apr. 8	Tony Musto, St. Louis	KO-9
May 23	Buddy Baer, Wash.	W-DQ-8
June 18	Billy Conn, New York	KO-13
Sept. 29	Lou Nova, New York	KO-6

1942

Jan. 9	Buddy Baer, New York	KO-1
Mar. 27	Abe Simon, New York	KO-6
June 5	Joined U.S. Army	

1946

| June 19 | Billy Conn, New York | KO-8 |
| Sept. 18 | Tami Mauriello, New York | KO-1 |

1947

| Dec. 5 | Jersey Joe Walcott, N.Y. | W-15 |

1948

| June 25 | Jersey Joe Walcott, N.Y. | KO-11 |

1949

| Mar. 1 | Announced retirement | |

1950

Sept. 27	Ezzard Charles, N.Y.	L-15
	For Heavyweight Championship	
Nov. 29	Cesar Brion, Chicago	W-10

1951

Jan. 3	Freddie Beshore, Detroit	KO-4
Feb. 7	Omelio Agramonte, Miami	W-10
Feb. 23	Andy Walker, S. Francisco	KO-10
May 2	Omelio Agramonte, Detroit	W-10
June 15	Lee Savold, New York	KO-6
Aug. 1	Cesar Brion, San Francisco	W-10
Aug. 15	Jimmy Bivins, Baltimore	W-10
Oct. 26	Rocky Marciano, N.Y.	L-KO-8

B.   EXHIBITION FIGHTS

1936

DATE	NAME	DECISION	CITY
Oct. 14	W. Davis	Exh. Won on KO in 3d Rd.	N.Y.
Oct. 14	K.O. Brown	Exh. Won on KO in 3d Rd.	S. Bend
Nov. 20	P. Williams	Exh. Won on KO in 2d Rd.	S. Bend
Nov. 20	T. Jones	Exh. Won on KO in 3d Rd.	N. Orleans

1941

DATE	NAME	DECISION	CITY
July 11	J. Robinson		Minneapolis
Nov. 25	G. Giambastiani		L.A.

1942

DATE	NAME	DECISION	CITY
June 5	G. Nicholson	Exh. 3d Rd.	Ft. Hamil-ton, N.Y.

Joe Louis Served in the United States Army 1942-1945

1944

DATE	NAME	DECISION	CITY
Nov. 3	J. Demson	Exh. Won on KO in 2d Rd.	Detroit
Nov. 6	C. Crump	Exh. Won on Dec. 3d Rd.	Baltimore
Nov. 9	D. Amos	Exh. Won on Dec. 3d Rd.	Hartford
Nov. 13	J. Bell	Exh. Won on Dec. 3d Rd.	Wash.,D.C.
Nov. 14	J. Davis	Exh. Won on KO in 1st Rd.	Buffalo
Nov. 15.	D. Amos	Exh. Won on Dec. 3d Rd.	Eliz., N.J.
Nov. 17	D. Amos	Exh. Won on Dec. 3d Rd.	Camden, N.J.
Nov. 24	D. Merritt	Exh. Won on Dec. 3d Rd.	Chicago

1945

DATE	NAME	DECISION	CITY
Nov. 15	S.L. Anderson	Two-Round Exh.	San. F.
Nov. 15	B.B. Brown	Two-Round Exh.	San. F.
Nov. 29	B.B. Brown	Two-Round Exh.	Sacramento

Nov. 29	B. Lee	Two-Round Exh.	Sacramento
Dec. 10	B. Frazier	Three-Round Exh.	Victoria
Dec. 11	B.B. Brown	Two-Round Exh.	Portland
Dec. 11	D. Johnson	Two-Round Exh.	Portland
Dec. 12	B.B. Brown	Three-Round Exh.	Eugene, Ore.
Dec. 13	B.B. Brown	Three-Round Exh.	Vancouver, B.C.

1946

Nov. 11	C. Everett	Four-Round Exh.	Honolulu
Nov. 11	W. Powell	Two-Round Exh.	Honolulu
Nov. 25	P. Daniels	Four-Round Exh.	Mexicali, Mex.

1947

Feb. 7	A. Godoy	Ten-Round Exh.	Mexico City
Feb. 10	A. Ramsey	Three-Round Exh.	San Salvador
Feb. 10	W. Haefer	Three-Round Exh.	San Salvador
Feb. 12	A. Ramsey	Three-Round Exh.	Panama City
Feb. 12	W. Haefer	Three-Round Exh.	Panama City
Feb. 19	A. Godoy	Six-Round Exh.	Santiago, Chile
Feb. 27	A. Ramsey	Two-Round Exh.	Medellin, Colum.
Feb. 27	W. Haefer	Two-Round Exh.	Medellin, Colum.
Mar. 10	W. Haefer	Two-Round Exh.	Havana
Mar. 10	A. Ramsey	Two-Round Exh.	Havana
June 6	R. Payne	Two-Round Exh.	San Diego
June 6	D. Underwood	Two-Round Exh.	San Diego
June 13	T.J. Fox	Four-Round Exh.	Spokane, Wash.
June 23	H. Wills	Four-Round Exh.	L.A.

1948

Jan. 29	B. Foxworth	Four-Round Exh.	Chicago
Sept. 30	P. Comiskey	Six-Round Exh.	Washington, D.C.
Oct. 28	B. Garner	Three-Round Exh.	Atlanta
Oct. 28	M. Wynn	Three-Round Exh.	Atlanta
Oct. 29	B. Garner	Four-Round Exh.	Norfolk
Oct. 31	B. Garner	Four-Round Exh.	New Orleans
Nov. 1	B. Garner	Three-Round Exh.	New Orleans
Nov. 3	B. Garner	Four-Round Exh.	Nashville
Nov. 8	J. Skkor	Four-Round Exh.	Boston
Nov. 9	B. Reynolds	Four-Round Exh.	New Haven
Nov. 17	J. Bivins	Six-Round Exh.	Cleveland
Nov. 19	V. Mitchell	Six-Round Exh.	Detroit
Nov. 23	K. Riviera	Six-Round Exh.	St. Louis
Nov. 24	R. Augustus	Exh. Won KO 2d Rd.	Oklahoma City
Nov. 25	C. Kennedy	Four-Round Exh.	Kansas City
Nov. 29	B. Smith	Four-Round Exh.	Cincinnati
Dec. 10	B. Conn	Six-Round Exh.	Chicago
Dec. 14	A. Godoy	Six-Round Exh.	Philadelphia
Dec. 16	P. Comiskey	Six-Round Exh.	Paterson, N.J.
Dec. 20	W. James	Four-Round Exh.	Lewiston, Maine

1949

Jan. 10	S. Ingram	Four-Round Exh.	Omaha
Jan. 11	O. Ott	Four-Round Exh.	Topeka, Kansas
Jan. 12	H. Hood	Four-Round Exh.	Wichita
Jan. 17	A. Swiden	Four-Round Exh.	Toledo
Jan. 18	D. Hagen	Four-Round Exh.	Moline, Ill.
Jan. 19	O. Ott	Four-Round Exh.	Rochester, Minn.
Jan. 25	E. Ray	Six-Round Exh.	Miami
Jan. 27	G. Fitch	Four-Round Exh.	Palm Beach
Jan. 28	N. Valdez	Four-Round Exh.	Tampa
Jan. 31	D.L. Oliver	Exh.Won KO 4th Rd.	Orlando
Feb. 1	E. Ray	Four-Round Exh.	Jacksonville
Feb. 3	B. Graves	Exh.Won KO 3d Rd.	Daytona Beach
Feb. 4	G. Fitch	Four-Round Exh.	Savannah
Feb. 23	E. Edward	Three-Round Exh.	Kingston, Jam.
March 1	Louis announces his retirement as heavyweight champ.		
March 1	E. Crawley	Four-Round Exh.	Nassau
March 4	O. Agramonte	Four-Round Exh.	Havana
March 5	O. Agramonte	Four-Round Exh.	Oriente, Cuba
March 16	E. Ray	Exh. Won KO 4th Rd.	Houston
March 18	T. Boddie	Four-Round Exh.	Dallas
March 22	H. Hood	Six-Round Exh.	St. Paul
March 22	A. Cestac	Four-Round Exh.	Washington, D.C.
Oct. 10	C. Sheppard	Four-Round Exh.	Baltimore
Oct. 24	B. Weinberg	Four-Round Exh.	Providence
Oct. 25	J. Domonic	Four-Round Exh.	Hartford
Oct. 31	B. Gilliam	Four-Round Exh.	Atlantic City
Nov. 14	J. Shkor	Ten-Round Exh.	Boston
Nov. 22	J. Chesul	Ten-Round Exh.	Newark
Nov. 28	J. Flynn	Ten-Round Exh.	Kansas City
Dec. 7	P. Valentino	Exh. Won KO 8th Rd.	Chicago
Dec. 14	R. Toles	Five-Round Exh.	Detroit
Dec. 14	J. Flynn	Five-Round Exh.	Detroit
Dec. 19	A. Hoosman	Exh. Won KO 5th Rd.	Oakland
Dec. 21	J. Lambert	Five-Round Exh.	Salt Lake City
Dec. 21	R. Layne	Five-Round Exh.	Salt Lake City

1950

Jan. 6	W. Bean	Six-Round Exh.	Hollywood
Jan. 10	J. Flood	Six-Round Exh.	Seattle
Jan. 12	C. Henry	Four-Round Exh.	Wilmington
Jan. 13	A. Spaulding	Four-Round Exh.	San Diego
Jan. 20	A. Walker	Four-Round Exh.	Stockton
Jan. 24	R. Layne	Four-Round Exh.	Salt Lake City
Feb. 1	G. Jones	Eight-Round Exh.	Miami
Feb. 7	N. Valdez	Four-Round Exh.	St. Petersburg
Feb. 8	C. McDaniels	Five-Round Exh.	Orlando
Feb. 14	J. Haynes	Four-Round Exh.	Tampa
Feb. 21	S. Peaks	Six-Round Exh.	Jacksonville
Feb. 23	D. Bolston	One-Round Exh.	Macon
Feb. 23	L. Jackson	Three-Round Exh.	Macon
Feb. 27	W. Johnson	Four-Round Exh.	Albany, Ga.
Feb. 28	D. Bolston	Four-Round Exh.	Columbus, Ga.
Mar. 3	L. Johnson	Four-Round Exh.	Waycross, Ga.

Mar. 18	K. Carr	Four-Round Exh.	Lubbock, Tex.
Mar. 20	S. Ingram	Four-Round Exh.	Odessa, Tex.
Mar. 22	J. Santell	Four-Round Exh.	El Paso, Tex.
Mar. 22	J. McFalls	Four-Round Exh.	El Paso, Tex.
Mar. 24	H. Hall	Four-Round Exh.	Austin, Tex.
Mar. 25	J.K. Homer	Four-Round Exh.	Waco, Tex.
Apr. 22	W. Haefer	Exh. Won KO 2d Rd.	Rio de Janeiro
Nov. 29	C. Brion	Won on Dec. 10 Rds.	New York

1951

Jan. 3	F. Beshore	Won KO 4 Rds.	Detroit
Feb. 7	O. Agramonte	Won on Dec. 10 Rds.	Miami
Feb. 23	A. Walker	Won KO 10th Rd.	S. Francisco
May 2	O. Agramonte	Won on Dec. 10 Rds.	Detroit
June 15	L. Savold	Won KO in 6th Rd.	New York
Aug. 1	C. Brion	Won Dec. in 10 Rds.	S. Francisco
Aug. 15	J. Bivins	Won Dec. in 10 Rds.	Baltimore
Oct. 26	R. Marciano	Knocked Out in 8th	New York
Nov. 18	U.S. Serviceman	Won KO in 4th Rd.	Tokyo
Nov. 18	U.S. Serviceman	Won KO in 4th Rd.	Tokyo
Nov. 18	U.S. Serviceman	Three-Round Exh.	Tokyo
Nov. 18	Cpl. DeCordova	Four-Round Exh.	Tokyo
Nov. 18	Cpl. DeCordova	Four-Round Exh.	Tokyo
Nov. 18	Cpl. DeCordova	Five-Round Exh.	Tokyo
Dec. 14	Sgt. Brooks	Three-Round Exh.	Sanda, Japan
Dec. 14	Chang Pulu	Won KO in 1st Rd.	Taipei, Formosa
Dec. 14	Sgt. Woodbury	Two-Round Exh.	Taipei
Dec. 14	D.H. Cantrell	Two-Round Exh.	Taipei
Dec. 14	Cpl. DeCordova	Three-Round Exh.	Taipei
Dec. 16	Cpl. DeCordova	Three-Round Exh.	Taipei

D
Joe Louis's Ring Earnings

1934

J. Kracken, Chicago	KO 1	$50
W. Davis, Chicago	KO 3	60
L. Udell, Chicago	KO 2	75
J. Kranz, Chicago	W 6	125
B. Everett, Chicago	KO 2	150
O. Borechuk, Detroit	KO 4	106
A. Winter, Chicago	W 10	200
A. Sykes, Chicago	KO 8	280
J. O'Dowd, Detroit	KO 2	111
S. Poreda, Chicago	KO 1	300
C. Massera, Chicago	KO 3	1,100
L. Ramage, Chicago	KO 8	2,200
		$4,757

1935

P. Perroni, Detroit	W 10	$4,200
H. Birkie, Pittsburgh	KO10	1,900
L. Ramage, L.A.	KO 2	4,354
D. Barry, S. Francisco	KO 3	3,270
N. Brown, Detroit	W 10	6,589
R. Lazer, Chicago	KO 3	11,212
P. Carnera, N.Y.C.	KO 6	60,433
K. Levinsky, Chicago	KO 1	53,752
M. Baer, N.Y.C.	KO 4	240,833
P. Uzcudun, N.Y.C.	KO 4	39,612
R. Toles, Flint	KO 6	1,250
B. Benton, Dayton	KO 2	750
W. Davis, Peoria	KO 2	750
G. Stanton, Kalamazoo	KO 3	750
		$429,655

1936

C. Retzlaff, Chicago	KO 1	$23,065
M. Schmeling, N.Y.C.	KO by 12	140,959
J. Sharkey, N.Y.C.	KO 3	36,506

Following his induction into the Army, Louis'
fighting career was temporarily halted.
Exhibitions while in the Army and on furlough
following his return from an overseas tour,
and until 1946

$$\overline{\$73,000}$$

1946

B. Conn, N.Y.C.	KO 8	$625,916
T. Mauriello, N.Y.C.	KO 1	103,611
Exh. in Hawaii		25,000
		$754,527

1947

Exh. in Mexico		$12,200
Exh. in Central America and S. America		120,000
J. Walcott, N.Y.C.	W 15	75,968
		$208,168

1948

L. Matriccani, Exh.		$2,600
B. Foxworth, Exh.		11,200
Exhibitions in England		40,000
Exhibitions in Brussels		6,000
Syndicated Articles		10,000
J. Walcott, N.Y.C.	KO 11	252,522
P. Comiskey, Exh.		5,860
Magazine Articles		10,000
U.S. Exhibition Tour		92,000
		$430,182

1949

U.S., Central and S. America, and Far East Exh. Tours	$242,000
U.S. Tour	62,000
	$304,000

1950

South American Exh. Tour	$38,000
E. Charles, N.Y.C.	102,840
	$140,840

TOTAL RING AND EXHIBITION EARNINGS	$4,292,162

A. Ettore, Philadelphia	KO 5	52,897
J. Brescia, N.Y.C.	KO 3	8,411
E. Simms, Cleveland	KO 1	20,000
		$281,838

1937

S. Ketchell, Buffalo	KO 2	$3,100
B. Pastor, N.Y.C.	W 10	36,000
N. Brown, Kansas City	KO 4	11,000
J. Braddock, Chicago	KO 8	103,684
T. Farr, N.Y.C.	W 15	102,578
		$256,362

1938

N. Mann, N.Y.C.	KO 3	$40,522
H. Thomas, Chicago	KO 5	16,659
M. Schmeling, N.Y.C.	KO 1	349,228
		$406,409

1939

J.H. Lewis, N.Y.C.	KO 1	$34,413
J. Roper, L.A.	KO 1	34,850
T. Galento, N.Y.C.	KO 4	114,332
B. Pastor, Detroit	KO 11	118,400
		$301,995

1940

A. Godoy, N.Y.C.	W 15	$23,620
J. Paycheck, N.Y.C.	KO 2	19,908
A. Godoy, N.Y.C.	KO 8	55,989
A. McCoy, Boston	KO 6	17,938
		$117,455

1941

R. Burman, N.Y.C.	KO 5	$21,023
G. Dorazio, Philadelphia	KO 2	18,730
A. Simon, Detroit	KO 13	19,400
T. Musto, St. Louis	KO 9	17,468
B. Baer, Washington, D.C.	W. disq. 7	36,866
B. Conn, N.Y.C.	KO 13	153,905
J. Robinson, Minneapolis	KO 1	5,000
L. Nova, N.Y.C.	KO 6	199,500
		$471,892

1942

B. Baer, N.Y.C.	KO 1	$65,200
A. Simon, N.Y.C.	KO 6	45,882
		$111,082

(Donated to Army Relief $36,146)

E
Poetry Inspired by Joe Louis

A SELECTED LIST

1. 1935

McLemore, Henry, "Joe Louis," New York World Telegram,
     September 6, 1935.

2. 1936

Davis, Ruth Olga Mae, "Lights and Shadows: A Little Bit of
     Everything," Chicago Defender, January 25, 1936.

Jordan, James Thomas, "Dedication to Joe Louis," Chicago
     Defender, June 20, 1936.

Kieran, John, "To Repeat," New York Times, June 19, 1936.

Razaf, Andy, "Personally to Joe Louis," Pittsburgh Courier,
     February 22, 1936.

Rice, Grantland, "Joe Louis," New York Sun, June 17, 1936.

Wegener, H. O., "Joe ist K.O.!" Box Sport, Berlin, Germany,
     June 22, 1936.

Vidmer, Richards, "Some of the Answers," New York Herald
     Tribune, June 30, 1936.

3. 1937

Bradley, Hugh, "Farr'll Get Lumps," New York Post, August 30,
     1937.

Moss, Morton, "Heroes and Zeroes," New York Post, June 16,
     1937.

_____, "The Pillow Is a Whole Lot Softer," New York Post, January 30, 1937.

_____, "Your Move, Bobby Pastor," New York Post, January 29, 1937.

_____, "Taps for Brave King Jim," New York Post, June 23, 1937.

Rice, Grantland, "A Few Lines to Tommy Far," New York Sun, August 20, 1937.

4.   1938

Kieran, John, "Owed to Joe Louis," New York Times, February 27, 1938.

_____, "Views of a Past Master," New York Times, July 2, 1938.

Seymour, Alexander, "To Joe Louis," New York Amsterdam News, May 28, 1938, p. 18.

Whitfield, Russell, "Prologue to a Fight (Louis vs. Schmeling)," New York Amsterdam News, May 28, 1938, p. 18.

5.   1940

Kieran, John, "Song for Joe Louis," New York Times, February 19, 1940.

Rice, Grantland, "The Superman and the Sucker Punch," New York Sun, June 20, 1940.

6.   1941

Cohane, Tim, "Frothy Facts," New York World Telegram, June 6, 1941.

_____, "I Am Young, Sir, and Do Not Fear the Bomber," New York World-Telegram, June 19, 1941.

_____, "Joe Louis," New York World-Telegram, June 19, 1941.

7.   1942

Byoir, Carl, "Joe Louis Named the War: Poem," Collier's, Vol. 109, May 16, 1942, p. 14.

F
Vertical Files, Scrapbooks, Newspaper Clippings, Dissertation, and Broadside

A SELECTED LIST

1. Scrapbooks and newspaper clippings, 1935-1941. University of Michigan, Michigan Historical Collection. Ann Arbor, Michigan. This collection includes over ninety bound volumes.

2. Scrapbooks and newspaper clippings. Schomburg Research Center on Black History and Culture, New York.

3. Newspaper clippings, letters and documents, Alexander Gumby Collection on The American Negro. Columbia University, New York, New York.

4. Verticle Files, Moorland Spingarn Research Center, Howard University, Washington, D.C.

5. Amsterdam News, Clipping Files, New York.

6. Vertical Files, Wake Forest University, Winston-Salem, North Carolina.

7. Vertical Files, Winston-Salem State University, Winston-Salem, North Carolina.

8. Young, Alexander Joseph, Jr. "Joe Louis Symbol. 1933-1949." Unpublished Ph.D. Dissertation, University of Maryland, 1968. 171 pp.

9. "Joe Louis Says Benjamin Davis Is My Number 1 Choice (as New York City Councilman)" 1945. Broadside.

G
Joe Louis in Films

1. FILMS

"The Spirit of Youth"   1938

"Colored Champions in Sport"   1939

"The Fight That Never Ends"   1946

2. DOCUMENTARY ON JOE LOUIS

"Sergeant Joe Louis on Tour"   1943

3. FILM BIOGRAPHY OF JOE LOUIS

"The Joe Louis Story"   1953
     (Starring James Edward)

H
Awards, Honors, and Namesakes

A Representative and Selected List

A. AWARDS AND HONORS

E. J. Neil Memorial Award

"Fighter of the Year" (1936, 1938, 1939, 1941)

Legion of Merit

"Man of the Century"

100% Wrong Award

Shalom Award

Special Deputy Sheriff of Wayne County, Mich.

B. NAMESAKES

Joe Louis Arena

Joe Louis Boulevard

Joe Louis Dude Ranch

Joe Louis Food Franchise Corporation

Joe Louis Milk

Joe Louis Super Market

Joe Louis Scholarship

Index

Including Authors, Joint Authors, and Editors.
Numbers refer to individual entry numbers.

ABOUT THE COMPILER

LENWOOD G. DAVIS is Associate Professor of History at Winston-Salem State University. He received both his B.A. and M.A. degrees in history from North Carolina Central University, Durham, North Carolina, and a doctorate in history from Carnegie-Mellon University. Dr. Davis has compiled more than seventy bibliographies. He is the author of ten books, *I have a Dream: The Life and Times of Martin Luther King, Jr.* (1973), *The Black Woman in American Society: A Selected Annotated Bibliography* (1975), *The Black Family in the United States: A Selected Bibliography of Annotated Books, Articles, and Dissertations on Black Families in America* (1978), *Sickle Cell Anemia: A Selected Annotated Bibliography* (1978), *Black Artists in the United States: An Annotated Bibliography,* coauthored with Janet L. Sims (1980), *Marcus Garvey: An Annotated Bibliography,* coauthored with Janet L. Sims (1980), *Black Aged in the United States* (1980), *Black Athletes in the United States: A Bibliography, coauthored with Belinda S. Daniels (1981),* A Paul Robeson Research Guide (1982), and *A Ku Klux Klan Research Guide,* coauthored with Janet Sims-Wood (1983).